THE DIRECTORY FOR BUILDING COMPETENCIES

THE DIRECTORY
FOR
BUILDING
COMPETENCIES

Written by
Dennis J. Kravetz

Kravetz Associates
671 Timber Ridge Drive
Bartlett, IL 60103   (708) 483-7300

THE DIRECTORY FOR BUILDING COMPETENCIES

by Dennis J. Kravetz

Copyright © 1995 by: Kravetz Associates
671 Timber Ridge Drive
Bartlett, IL 60103   1/03

Library of Congress Cataloging-in-Publication Data

Kravetz, Dennis J., date.

The directory for building competencies.

Bibliography: p.
1. Performance.   2. Success in business.
I. Title.
HF5386.K834   1989   650.1   89-8011

ISBN   0-927764-00-8

Manufactured in the United States of America

Third Edition

C. 7

CONTENTS

The following chapters are intended for those in supervisory positions:

PREFACE

Building job competencies is something that all of us need to do. We need to be as competent as possible to be successful in a competitive world. For those of us who are managers, we need to be concerned not only about our own competence but that of our employees as well. Every manager knows the value of having a highly competent work force versus one that is just average. But how do you help the employee who has poor interpersonal competence, is poor at planning, or needs improvement in any one of many other areas?

The dilemma that managers and employees have is knowing what day-to-day activities will build competencies. Many managers have painfully avoided performance coaching because they do not know what activities to suggest for improvement. Yet, these same managers recognize that performance improvement is more than just **telling** the employee that they need to improve. Managers no longer need to fear this problem. This book provides you with the day-to-day activities that build competencies and have been proven to work.

Purpose of This Book

The Directory was created to help employees build new competencies or improve existing ones. Employees can select actions from the book which will build competence and apply these actions on their own. Managers can use the book for self improvement and to suggest actions that their employees can take. This will help managers do a better job at performance coaching. The Introduction of this book provides further details on how to do performance coaching and should be read first by managers.

Each chapter of this book represents a different job competency. Individuals merely need to turn to the appropriate chapter and scan through the list of action items to find those that will help them most. They then apply these action items on a day-to-day basis.

Similarly, employees or managers can read the practical articles or books that will help them build competencies and apply what is learned.

Bottom-Line Improvement the Goal

Used appropriately, the action items and readings suggested in this book will bring about bottom-line competency improvement in employees. We have kept the action items easy to understand and implement to ensure that employees will use them. Our focus is on bottom-line performance improvement and change. We have eliminated abstract discussions, and instead zeroed in on suggestions that can be put into practice the next day if needed.

Where did the actions in this book come from? For nearly twenty years we have been working with managers and employees to help them build competencies (see a description of Individual Management Development in the pages that follow). We found that changing individuals is both easy and difficult at the same time. It is easy if you can suggest very specific, job-related activities that build competencies. It is very difficult if you give the employee only vague suggestions on how to improve or expect them to figure it out on their own. One of the limitations of traditional upwards evaluation programs is that they merely tell employees what is wrong, not how to fix it.

In short, the actions that worked with employees over the years are the ones we reproduced in the book. The ones that did not work you will never see. When the employee uses the effective actions over and over again, they become an ingrained part of that person's behavior. This is another way of saying that the person has become competent in that particular area.

Intended Audience

The suggestions offered in this book will be of benefit to any type of employee—be it an executive, manager, professional, production employee, or office support personnel. Regardless of the type of job the employee holds, they can benefit from the suggested action items and readings. We have kept in mind the large diversity of jobs in the workplace in creating this Directory. There is something for everyone within these pages. While most ideas and readings apply to all, some are more appropriately geared to one group, such as managers.

Anyone who supervises others will likely want to have this book on their bookcase as a handy reference source. Several large companies have distributed copies to each and every manager at the company. Some have given the book to each and every employee. The book will come in handy whenever helping employees get better at what they do, regardless if the employee is a superstar, marginal performer, or average performer. All can benefit from improved competencies.

Self-Development Use as Well

Not only will this book help managers build the competence of their employees, but can be used for self-development as well. Managers who become aware of areas for personal self-improvement will find the Directory of great value. The ideas can be applied just as easily by managers for their own development as for use with the manager's staff.

We are not suggesting that managers replace good performance coaching with a book, but that by giving a copy of the Directory to each employee, individual employees may self-improve in areas that the manager may not actively coach in. Once again, the focus should be on bottom-line improvement, regardless of how that improvement comes about. Much of the ultimate competence building which takes place comes from our own initiative. We simply need the tools to help us.

Tie-In With Other Products

Kravetz Associates can assist individual managers and companies with many competency improvement issues. Say for example, that an executive is unaware of the exact set of developmental needs a given manager might have. Or the executive does not have the time or skills to bring about the desired change. We have a service called "Individual Management Development" that helps to identify and correct any manager's competency needs.

The Individual Management Development process starts with one-on-one meetings with members of the manager's staff, the manager's peers, and boss (surveys can be used in place of meetings if needed). As a result of these confidential conversations, and our own assessment of the manager, we develop and prioritize the developmental needs for that manager. We then put together a customized developmental program, including on-the-job activities, readings, and seminars that provide the needed development. Through coaching, we build any needed competencies.

Kravetz Associates also helps companies define the technical and other job competencies that their organization needs. We link together this competency database with many other human resources activities. For example, companies can design training course curriculums that build the same competencies identified in the job analysis. They can also design performance appraisal systems and pay-for-competency compensation systems which measure and reward the same job competencies. Selection procedures, career development systems and many other human resource programs can likewise draw upon the same competency database. It is helpful to have a competency language that cuts across the entire organization.

A Unique Sourcebook

While a number of books exist for helping build a specific skill (e.g, presentation skills, planning skills), we know of no single volume which can help with such a large number of competencies, and was written for the entire workforce. Yet this is exactly what employees need—a sourcebook which contains advice on how to build competencies in many different areas. Regardless of the employee or the particular competency improvement need, The Directory for Building Competencies contains suggestions that can help.

We encourage you to take your development seriously. Look openly at the strengths and developmental needs that you have. And use this book to help build the competencies which need strengthening.

That is in your long-term interests regardless of what organization you work for.

Bartlett, Illinois   Dennis J. Kravetz
March, 1995

THE AUTHOR

Dennis J. Kravetz received his B.S. in psychology from Purdue University and his M.S. and Ph.D. degrees in industrial psychology from the University of Illinois. He is founder and president of Kravetz Associates, a human resources consulting firm located in Bartlett, Illinois which specializes in the training and organizational development areas. Formerly, he was vice-president of human resources and training director at the Fuji Bank of Japan, the world's largest bank. He also spent thirteen years in other human resources positions with large corporations.

Dennis has written over thirty articles in management and human resources. He twice received the Creative Application Award from the Society for Human Resources Management. This national award is given annually for the most outstanding creative application in the human resources field. He also received an Excellence in Training Award from the American Society for Training and Development.

Dennis formerly served on the Board of Directors for the Society for Human Resource Management and the Society's Foundation. He also was on the board of Commerce Clearing House Publishers. Dennis is the author of the following books:

Kravetz, Dennis J. *Training Best Practices*. Bartlett, IL: Kravetz Associates, 1995.

Kravetz, Dennis J. *The Human Resources Revolution: Implementing Progressive Management Practices for Bottom-Line Success*. San Francisco: Jossey-Bass, 1988.

Kravetz, Dennis J. *Getting Noticed: A Manager's Success Kit*. New York: John Wiley and Sons, 1985. Also published as an audiocassette series by Nightingale-Conant, Chicago, 1987.

KRAVETZ ASSOCIATES

Kravetz Associates was founded in 1976 to assist companies in establishing state-of-the-art human resources programs and services. Each principal with the firm has headed up various human resources functions with large corporations as well as had significant consulting experience. All consultants hold graduate degrees in industrial psychology or related areas and are leaders in the profession. The firm has won several national awards for outstanding human resources innovations. Our human resources consulting services fall into the falling categories:

1. Customized training courses.

We design courses from scratch in the areas of management development, sales training, customer service, communications, and technical education. We handle all aspects of the course design work, including video production, participant's manuals, leader's guides, skill practices, simulations, business games, and all other needed materials. We do cutting-edge work in this area, and have designed courses not only for corporate clients but also for some of the largest off-the-shelf training vendors.

We can provide train-the-trainer assistance for companies, and actually instruct some of the courses we design on an ongoing basis. Our instructor's not only have excellent platform and communications skills, but business savvy from having worked in large corporations.

2. Organizational development work.

Our most successful service involves assessing how companies manage the people-side of the business. Our work to date has identified eighty different people-management practices that predict company financial success. Our database of norms and best practices includes over 300 large corporations and over half of the largest 500 companies. The assessment process involves surveys, focus groups and a direct examination of the organization's people-management practices. We provide clients with a specific road map of how to improve and they receive benchmarks of what the leading companies are doing in any area where they need to improve.

We define technical and other job competencies for organizations. The competency database we develop is used to tie together many human resources activities such as performance measurement, training courses, selection, career development and compensation. We have a unique process for defining job competencies which permits a one-time job analysis to serve many purposes.

Other organizational development work includes building and changing company culture, changing management styles, and improving people-management practices. We also establish customer satisfaction programs through designing surveys, training and other systems to make this an effective initiative.

3. Individual management development.

Our individual management development service helps managers build competencies in any needed area. By meeting with the target manager, and those familiar with the manager, we identify the top priorities for development. Working with the manager one-on-one, we put together a set of action items that will build managerial competence or change behavior. This ensures that the manager knows what to do on a daily basis to build competence. We also provide readings or other outside resources to help with the development. We serve as a coach for the manager and stay with them to ensure improvement. This service is the ultimate in improving the performance of individual managers and goes far beyond upwards evaluation programs.

4. Career development programs.

We have a unique career development system called Career Match. It enables individual employees to assess their competencies, job interests, and personality traits. As a result of this assessment, the employee receives a summary score on each of six "career orientations." By plugging the summary code into the Career Match software, the program finds every job at the company that matches the employee's code. Company information on their jobs, such as the job's competencies, is stored on our software. The system ensures that employees know which jobs are matches for them and what competencies they need to build to hold such jobs. It enables career development efforts to be very focused for individual employees by linking their competencies to specific company jobs.

5. Selection procedures.

We design, develop, and validate selection procedures for companies. As in other work, we focus on the cutting edge, which in this case is job simulations. Job simulations, as the name implies, are structured exercises that simulate portions of the target job. These exercises are practical to use, and have excellent "face validity" for candidates (each takes twenty minutes to two hours for candidates to complete). Simulation exercises enable companies to know with certainty if job candidates have the competencies needed for various jobs. We also design behavioral interview programs, tests and other selection procedures needed by clients.

INTRODUCTION

This introductory chapter is intended for managers who may need to coach and counsel their employees. We want to cover two main topics. The first pertains to the proper use of this Directory in helping employees with various competency improvement needs. The second topic deals with how to run an effective performance coaching session with an employee. Managers who have had limited training in performance coaching will find it particularly beneficial to read this second part of the introduction.

Contents of the Directory

The Directory for Building Competencies was compiled based upon our experience with hundreds of managers and employees in a large number of leading organizations. Having done a large number of job competency studies, we compiled a list of virtually every type of competency we had run across over the years. We then categorized the competencies into groups, with each group representing a chapter in the Directory. The chapter groupings were intentionally kept broad to make it easy to access the information via the Table of Contents.

The competencies covered in each chapter are relevant to any level of employee, (the exception being the last few chapters). For example, our second chapter deals with interpersonal competence. Virtually any level of employee, from senior manager through entry level office personnel, could potentially have problems in the interpersonal area. Any of these employees could also benefit by implementing the action items suggested in that chapter. They are, for the most part, just as applicable for senior managers as they are for entry-level personnel. A manager needs to merely identify those that are most appropriate for a given employee.

The last several chapters have a more targeted audience. These chapters deal with topics (e.g., leadership style, staff selection) that are likely to fall in the domain of managers or team leaders. Therefore, the use of these chapters will be more appropriate for those who currently supervise others, or are likely to move into a supervisory position.

We also would like to say a word about the chapter on technical competence. We did not include any readings in this chapter since this would require listing virtually every important technical article or book in every profession—well beyond the scope of this book. Our experience has shown that managers have little difficulty in coming up with technical articles and books in their field—accounting managers know of good accounting publications, engineering managers know of good engineering publications, etc. For this reason, we felt it unnecessary to list out specific references in the technical chapter.

The action items in the chapter on technical competence pertain to staying current in one's field and having a high level of professionalism. Once again, we did not list specific suggestions such as how an accountant can master accounts payable, or how a manufacturing engineer can master computer-based design, since we would have to do this for every profession. Managers in these areas can easily come up with suggestions on how employees can take certain actions to learn more about the technical aspects of their jobs.

Where we **did** concentrate our action items and readings was on the wide range of developmental areas that cut across many jobs—areas where managers may not feel like experts in changing employee performance. For example, an accounting manager may not know how to improve an employee's interpersonal competence or verbal competence. It is here where managers and employees greatly need a sourcebook, and for this reason, these non-technical action items and readings make up virtually the entire Directory.

Use of the Directory

The use of The Directory for Building Competencies is very simple. The following steps can serve as guidelines:

1. Clearly Identify the Competency Area(s) for Improvement.

The starting point is to identify the area(s) where the employee needs to build competence. This might be known from personal observation, work samples, the comments of others, or the employee's own suggestions. For those employees with several areas for improvement, we recommend rank-ordering the developmental areas and pursuing the highest two or three on the list. You can always go back and improve the others later.

2. Turn to the Table of Contents.

Use the Table of Contents to determine which chapter is most closely related to the competency improvement need. We have kept the chapters distinct to avoid having to look in more than one place to solve a particular improvement need. More than one chapter will need to be accessed only when there are multiple developmental needs for an employee.

3. Scan the Action Items and Readings.

After locating the appropriate chapter, scan the action items presented in that chapter. Some will be more appropriate than others for use with a particular employee. Think of presenting four or five action items to the employee in a coaching session.

Employees may vary greatly in their ability and interest in reading. Keep this in mind when examining the readings for that chapter. Use brief articles for those who are less inclined to read, and refer books or several articles to those who are active readers.

4. Present the Suggestions in a Coaching Session with the Employee.

Once the action items and readings have been identified, a coaching session should be set up with the employee. The guidelines and steps for running this coaching session are presented later in this chapter. In general, the manager should try to recommend action items to the employee and gain a commitment to implement the best actions. This should be accomplished by means of discussion and agreement rather than demanding that the employee use them. This will ensure a sincere employee commitment to implement the suggestions.

5. Follow Up on the Progress Made.

Continue to follow up on the employee's progress. When improvements are noticed, be certain to recognize and reward the improvements. This will ensure that the actions are continually used. If no change is noted or only modest change has occurred, ask the employee to review what they have done. Inspire them to do more where needed. You might also return to the Directory to determine other action items and readings for the employee to implement.

The Directory and Self-Improvement

Many of you might be using the Directory for your personal self-improvement. Perhaps your manager has mentioned to you in a performance appraisal or coaching session the need to improve in certain areas. Or you may simply want to get better at certain competencies in your own mind. Whatever the case, the Directory can help you in your personal development. Start out by defining your improvement needs, find the appropriate chapter through the Table of Contents, and note those action items and readings that are best for you.

The biggest difference with self-improvement is the tracking and rewarding of progress. We recommend that you keep a log or diary of how you are doing in your targeted areas. Or ask a trusted colleague to give you feedback on any changes they have seen in you. If improvements have been made, be certain to reward yourself in some way for the progress you have made. It will no doubt be noticed by others eventually, but you should reward yourself in the early stages and continue your progress.

Performance Improvement Coaching

Of all of the different types of coaching that managers can do with employees, performance improvement coaching is the most difficult. That is because many managers are uncertain as to how employees will react and do not know precisely what to suggest to fix the problem. Since some employees may react negatively to perceived criticism or discipline, the session can be a negative one. Both manager and employee would rather avoid it.

Today, effective managers do not view performance coaching as criticism and discipline. Instead they see performance coaching as a means to guide and assist employees, a way for people to learn and get better at what they do. That change in attitude makes all of the difference between a successful and unsuccessful coaching session.

Let's contrast the prior style of management with the current management style regarding performance coaching:

Performance Coaching Attitudes

Prior Style of Management	Current Management
Coaching is discipline	Coaching is way to solve problem
Manager should criticize and blame	Manager should work toward solution
Session should focus on past	Session should focus on future
Problem is due entirely to employee	Problem is shared
Coaching done only late in game	Coaching done all the time
Only problem performers need coaching	Everyone benefits from coaching
Employee is on own in solving problem	Manager helps employee solve problem
Coaching is a negative experience for all	Coaching can be fun and upbeat
Employees can't or won't change	Employees can learn and change

The New Outlook on Performance Coaching

As you can see, there is quite a bit of difference between the current and prior way of managing when it comes to coaching. Let's expand on the outlook effective managers have about coaching:

1. Everyone can benefit from coaching.

Today's managers recognize that all employees benefit from coaching. Even outstanding performers can learn, grow and benefit from performance coaching. Since everyone receives coaching, these meetings do not stick out as discipline hearings.

2. The focus is positive and win-win.

Managers who are particularly good at coaching do it in such a way that the employee may not even know they had a coaching session. The manager will talk about how to improve in a positive way. The manager is open to the employee's ideas and remains positive and helpful. Performance change helps both employee and manager and in this way becomes a win-win session.

3. Future orientation to coaching.

Rather than dwell on the past, the manager keeps things focused on the future. The emphasis is on better success down the road, not criticizing prior performance. This keeps the discussion positive.

4. The focus is on the problem, not the person.

This is a subtle, yet very important point. When managers focus on the person and the traits the person lacks ("you are lazy,"), the employee becomes defensive and uncooperative. When the focus is on the problem ("you have been late the last three days"), there is a much better chance of cooperation. More about this later.

5. We are "in this together."

Today's manager will see a problem as shared between both manager and employee. When you stop to think about it, a competency deficiency reflects poorly on your department and you as the manager. Improving the deficiency helps both you and the employee. A manager can help the employee work out a solution and have an ongoing role in the process. The role is much more than "describe the problem and leave."

6. Employees can and will change.

You must think positively about the employee's ability to build additional competence. Without your confidence and support nothing will happen. Would you be motivated to build additional competencies if your boss felt it was hopeless? Your employee will feel the same way. We are not suggesting that **every** competency improvement problem can be cleared up, but studies have shown that the majority **can** be corrected. But this all starts out with you believing it can be corrected.

7. Get employee's ideas.

Most of us will commit to a plan if we have input. In improving competence, it is best to let employees suggest solutions. Managers need to share out their ideas as well but should not do all of the talking. When both manager and employee have input, the employee is more likely to do what is needed. The plan for improvement becomes "our plan," not "your plan."

Performance Coaching Steps

We would now like to introduce a series of steps that can be used in performance coaching. These steps can serve as a guide for running the coaching session itself. Though each of the steps is described separately, they flow together in an actual coaching session. In certain cases, the steps may even be moved around where needed. The order shown is the most likely way to use the steps in a performance coaching meeting. The steps are as follows:

Performance Coaching Steps

1. Maintain or strengthen the employee's self-esteem.
2. Describe the problem.
3. Discuss solutions to the problem.
4. Agree on actions.
5. Set follow-up.
6. Express confidence in the employee.

1. Maintain or strengthen the employee's self-esteem.

Self-esteem should be maintained throughout the session, so this step can be used whenever needed. By maintaining the employee's self-esteem, cooperation and help will be given.

How can you maintain or strengthen someone's self-esteem when you want to discuss a performance deficiency? It sounds impossible but can be done. You simply recognize their work in other areas, or ask for their help in solving this problem. If you cannot do this, at least open on a neutral note, making some small talk to relax the employee.

Ways to maintain self-esteem at the beginning of a coaching session are as follows:

- "You always put forth a great deal of effort. I would like your help in solving a problem I have been noticing lately."

- "You always have a lot of good ideas. I wonder if you can help me with this problem."

- "Thanks for sending me a copy of that report. I'm glad you gave me a copy. What I wanted to talk about today is . . . "

2. Describe the problem.

The manager's description of the competency deficiency should be clear and straightforward. Cite **specific** performance examples and compare those with what you expect. Avoid fault-finding or accusations. Avoid drawing conclusions about the person based on the problem at hand. Focus on the problem itself, not the person.

Wrong Way	Right Way
"It appears to me that you don't want to work hard."	"I've noticed that your volume of work has dropped off."
"You just can't seem to get along with anyone."	"I noticed that you had an argument with Dan yesterday."
"It seems to me that you can't learn how to code our billing forms."	"I've become aware that some of our billing forms have been coded incorrectly."

3. Discuss solutions to the problem.

After describing the problem, it is best to ask for the employee's help in solving the problem. See what suggestions the employee has before offering your own. Resist the temptation to offer your solution too quickly. Use the "silence technique" if you have to in order to get the employee's thoughts out into the open. Do not criticize their ideas—if the idea is not good, ask for other solutions.

Next, offer your own solutions to the problem. Base these on your use of the Directory for Building Competencies. Keep an open mind on what might work.

Examples of how to discuss solutions to the problem include:

- "I need your help in getting the work volume back up to where it should be. What do you think we can do?"

- "We need to reduce the number of arguments within our department. What can you do to work better with the others."

- "I like your idea on spending time with someone in the Billing Department to help reduce coding errors. I also feel that if you . . . it will help reduce errors."

4. Agree on actions.

Coaching sessions should end with a clear understanding of who is going to do what. This creates a "contract" between manager and employee to work together to solve the problem. In some cases you might summarize the actions agreed to in writing so the employee can have a copy.

Action items from a coaching session can apply to **both** the employee and the manager. The employee is ultimately responsible for improving performance, but the manager can take certain actions as well. For example, the manager might agree to:

- Provide some training for the employee.

- Make certain materials available (equipment, policies, articles).

- Set up meetings between the employee and an in-house "expert."

- Identify outside programs that can help the employee.

Examples of agreeing on actions are as follows:

- "You are going to watch your performance volume against the goal we set. I am going to have Bill Smith spend some time with you to help you increase your speed."

- "You are going to double-check the billing codes against the chart. I am going to have a new chart made up so it is easier to use."

5. Set follow-up.

This step involves setting a time to re-visit the performance problem. You want to check and see how things are going. Agree to a specific time with the employee. Avoid vague statements like "we will discuss this later." Use specific dates instead.

Specific examples are as follows:

- "Let's meet two weeks from today at 1:00 to see how things are going."

- "I'd like to sit down and review your progress on the 28th. Is 10:00 okay with you?"

6. Express confidence in the employee.

This last step is extremely important to make the employee feel that you believe in them. For if you do not think they can improve, who will? This show of confidence must be genuine and not phony. You should really believe the employee can get better unless they prove otherwise.

Here are examples of how to express confidence in the employee:

- "I know you can get your volume up. You have done it before and I know you can do it again."

- "I'm confident you can eliminate these coding errors. I know you like to be accurate in your work and can make the needed improvements."

Performance Coaching Form

Performance Coaching Steps

1. Maintain or strengthen the employee's self-esteem.

2. Describe the problem.

3. Discuss solutions to the problem.

4. Agree on actions.

5. Set follow-up.

6. Express confidence in the employee.

Describe the performance problem in the space below (note examples & dates):

Solutions to the performance problem (taken from the Directory for Building Competencies):

How will this employee react to the coaching? If negative, note what can be done to resolve.

Date of coaching session _____ **Date to follow up** _____

Notes on the coaching session (note how the session went, things to do, etc.):

1

Verbal Communication Skills

This chapter helps improve performance in the following areas:

- Speaking skills.
- Presentation skills.
- Keeping others informed.
- Conversational skills.
- Participating in meetings.
- Non-verbal communications (body language).
- Telephone skills.

Action Items for Increasing Verbal Communication Skills

1. Avoid the use of jargon.

Employees with technical backgrounds are apt to use jargon very easily. This can be a serious problem when communicating with others who are not familiar with such terminology. It can cause the employee to be seen as "too technical" or "too academic." Become conscious of your use of jargon and avoid it whenever you can, even with peers who understand the terms. Speaking in "plain English" is an asset, not something that will make you seem less knowledgeable. If you must use jargon with people outside your field, clearly define the terms you are using.

2. Use effective vocal quality and animation.

Effective speech is not only what you say, but how you say it. Quiet, monotone speech is not very exciting to listen to. If that is the way you speak, increase the volume and pitch of your voice when emphasizing your main points. Use variety in your speaking—with more animation on key points and less animation on minor details. Vocal quality is also effected by the proper breathing. Deeper breaths enable you to project your voice better. Try to breathe more deeply when speaking to larger audiences.

3. Keep others more informed.

Part of effective communication involves passing along important information to others. Whenever you become aware of new information, verbally or in writing, think of who else would benefit from the information. If you change procedures or policies in your area, think of who else is impacted by the change. Take the initiative to inform others of these changes. You can never over-communicate, but can easily run into problems by not communicating enough.

4. Use notes or bullets when presenting ideas.

When called upon to share out your ideas, do this by using notes or bullets. Some people make the mistake of "winging it" and not organizing their ideas. They may ramble or forget their important points. Others may error by reading a speech, which can sound canned and formal. The best way to handle a presentation is to organize your ideas into bullets or brief notes, then turn each bullet into several sentences that you say in your own words. Whether it be a staff meeting or formal presentation, the use of organized bullets and thoughts will make for more effective communication.

5. Use body language to communicate.

Much of what we communicate to others comes through non-verbal communications, commonly called "body language." Become conscious of your body language when you speak, and improve where needed. For example, make sure you use gestures when expressing your ideas. Lean forward to show interest in a subject. Use facial expressions which coincide with the ideas you are trying to get across. Maintain eye contact with those you are speaking to. When used effectively, body language adds immensely to your message.

6. Be concise when speaking to others.

Some people have a tendency to ramble and get off on tangents when speaking to others. Ask yourself after a meeting or presentation whether you kept to the main points or strayed into other areas. Get feedback from others if your uncertain. If you have a tendency to stray, stick to the notes or bullets that you prepared beforehand.

Resist the temptation to tell war stories or anecdotes that are not essential to making your key points. Say what you have to say in simple sentences and clear thoughts.

7. Become conscious of "ums" and "ahs" in your speech.

When speaking, many people fill in the normal pauses between thoughts by saying "um," "ah," or "you know." When used infrequently, these expressions do not detract from your speech. The problem occurs when they are used too often and cause the audience to focus on the "um" more than the rest of the words. Listen to your own speech to see if you use these expressions too often. The key to eliminating them is to simply let there be a pause between thoughts—do not fill in the blank space with a word such as "um."

8. Adapt what you have to say to your audience.

Effective communication is based in part on adapting what you have to say to your audience. That audience can be just one person—perhaps your boss—or an entire room full of people. Try to walk a mile in the shoes of your audience. Ask what they know about your subject? What is their interest level? What do they value and want to get from what you have to say? Then present what you have to say with the answers to these questions in the back of your mind.

9. Speak out more (or less) at meetings.

Some employees may have too little or too much to say at meetings. Ask yourself after meetings whether you said too little or too much. Seek feedback from others if you need it. If too little, feel confident in yourself and your ideas, and recognize that others are interested in what you have to say. Build up the confidence to say what you feel and express yourself. If you are too talkative, try to hold back from doing most of the talking. Encourage others to say what they feel. Focus on listening as much as speaking out.

10. Improve grammar where needed.

Those employees with less formal education may have difficulty with grammar. If you have difficulties in this area, there are several ways to improve. You may want to take a high school or college course on grammar or speaking. Another option is to buy a book on proper grammar and put the ideas into practice. Still another option is to have a trusted friend with good grammar point out to you when your grammar is poor and to correct you in private. By putting these ideas into practice, day-to-day grammar can be improved.

11. Use effective visual aids.

We have all heard the expression that ''a picture is worth a thousand words.'' And this is true when presenting your ideas. On many occasions a table, chart, drawing, or overhead will help you get your ideas across. Think of using some sort of visual aids when presenting your ideas, particularly in group settings.

12. Take a public speaking course.

To help you present your ideas better, and build confidence, enroll in a public speaking course. A number of private companies, as well as colleges and universities, offer training in this area. Many courses give you a chance to see yourself on videotape several times as part of building presentation skills. By enrolling in such a course, and putting the ideas into practice, you can get your ideas across better to your boss and co-workers.

13. Enroll in a public speaker's bureau.

You can build presentation and communications skills by practicing away from work as well as on the job. Public speaking organizations such as Toastmasters help people develop presentation skills and give them a means for expressing themselves away from the job. By seeing others speak, and getting feedback on your own talks, you can improve your skills in this area. You can then transfer what you have learned back to the job.

14. Increase eye contact with your audience.

Some employees are unable to look people in the eye when they talk to them. This creates a feeling of being impersonal, not caring about people, or not having the confidence to look at others. The solution is to maintain eye contact when speaking with others. Alternate eye contact with each member of the audience if more than one person is present. To avoid darting glances, hold the eye contact for five seconds or more with each person.

15. Build your vocabulary.

Some people have a limited vocabulary and may have a hard time finding the right words to express themselves. If you have this problem, it can be corrected by working on building your vocabulary. Do this by working crossword puzzles and playing word games such as Scrabble. Increase your reading and take the time to look up words you are uncertain of. Maintain lists of new words, review them periodically, and work them into your everyday language. Though it may sound strange, some people have been known to read a dictionary as a means of increasing vocabulary. If you try this, avoid technical jargon and concentrate on the more practical words that can be used every day.

16. Rent a video camera and tape yourself.

The best way to see how you communicate with others is to see yourself on tape. Most homes have video recorders these days. By merely renting a camera you can tape yourself and evaluate your communications skills. Tape your self giving a stand-up presentation, and also speaking while sitting down as you might do in a meeting. Focus on your delivery more so than your appearance. Was your speech clear and concise? Did you vary your voice pitch and volume to get across key ideas? Did you use gestures and have good posture? All of these areas and many more can be noticed and improved upon by taping yourself. Do it several times and try to improve each time.

17. Give yourself time to think when answering questions.

Some employees get flustered when they are asked a tough question. They are worried about giving out the wrong answer on the spot. If you have this problem, there is a way to correct it. Learn how to restate someone's question (e.g., "You want to know. . .") to give yourself time to think of the answer. By doing so you will show your questioner that you understand what they are saying, and give yourself time to think through your answer. You can then reply with the answer that you want to give.

18. Read the body language of others.

Just as it is important for you to use appropriate body language when speaking, it is also important to read the body language of others. For example, people who lean forward, maintain good eye contact, have an "open" body language, and nod in agreement are telling you they like hearing what you have to say. People who lean back, avoid eye contact, or have a "closed" body language (arms folded) are telling you they are bored or in disagreement with what you are saying. Adjust your presentation based upon what you read in others—keep going if you see positive signs, and take a break or get people more involved if you see negative signs.

19. Anticipate questions or challenges to your ideas.

Effective communicators give advance thought to the questions people might have of them, or challenges that might be made to their ideas. They envision themselves speaking and then try to envision what types of questions or challenges might come up. By thinking through the answers to these questions, you are better prepared to deal with them. Some go even further by actually presenting criticisms to their ideas when speaking. By doing this, they can "steal the thunder" from critics and prevent the meeting from getting bogged down on negative ideas. Try to do as much of this as you can in anticipating others.

20. Avoid becoming devensive or arguing with others.

Some employees take any questioning of their ideas personally. They regard the comments of others as a personal attack on them, and they try to attack back by being defensive or arguing. If you have a tendency to do this, see the comments of others as merely their opinion, not an attack on you. Everyone is entitled to express their feelings in the interest of hearing all sides of an issue. When someone challenges you, try to remain calm and merely acknowledge the person for speaking out. If necessary, offer additional information or restate your opinion in a non-argumentative way.

21. Better organize the flow of your ideas.

Every presentation, even an informal meeting, has a common structure if it is to be done effectively. First, write down the main message (theme) of what you want to communicate. Then think of the main points which support your message and write these down. Organize the ideas in a way that creates the best flow to get across your message. Then add in any supporting details that are needed. As pointed out earlier, by working with notes or bullets of the main ideas and supporting details, you will get the ideas across more effectively. Stick to your organization as you go through the presentation.

22. Make your communications more persuasive.

Some employees have the right ideas, but are not particularly effective at persuading others. Persuasive communications make up perhaps 90% of all meetings and formal presentations. Even if we are not selling directly, we are at least trying to get others to buy our ideas and our professionalism. Part of being persuasive is the mechanics of speech and body language (see earlier action items). Also, persuasive communications are enhanced by organizing your ideas so they lead to a certain conclusion. Most important, you must recognize up front that you are trying to persuade others (even if it is subtle persuasion), and be emphatic in convincing others of your ideas.

23. Make audiotapes.

Listening to audiotapes of yourself, like using videotapes, is an effective way to improve communications. Small recorders can easily be used in meetings or at the dinner table without distracting others. While audiotapes do not enable you to see gestures or body language, they do help with vocal delivery. They enable you to assess clarity, speed of conversation, use of voice animation, and so on. Try using audiotapes periodically and see how you sound to yourself (and others). The use of audiotapes can help in improving your delivery.

24. Be more relaxed then presenting ideas to others.

Many people get nervous when presenting to others, particularly when the group is large. Some individuals are even nervous at one-on-one meetings. If you have this problem, try using relaxation techniques to calm your nerves. The single most effective technique is to take deep breathes before your meeting. This relaxes you and ensures that you are not gulping air when speaking. Other relaxation techniques involve thinking of a very relaxing place for you where things are calm and peaceful. You concentrate on this place before your meeting and this has a way of making you calm and relaxed.

25. Develop an informal style when communicating with others.

Some people seem very formal and stiff when they communicate, particularly at meetings and stand-up presentations. If you have this problem, there are ways to improve upon it. First, make sure you avoid jargon in the presentation itself. Second, use the relaxation techniques mentioned above. Third, when presenting, imagine yourself as having a one-on-one conversation with each person in the room. This psychological attitude of talking with individuals rather than a room of people will do more than anything else to help you appear less formal. Alternate eye contact, holding it for at least several seconds with each person.

26. Be more direct and forceful.

Some employees are hesitant to express their ideas in front of others. They may preface their ideas by saying, "It's only my opinion, but. . ." or "Well, I don't know how everyone else feels, but it seems to me. . ." When using phrases such as these, your ideas get weakened. It is as if you are afraid to say what you really feel. Review your communications with others to see if you use these phrases too often. If you do, eliminate them and be more direct and confident in expressing how you feel.

27. Obtain the feedback of others.

Be on the lookout for feedback on your communications. After a meeting or other presentation, ask a co-worker or boss how it went. Find out what they think could have been done differently to get your ideas across better. Look at their suggestion with an open mind—your goal is to get better, not defend the way you spoke. Incorporate their ideas if they make sense. Tape yourself periodically and critique your own communications. Communications is an area where no one ever gets perfect, but we all can get better and better.

28. Repeat the phone messages of others.

One way to increase the accuracy of phone communications is to repeat phone messages when writing them down. For example, summarize out loud the phone number and message that someone is leaving. They can correct you if any of the message is incorrect. For lengthy conversations, periodically jump in to summarize what you think are the person's most important points. By repeatedly checking for accuracy, you can ensure that you are helping others and getting the correct information.

29. Use the caller's name in phone conversations.

It is more professional and personal if you use the caller's name in a phone conversation. Periodically use their name, preceded by Mr., Mrs., or Ms. For example, you might say, "Mr. Smith, we look forward to seeing you Monday at 3:00." Do not use the caller's first name unless you know them personally. By saying the caller's name at various points in the conversation you will provide friendlier and more personal service.

30. Practice the basics of phone answering.

Phone conversations with others will be more successful if employees would follow the basics. We all know how upsetting it is to get poor service when we call another company. The basics of phone answering are as follows:

- Answer before the third ring.
- Put a smile in your voice—take on a more friendly, helpful tone as if greeting someone in person.
- Offer assistance after identifying your area.

By continually using the phone answering basics, you can ensure that the other party feels they are getting good service. This is a more effective way to communicate with others.

31. Transfer phone calls in an effective way.

Everyone has had the experience of being disconnected when being transferred, or being transferred from place to place with no end in sight. This can be very frustrating and upsetting. The transferring of phone calls can be helped by practicing the following guidelines:

- Try to handle calls yourself rather than transferring.

- Ask the caller if it is alright to put them on hold or transfer their call.

- Check with people on hold every thirty seconds.

- Stay on the line until a transferred call is completed.

Examine how often you use the above practices. If you do not use them all of the time, change your way of transferring calls or putting callers on hold. This is still yet one other way to improve communications skills.

32. Imagine a phone caller is standing in front of you.

Many people have a phone voice which is different from their natural voice, the phone voice being more monotone and boring. This is because they treat phone calls as interruptions, and do not think of phone calls as visits. Many people have found that an effective way to change your phone voice is to imagine that the caller is standing there in front of you. Somehow, we put more energy and enthusiasm into personal visits, and treating a phone call in the same way can help accomplish this. Many sales people even stand up when on the phone, finding that this gives their voice more energy and enthusiasm than when sitting down. Try these techniques if you want to get the most out of your phone conversations.

Recommended Readings

A Survival Guide to Public Speaking. *Training and Development*, September, 1990, p. 15-26.

Baskin, O.W., and Arnoff, C.E. *Interpersonal Communication in Organizations*. Santa Monica, CA: Goodyear Publishing Company, 1980.

Becker, Christine. Improving Communication Skills. *Public Management*, April, 1987, 69, p. 12.

Cohen, William A. and Cohen, Nurit. *Top Executive Performance: 11 Keys to Success and Power*. New York: Wiley, 1984.

Dellinger, Susan, and Deane, Barbara. *Communicating Effectively: A Complete Guide for Better Managing*. Radnor, PA: Chilton Book Company, 1982.

Denton, Keith D. If You Want Your Ideas Approved. *Management Solutions*, September, 1986, 31, p. 4-11.

Frank, Ted, and Ray, David. *Basic Business and Professional Speech Communication*. Englewood Cliffs, NJ: Prentice-Hall, 1979.

Hunt, G.T. *Communication Skills in the Organization*. Englewood Cliffs, NJ: Prentice-Hall, 1980.

Lovett, Paul D. Meetings that Work. *Harvard Business Review*, Nov-Dec, 1988, 66, p. 38.

McKay, Matthew; David, Martha; and Fanning, Patrick. *Messages: The Communication Book*. Oakland, CA: New Harbinger Press, 1983.

Nirenberg, J. *How to Sell Your Ideas*. New York: McGraw-Hill, 1984.

Sheppard, I. Thomas. Silent Signals. *Supervisory Management*, March, 1986, p. 31-33.

Smith, Terry C. *Making Successful Presentations: A Self-Teaching Guide*. New York: Wiley, 1984.

Snyder, Elayne. *Persuasive Business Speaking*. New York: AMACOM, 1990.

Sutton, Suzy. Our Telling Gestures. *Executive Female*, September/October, 1983, p. 34-35.

Swets, Paul W. *The Art of Talking So That People Will Listen: Getting Through to Family, Friends, and Associates*. Englewood Cliffs, NJ: Prentice-Hall, 1983.

Townsend, John. How to Master Meetings. *Management Today*, July, 1987, p. 80.

Weigand, Richard. It Doesn't Need to Be Dull to Be Good: How to Improve Staff Presentations. *Business Horizons*, July-August, 1985, 28, p. 54.

2

Interpersonal Skills

This chapter helps improve performance in the following areas:

- "People" skills.
- Ability to get along with others.
- Ability to work as part of a team.
- Ability to relate to others.

Action Item For Increasing Interpersonal Skills

1. Show a personal interest in others.

Some employees show very little interest in others beyond work-related matters. If you are like this, gradually increase your personal interest in others. Use breaks, lunches, and conversations in hallways to find out more about the hobbies, families, and goals of others. Ask open-ended questions and be a good listener. Increasing your interest **gradually** will ensure that you are not seen as prying into someone's personal life.

2. Share out more information about yourself.

Forming good interpersonal relations with others is a two-way street—both parties need to share information with each other. You should evaluate how often you share out personal information about yourself to others. Be willing to share out some of your hobbies, goals, and family situation with others. Take the opportunity to open up a bit more if you are reluctant to share out information about yourself. Employees will share more with you if you are willing to do the same.

3. Become more visible to others.

Some employees remain isolated in an office all day long, making it difficult for others to interact with them. This causes others to see these people as inaccessible and not very people-oriented. Review whether you keep yourself isolated in meetings or in your office with your door closed. If so, practice "management by walking around" and increase the number of informal visits with others on their turf. Increasing your visibility will help you build interpersonal skills by being "out there" more often.

4. Use the open door policy.

Some employees feel uncomfortable approaching others. They feel they are always interrupting something more important. Minimize this by keeping your door open and showing you are glad that the employee stopped by. If you are on the phone and cannot talk at the moment, motion the person into your work area. Show the person that their visit is more important than paperwork or other activities.

5. Use social events more often.

Away-from-work activities such as breaks, lunch, dinner, or sports events can be an effective means to build interpersonal skills. Employees are often more relaxed and open away from work. You can get to know each other from a different perspective in an away-from-work situation. Care needs to be taken in this area—there are certain lines that need to be drawn on how many and what kinds of social events to use with others you work with.

6. Keep an open mind.

Having a closed mind or being very opinionated can cause others to not want to interact with you. When others share some of their feelings or concerns with you, avoid being defensive or arguing. By doing so, you will encourage future conversations. Listen to their ideas and be willing to keep an open mind. It will encourage people to candidly discuss more with you and you can always learn from this.

7. Make small talk more often.

Some employees are strictly business and reluctant to make small talk. You should evaluate if this applies to you. If so, bring up events on the outside with others such as the recent football or baseball game, the weather, or events in the news. Use these as conversation starters (e.g., "What did you think of the football game on Sunday?"). From this you can branch to other topics or events in the workplace. Small talk is an effective way to be more personal and friendly with others.

8. Reduce your criticism of others.

Some individuals are quick to criticize others. They shoot down ideas or make sarcastic remarks if people do not think the way they do. As a result, others get offended and do not want to deal with the individual. Try to reduce your tendency to criticize others if you have this problem. Hold back your initial negative reaction and say nothing instead. Instead, focus on the positive side of people and what is good in them rather than the negative. Let the tone of your conversation be more positive than critical.

9. Smile and be more friendly.

It sounds simple, but many employees forget to do this. When meeting someone new, be quick to smile and warmly greet the person. Smile and say hello to others you pass in the hallway. Say good morning and good night to your boss, peers or staff each day. These small but important matters make a difference in how others see you and your interpersonal skills.

10. Reduce the need to control too much.

Some employees, particularly some managers, are very forceful in running their areas. They restate their opinions over and over, interrupt others, and discourage any ideas different from their own. If you do this, let others speak their ideas more openly. Ask for the opinion of your staff or peers and let them have their say. Don't judge their ideas too quickly. Keeping your need to control in check will help in building interpersonal relations with others.

11. Compliment others for a job well done.

Some people forget to compliment others for a job well done, and this hurts their working effectively with that person. Assess how often you take the time to compliment a co-worker for doing something well. If you do not do this, try to remind yourself of the need to do so. Take the time to say something nice to your peers, staff or boss when they deserve it. There is probably no better way to build interpersonal relationships with others than to say nice things about them. We are not suggesting that you be phony, but merely that you give a compliment when it is due.

12. Focus on problems, not people.

If you need to bring up a problem with someone else, focus on the problem itself instead of criticizing the person. Describe the problem as objectively as you can without blaming, and ask for the other person's help. People will work with you in solving a problem, but you may burn your bridges with someone if all you do is blame them. Keep the discussion positive and friendly as much as you can. Work for solutions rather than blaming and criticizing for things already done.

13. Do less judging and evaluating of people.

Employees with technical backgrounds are used to judging and evaluating things every day. But what might work for judging equipment or numbers does not work in judging people. If you have a tendency to judge and evaluate people all the time (e.g., "he is only interested in money" or "she never works hard on Friday"), try to tone this down. Regard people as complex and if you have to judge, focus on the positive.

14. Show more sensitivity when needed.

Some employees are reluctant to show sensitivity when it is needed. This makes others see them as cold and uncaring and someone to avoid. It is helpful to express concern or sorrow when a co-worker or staff member is dealing with illness or a death in the family. Say the right words to show your feelings. Apologies are sometimes in order if you have offended or hurt someone. The employee who cannot show sensitivity when needed will have a difficult time relating well with others.

15. Recognize anniversary dates and birthdays.

When one of your peers or staff celebrates an anniversary date with the company or has a birthday, recognize this. Congratulate the person verbally or drop them a brief note. By doing so, you show your concern and interest in others. This helps build a positive relationship with that person.

16. Pay attention to feedback on your interpersonal skills.

Others may give you feedback on how you are doing in the interpersonal skills area. Listen to what co-workers, family and friends have to say. Implement their suggestions. You might even ask a trusted friend to let you know if you aren't being friendly, sounding too critical, etc. By using such feedback you can learn and grow in this area.

17. "Look for" interactions with others.

In an active workplace it is easy to avoid interactions with others. We can all look busy with paperwork and avoid making eye contact. Employees who do this will be seen as less approachable and less people-oriented than those who will at least nod or wave. If you are guilty of looking busy all of the time, try changing your approach. Look people in the eye and say hello as you pass them in the hallway. When at your desk, look up and make eye contact with those who pass near your office. By doing so you are telling others you are friendly and approachable.

18. Make interactions a win-win situation.

Some individuals see meetings and discussions as a means for them to get across their ideas in favor of others. This "contest" produces winners and losers. And may also cause the losers to not want to deal with the winners. When in situations like this, try to make them win-win by encouraging others to speak. On occasion, push the ideas of others, not just your own. This will lead to better interpersonal relations.

19. Be less defensive about your decisions.

Some employees become defensive if a co-worker or staff member suggests they were wrong. As a result, the co-worker will not want to interact with the person since they never listen to feedback. If you are receiving feedback from someone else, try to minimize answers like "Yes, but. . ." and instead listen more to what the person says. Then try to see if there are ways to make things better in the future. Be willing to accept responsibility for your actions, and own up where needed. Too much defensiveness will discourage others from ever giving you suggestions or ideas.

20. Be more accepting of others.

We are all different and unique, and for some people this becomes a problem. They avoid people who they see as different. Avoid this trap by accepting others who may be different than you, looking for their good qualities, and trying to build a solid working relationship. Others should not be looked down upon just because they have different backgrounds, hobbies, or interests than your own.

21. Be more relaxed and open.

When the workplace is busy, it is easy to forget people and interacting with them. We may focus so much on tasks that we take little note of people. Try to communicate an image of being relaxed and open even when you are busy. Make people feel you really want to get to know them and that this isn't at the bottom of your priority list. If you are too busy right now, then arrange another time to meet, have lunch or go on a break together. Show a genuine concern for the "people side" of business.

22. Get involved in more away-from-work social activities.

Many of us have a busy work life and a busy home life. To ensure that we do not become too self-centered, we should broaden contacts away from work. By increasing friendships on the outside, the skills learned can be brought back to the job. These contacts can be made in pursuing hobbies, clubs, church activities, or community events. You can broaden you circle of friends and increase interpersonal skills by volunteering for some of these activities.

23. Keep a scorecard on your interpersonal relations.

Try to keep track of how you are doing in interpersonal relations with others. For example, how often have you given out positive comments to others in the past week versus being critical or sarcastic. You may be surprised at the pattern. By keeping track, you can gauge your progress and make improvements where needed. When changes have been noted, be certain to reward yourself for improving in the interpersonal skills area.

Recommended Readings

Bolton, Robert and Bolton, Dorothy Grover. *Social Style/Management Style: Developing Productive Work Relationships*. New York: AMACOM, 1984.

Boyer, Glen L. Are You User Friendly? Learn to Effectively Use People Resources for More Effective Management. *Administrative Management*, August, 1986, 47, p. 11-14.

Brinkman, Rick and Kirschner, Rick. *Dealing with People You Can't Stand: How to Bring Out the Best in People at Their Worst*. New York: McGraw-Hill, 1994.

Buzawa, Dorothy J. Working with Difficult People. *Management World*, Jul-Aug, 1988, p. 17-19.

Carnegie, Dale. *How to Win Friends and Influence People* (Rev. ed.). New York: Simon and Schuster, 1981.

Clinard, H.H. *Winning Ways to Success with People: Seven Powerful Skills*. Houston, TX: Gulf Publishing Company, 1986.

Costley, Dan I., and Todd, Ralph. *Human Relations in Organizations* (3rd ed.). St. Paul, MN: West Publishing Co, 1987.

Fernandez, John P. *Managing a Diverse Workforce: Regaining the Competitive Edge*. Lexington, MA: Lexington Books, 1991.

Garner, Alan. *Conversationally Speaking: Tested Ways to Increase Your Personal and Social Effectiveness*. New York: McGraw-Hill, 1991.

Harris, Philip and Moran, Robert. *Managing Cultural Differences*. Houston: Gulf Publishing, 1987.

Kruper, Karen R. and Kruper, Joseph J. Jerks at Work. *Personnel*, June, 1988, 67, p. 68-75.

Nelton, Sharon. How to Win Friends for Half a Century. *Nation's Business*, Dec, 1986, 74, p. 40-41.

Turner, Steve and Weed, Frank. *Conflict in Organizations: Practical Solutions Any Manager Can Use*. Englewood Cliffs, NJ: Prentice-Hall, 1983.

3

Writing Skills

This chapter helps improve performance in the following areas:

- Writing memos and letters.
- Writing reports and manuals.
- Writing mechanics—organizing ideas, writing style, grammar, etc.

Action Items for Improving Writing Skills

1. Write with a specific audience in mind.

As with verbal communications, writing is more effective when a specific audience is kept in mind at all times. Who are you writing for? What do they know about the subject? What is their level of interest? What will they want to get out of your written information? By answering these questions in advance you can ensure effective communications. Walk a mile in the shoes of your audience before writing. Put in the appropriate facts, details, and amount of information that your audience would like to hear. Do not write a memo or report that pleases you, but one that will please your readers. Keep the audience in mind at all times when writing.

2. Keep jargon to a minimum.

Probably one of the most serious errors in writing is to write above the heads of your audience—to use jargon that they are not familiar with. Writers commonly use words that are in their everyday vocabulary. However, just because you are familiar with the terms is no assurance that your readers know the words. You may end up confusing the reader rather than clarifying matters.

A simple rule of thumb is to avoid all jargon or technical terminology that your audience is not familiar with. If you absolutely must use a jargon term, then define it for your readers. It is also useful to have a non-technical person, such as a staff assistant, critique your writing. Have this person let you know if you are using terms that people outside the department are unfamiliar with. Make changes where needed to eliminate jargon.

3. Keep written communications brief.

With the pace of work being so rapid, many complain that there just is not enough time to do everything necessary. In-baskets easily get overloaded with paper. Keep this in mind when preparing written communications. That beautifully detailed report of yours may never be read by someone else because it is too intimidating to even **start** reading. And you may later wonder why someone has not implemented the actions you laid out at the end of the report. The simple solution is to keep written communications brief. Offer people the opportunity to discuss the rationale, details, etc. with you if they desire, but do not put this into your write-up.

4. Use outlines to help organize ideas.

Many writers complain that they just do not know where to begin. As a result they struggle for a long time with that first sentence and first paragraph. It is always useful to start your writing by creating a brief outline of what you want to cover. If nothing else, brainstorm a "laundry list" of all of the topics you need to address. Then go back and organize these ideas into an outline. Your actual writing is nothing more than expanding each idea in the outline into several sentences. The writing will come much easier if you know where you are going with it by using an outline.

5. Make use of headings and sub-headings.

Lengthy memos or reports can be very confusing if the reader does not know where the writer is going. Break up any material longer than one page into sections. These sections may correspond to the outline you have compiled. Then write in headings or sub-headings to title each section. This will make it easier for the reader to follow and will be particularly useful if the reader wants to go back and reference a certain section of the write-up. Limit the length of each section to no more than four paragraphs.

6. Keep paragraphs short.

Lengthy paragraphs are difficult for readers to follow. Readers can easily get lost in lengthy paragraphs and such reading appears intimidating. Some professions (e.g., attorneys, scientists) have a habit of writing in lengthy paragraphs since most of the articles or technical materials they see are written this way. Yet most business correspondence that managers and other employees see is written very differently—short paragraphs being the norm. To make your writing as effective as possible for people in the workplace, keep paragraphs brief—no more than four sentences per paragraph unless the sentences are very short. This will increase the likelihood that your writing is read and understood by your audience.

7. Use simple, declarative sentences.

Some materials (e.g., legal documents) are famous for having extremely lengthy sentences that must be re-read several times to comprehend. Many technical manuals and reference works are also written this way. Once again, this style is not appropriate for most readers outside of the technical area. Short, simple sentences tend to be the norm for most business memos and letters since they make for quicker reading and comprehension. If you are someone who writes in very lengthy sentences, break up a long sentence into two or more individual sentences. Try to eliminate clauses linked together with semi-colons. Instead, keep sentences simple and direct.

8. Use visual aids in your writing.

Visual aids often help explain ideas that are hard to get across in words. A table or graph can illustrate numbers and trends better than explaining them in words. Evaluate your own writing to see if it can be helped by some sort of visual aids. Keeping the visual simple will make it easy to prepare and easy for your audience to understand. Only the necessary facts and figures should be included in your visual aid.

9. Use a personal computer for writing.

Many employees have adapted to computers and use them in their everyday work. Others are reluctant to try a personal computer for writing and this can actually hamper their writing effectiveness. First of all, computers make it easy to store form letters and common tables that can be modified for a specific application. This saves time in not having to write these materials from scratch. Second, many word processing software packages have a spelling checker, thesaurus, and even grammar checkers. This can not only help correct errors, but make you a better writer as well. In addition, the use of PCs by all can save staffing since secretaries will not have to type memos, letters, etc. from handwritten copies. Last, the PC makes it easier to edit than when "cutting and pasting" with handwritten material. Everyone in the workplace today, even managers, should try using PCs for their writing if at all possible.

10. Copy the writing style of someone else.

Writing technique can be improved by copying the writing style of someone else. If a memo or letter comes across your desk that you really like, take time to evaluate it. What makes it effective? How were the ideas organized? What sort of writing style was used? By answering these questions, you can identify how to improve your own writing. Ask your boss or peers for a memo, report, or letter that they felt was very well done. After you find a good model, try to write in a similar way.

11. Include completed samples in your writing.

Written matter is always improved if you can include completed samples. For example, it is very useful to show a completed form rather than just tell people how to fill out the form. If the letter or memo you are writing encourages people to fill out some materials, think of including a sample which is already completed for their reference. They can then use the sample as a model for completing their own.

12. Use an "executive summary" for longer materials.

Some employees make the mistake of not summarizing longer reports, memos, policies, etc. Given that many managers have a limited time to read, it is best to include a brief summary page at the beginning. In this way the manager can understand what is in the report or memo without having to read all of the details. If they are interested in the details, they can go through the remainder of the write-up or request the entire write-up from you. Think of including an executive summary for any write-up that exceeds two pages. Use this for **all** people that you write to, not just senior managers.

13. Spend more time proofreading written materials.

Some employees are good at writing, but do not take the time to carefully proofread materials before they are sent out. The result may be typos, incorrect facts, or other problems. Readers may conclude that the person who wrote the material cannot spell, is not very smart, etc. Care should be taken to ensure that all written materials are accurate before they are sent out. You should check the materials personally and have someone else do likewise if possible. The net result will be a higher-quality product.

14. Increase your vocabulary.

As mentioned earlier, jargon and technical terms should not be used in your writing if at all possible. However, some people may have difficulty finding the right words for getting their ideas across— they need to build their vocabulary without sounding too technical. This can be done by working crossword puzzles, playing word games like Scrabble, using a thesaurus, and looking up and writing down new words that are encountered. Vocabularies can be built up by adding a few words each day.

15. Use care in deciding who to send memos to.

There are two possible errors that can be made in sending out
materials: (1) sending a copy to people who do not need it; and (2)
not sending a copy to those who do need it. Our experience has
been that the second mistake is more common than the first one,
though both can occur in the workplace. The solutions are the same
in both cases: carefully think through who needs to have a copy
of what you just wrote or received. Questions that should be asked
include:

- Who needs to see this?

- Whose area does this impact?

- Will I be adding irrelevant paper to someone's in-basket if I send
  them this?

- Will others be able to do their job more effectively by seeing this?

Think of potentially sending the material to a variety of people—
your boss, staff, peers, those in other parts of the company. Work
up the final list based upon those who would really benefit from
the material. Follow up if you are unsure of someone's interest in
receiving such material.

16. Build more persuasive, logical arguments.

The majority of written reports, memos, and letters have the intent
of persuading someone else. That persuasiveness may be subtle, but
should be there in most written communications. We are at least
trying to persuade others of our knowledge and expertise if we are
not trying to persuade them to undertake a certain course of action. Increase the persuasiveness of your written materials if they
currently do not lead to conclusions and recommendations.
Organize the flow of your ideas to lead to a logical conclusion. Include a recommendations section if it is unclear on what should
be done. Use cost/benefit arguments to support your recommendations.

17. Make periodic follow-ups to your written material.

One way to continually improve your writing is to follow up on it with others. Ask those on your mailing list how they felt about your recent memo or report. Was it clear? Concise? Did they read all of it? Was there anything that could have been improved upon? Ask people to be very candid with you—tell them you are always interested in feedback. Look at their suggestions with an open mind. Make changes that will improve the quality of your writing.

18. Add transitions to your writing.

The writing of some individuals has no flow. The text seems to jump abruptly from idea to idea. What this writing lacks is the use of transition statements to end one section and begin the next. Sample transition statements are the following:

- The third factor affecting our profits is . . .

- Next, our committee looked at offices outside of the metro area.

- . . . suggests that we purchase the new company. As for financing the purchase, . . .

Transition statements give organization to the reader—they are like signs that tell you where you are going. They make the reading more easy to follow. Review your own writing to see if you use them, and incorporate changes where needed.

19. Break long writing projects into several pieces.

Lengthy writing projects, such as training manuals, can be difficult for many to undertake. Those who struggle with longer writing assignments should think of breaking such work into manageable pieces after creating a general outline. Then treat each segment as a stand-alone piece with targeted beginning and completion dates, and its own outline. The execution of the entire project will be easier if it is seen as a series of separate pieces rather than one large project. Use this approach with any lengthier, long-term writing projects that you have.

20. Use away-from-work writing to build skills.

Some employees, perhaps those in the production area, may have little, if any, opportunity to do writing on the job. Upon being promoted to a new area, writing may be a part of the new job responsibilities, making for a difficult transition. To aid in the transition, employees might want to practice writing at home to build additional skills. Keeping a diary or log of recent activities is a good way to practice writing simple, declarative sentences. Doing this daily will help build many of the skills that can be transferred to the job in writing letters or memos. Employees with limited writing experience should think of this as well as classroom training.

21. State clear actions in your writing.

Many types of business communications request that certain actions be taken. Some writers forget to call for actions or bury the actions at the end of a paragraph. If this is true in your writing, be certain to clearly state what these actions should be. Have a stand-alone section calling for the next steps or action items and label it as such. Use bold type or capital letters to make the actions stand out from the rest of the text. In longer reports, you will want to be certain to have the action items in your summary which is presented in the cover materials. It is best to clearly state what actions should be taken, rather than leave it to the reader to figure this out independently.

22. Ask others to critique your writing.

One way to ensure that your writing improves is to have someone critique it for you periodically. Think of someone at your company who writes well. Seek them out and compliment them on their good writing. Tell them you are trying to improve your writing and would like to have some feedback. This person might periodically review your written material and recommend changes. Be certain to learn from their comments by finding out not only what they recommend changing but why it should be changed.

Recommended Readings

Anastasi, Thomas E. *Desk Guide to Communication* (2nd ed.). New York: Van Nostrand Reinhold, 1981.

Brooks, Julie K. and Stevens, Barry A. *How to Write a Successful Business Plan.* New York, NY: AMACOM, 1987.

Brusau, Charles T.; Alred, Gerald J.; and Odiu, Walter E. *The Business Writer's Handbook* (3rd ed). New York: St. Martin's Press, 1987.

Carr-Ruffino, N. *Writing Short Business Reports.* New York, NY: McGraw-Hill, 1979.

Ceccio, J.F. *Communication in Business* (4th ed). New York: Wiley, 1986.

Cole, Diane. Putting Word to Work: A Persuasively Penned Memo Can Sell Your Ideas and Boost Your Career. *Savvy,* July, 1985, 6, p. 32-33.

Corbett, E.P.J. *The Little English Handbook: Choices and Conventions* (2nd ed.). New York: Wiley, 1977.

Dumaine, Deborah. *Write to the Top: Writing for Corporate Success.* New York: Random House, 1983.

Holtz, H. *Persuasive Writing: Communicating Effectively in Business.* New York: McGraw-Hill, 1983.

Lamphear, Lynn. *Short Cuts to Effective on the Job Writing: How to Achieve an Immediate Improvement in Your Business Letters, Memos, and Reports.* Englewood Cliffs, NJ: Prentice-Hall, 1982.

Murray, Donald. *Write to Learn.* New York: Holt, 1987.

Poe, R.W. *The McGraw-Hill Handbook of Business Letters.* New York: McGraw-Hill, 1988.

Roddick, Ellen. *Writing that Means Business: The Manager's Guide.* New York: MacMillan, 1984.

Smith, Leila R. *English for Careers.* New York: Wiley, 1981.

Strunk, William, and White, E.B. *The Elements of Style* (3rd ed). New York: MacMillan, 1979.

Westheimer, Patricia. *The Perfect Memo*. Glenview, IL: Scott, Foresman, 1990.

Westheimer, Patricia. *The Perfect Letter*. Glenview, IL: Scott, Foresman, 1990.

4

Listening

This chapter helps improve performance in the following areas:

- Ability to comprehend directions.
- Ability to remember what was said.
- Paying attention to others.
- Ability to listen effectively.
- Communicating with others more effectively.

Action Items for Listening

1. Show others you are a good listener through body language.

Part of being a good listener is showing others that you are interested in what they have to say. If you are mentally interested, but your body language says something else, the speaker will think you are not paying attention. The following are ways that you can show effective listening through body language:

- Maintain good eye contact.

- Lean forward to show interest.

- Face the person directly instead of turning to the side.

- Vary your facial expressions at points in the conversation.

- Nod your head periodically to indicate understanding.

- Make notes on what someone has said.

- Have an "open" body posture—relaxed, arms not folded.

These subtle, yet very important, indicators tell someone that you are listening to them. Evaluate your use of all of the body language signs. If you are not using the right body language, make changes accordingly.

2. Focus on the main points in a conversation.

Some individuals may pay attention in a conversation, but do not pick up the main points correctly. This can be a particular problem when the person speaking tends to ramble or give too many details. The solution is for the listener to focus on just the main points in someone's conversation. By searching for and retaining the main points, effective listening will be ensured. If unclear on what the speaker's main points are, simply ask the person to clarify during the conversation itself.

3. Restate the speaker's main points.

Those who have trouble remembering the main points of a conversation should try to periodically restate the speaker's main points. This is perhaps the single most important activity to aid in retention. Your restating of someone's ideas can be done mentally to yourself or out loud. The important point is to do this throughout the conversation to have better retention. The same technique can be used to remember someone's name. Upon meeting someone new, restate their name several times to yourself and link it to their face. You are more likely to remember them later if you restate the name.

4. Spend at least 50% of your time listening in a conversation.

The reason why some people are not good at listening is simply that they spend more time talking than listening. Many managers have this problem in particular since they frequently feel the need to give an opinion or make a decision. Evaluate how much time you spend listening versus talking in a conversation. Cut back the amount of talking that you do if you have a tendency to dominate the conversation. Try to have a balance in the amount of time spent listening versus talking. Managers may want to "error" in the direction of more listening than talking when interacting with their employees since studies have shown that effective managers spend 60% or more of their time listening.

5. Minimize distractions when talking with others.

Some people do not listen well because they let themselves get distracted during a conversation, making it hard to concentrate. Such people might take phone calls, or let people come into the office when they are conversing with someone else. Or they might shuffle papers, play with the phone cord, or in other ways distract themselves during a conversation. The net result: less retention of what was said and perhaps an unhappy speaker. The solution is to not let yourself get distracted during the conversation. Keep your hands free unless you use them to make notes. Try to resist taking phone calls or visits when talking with someone. The result will be better listening and comprehension.

6. Allow pauses in a conversation.

Some individuals, due to limited time, are uncomfortable with any pauses in a conversation. This brief time is seen by them as "down time" and they feel the need to fill in the void by speaking. Yet in many conversations, the speaker may need a moment to think, particularly if they have to make a decision or are concerned about something. Effective listeners recognize that brief pauses in conversations are normal and do not try to speed things up. Evaluate whether you tend to fill in these brief pauses, and if so, try to use more patience. Give the speaker a chance to say everything that is on their mind.

7. Read the body language of the speaker.

Just as it is important for the listener to use effective body language, it is also important to read the body language of others. Much of what we communicate comes through non-verbal communications. When verbal and non-verbal signs conflict, the non-verbals usually win out (consider your spouse storming around the house and slamming doors and cabinets while saying "I'm not mad"). Since body language is important, you must pay attention to it in a conversation. It may be more important than the words someone is saying.

When the speaker is upset or frustrated, you might see arms folded tightly, fists or teeth clenched, frowning, limited eye contact, or not facing you directly. Someone who is relaxed may show just the opposite. Paying attention to the signs is an important part of being a good listener. Learn to read body language accurately.

8. Verbalize your understanding of what someone has said.

Effective listeners make statements throughout a conversation to indicate that they understand. Samples of these statements are "I understand," "I see," or a simple "um-hum." It is still one other way to let people know that you are listening and understanding what they say. Evaluate whether you say statements to indicate you are listening to others. Add them if you do not use them now.

9. Focus on what is being said, not your next comment.

Poor listeners cannot wait to get their words in. While someone is still talking, these individuals are thinking about what they are going to say next instead of listening. The better approach is to wait till the other person is finished, then reply as needed. That way you are more likely to recall all of what was told you. Take the time to examine what you think of when others are speaking. Focus on them rather than your next reply.

10. Increase the empathy you have with others.

In some conversations, the speaker will share out concerns, frustrations, anger, or other emotions. Poor listeners do not react to this other than noting it. Effective listeners make an empathy statement whenever they detect emotion in what someone has said. Examples of empathy statements are as follows:

- "I can understand why you are upset about this."
- "I know it can be frustrating to not get promoted."
- "It must really be exciting to have won the award."

Empathy statements indicate understanding of what someone is feeling, not necessarily agreement. The failure to show empathy is like telling the other person you do not care, or you are not listening to them. You should use empathy statements throughout a conversation to indicate you recognize someone's emotional feelings.

11. Minimize your emotional reactions in a conversation.

Poor listeners let their emotions carry them away when they hear something upsetting. As a result, much of the conversation is forgotten, except the emotionally upsetting part. If you have a tendency to react very emotionally, try to reduce this during the conversation itself. Focus on getting all of the information and facts that are necessary.

12. Increase the use of open-ended questions.

The use of closed questions (questions that can be answered yes or no) reduces the amount of talking from the speaker. As a result, you will be doing most of the talking with the other person saying just a few words. If done repeatedly, conversations become a monologue rather than a two-way discussion. Good listeners try to draw out the other person. They ask open-ended questions to get at all of the ideas and feelings the other person has. Open-ended questions require someone to answer with many words. Examples of open-ended questions are as follows:

- "Tell me all about what you found out."

- "Describe the problem for me in your own words."

- "Tell me more about why you feel the way you do."

Examine the types of questions you ask during a conversation. If you ask only closed questions (or none at all), the conversation will be one-sided and you will not be seen as a good listener. Try to use more open-ended questions.

13. Summarize and clarify more often.

Good listeners use gaps in a conversation to summarize what someone has said. This is an excellent way to show an understanding of the other person. If you did not understand them correctly, they can clarify what they meant. This saves going further in a conversation with a misunderstanding. Try to summarize what the other person is saying periodically throughout a conversation.

14. Avoid jumping to conclusions.

Some people are quick to draw conclusions about what someone has said. Before they have obtained all of the information, they already have it figured out. Maybe this is because people who do this think they "have heard it before." On many occasions they may not have heard it before, and even if they have, the speaker feels they are not being paid attention to. It is better to listen to everything the person has to say and summarize what you think they are saying. Then draw conclusions and take any necessary action.

15. Read the other person's feelings as well.

Effective listening is not only hearing the words, but understanding the feelings behind the words. Many times people want us not only to understand the facts, but understand how they feel, what they are going through. Failure to understand this can limit communications. Body language will give you many clues to the person's feelings. If uncertain, try to draw out the person's feelings through open-ended questions. Don't be content with just knowing the what, but also the why.

16. Set up an open climate for listening.

People are more inclined to share out what they feel when the climate is open and friendly. We all enjoy talking with others who encourage us to say what we think. Poor listeners can discourage others from saying what they feel by criticizing what the other person says, downplaying their feelings, or not devoting their full attention. Evaluate the type of climate you set up when listening to others. Hold back until later a tendency to criticize or evaluate what someone has said. Draw the other person out by showing a genuine, sincere interest in what they have to say. Thank them for being candid, even if you disagree with their feelings. By doing this, you will be practicing better listening skills.

17. Avoid interrupting others when they are talking.

Probably the most aggravating thing a poor listener can do is interrupt someone while they are talking. We have all had this experience and know how frustrating it can be. There is no better way to show a lack of interest in what someone has to say than by constantly interrupting the person. Take stock of how often you interrupt when in a listening role. Try to eliminate this and allow the other person to finish what they have to say. Show more patience as a listener.

18. Try to view what someone says from their perspective.

Good listeners try to "walk a mile in someone else's shoes"—they try to understand the situation from the other person's perspective. This can be difficult to do, particularly if you disagree with the other person's position. Notice, however, that all these good listeners are doing is developing an **understanding** of someone else's feelings, not necessarily agreeing with them. Try to use this approach when you listen to someone else speak. Think of what they are saying from their perspective, and why this causes them to feel a certain way.

19. Make notes on what is being said.

Good listeners not only verbally show that they understand what someone is saying, but may write down important points as well. This is an excellent way to visibly show others that you are listening to them. It also ensures that you will more easily remember what was said since you can always go back and review what you wrote down. Ask yourself if you typically make notes if a peer, staff member or boss visits you and shares out information. If not, try to do more of this in the future.

20. Take a course on better listening.

Many colleges have continuing education courses that deal with listening skills. Such courses are also offered by some private training firms. These courses can help you learn more about listening in a positive environment. You may want to consider such courses after implementing the suggestions in this chapter and pursuing the readings at the end of this chapter.

21. Practice good listening at home.

One way to improve listening skills at the workplace is to practice such skills at home. Try to be a better listener with family and friends and see if it makes an impact on them. Practicing at home is usually easier than at the workplace. You may also get feedback more easily. Though it may sound strange, one way to practice better retention is by listening to talk shows on television. Pretend the speaker is talking to you, and pay attention to their main points by restating them as suggested earlier. See how much you can recall afterwards. It is an easy way to practice retention since you do not have to carry out a conversation with the person. Practice your new listening techniques at home, then apply them on the job.

Recommended Readings

Atwater, Eastwood. *I Hear You: Listening Skills to Make You a Better Manager*. Englewood Cliffs, NJ: Prentice-Hall, 1981.

Becker, Christine. Improving communication skills. *Public Management*, April, 1987, 69, p. 12-15.

Burley-Allen, Madelyn. *Listening: The Forgotten Skill*. New York: Wiley, 1982.

Glatthorn, Allan, and Adams, Herbert T. *Listening Your Way to Management Success*. Glenview, IL: Scott, Foresman, and Company, 1983.

Hulberg, Jack. Cultivating the Art of Listening. *Business Education Forum*, December, 1986, 11, p. 20.

Kiechel, Walter. Learn How to Listen. *Fortune*, August 17, 1987, 116, p. 107-108.

Lewis, David. The Art of Active Listening. *Training and Development*, July, 1989, 21-25.

McKay, Matthew; David, Martha; and Fanning, Patrick. *Messages: the Communication Book*. Oakland, CA: New Harbinger Press, 1983.

Nichols, Ralph G. Listening is a 10-part Skill. *Nation's Business*, September, 1987, 75, p. 40-41.

Reed, Warren H. How Well Do You Listen? *Savvy*, January, 1986, 7, p. 16-18.

Your Attention, Please. *Changing Times*, October, 1986, 40, p. 127-129.

5

Planning

This chapter helps improve performance in the following areas:

- Developing work plans.
- Planning the day's activities.
- Making long-range plans.
- Using goals and objectives.
- Strategic planning.

Action Items for Planning

1. Start with daily work plans.

Those who have limited experience in planning may find it easiest to begin by making daily work plans. Think of all the activities that need to be accomplished for each day, and ensure that the more important activities receive consideration. Put together a list of those activities that need to be done and use a check-off system as the day progresses. Many find it best to make daily work planning the very first activity they do each morning. If the rush of business prevents you from doing this, then come in earlier in the morning or stay late in the evening to make plans for the next day.

2. Extend planning to longer ranges.

Those who get in the habit of making daily work plans should try to extend the range of their plans. Think of longer-term plans for accomplishing goals for the department. Such plans might span a week, month, year, or even multiple years. The mechanics are the same as daily plans—think of what needs to be done, who will do it, target completion dates, etc. The challenge with long range plans is to monitor their ongoing achievement and ensure that they get accomplished. You need to periodically monitor your progress toward accomplishing longer-range goals.

3. Use a charting system for planning activities.

Poor planners try to keep plans "in their head" as they work along. This might work for just one person but makes it difficult to communicate the plans to others when needed. A charting system, such as a Gantt Chart, helps communicate the plan to others, be it peers, staff, or the boss. While there are many different planning charts, the most common would have columns with the following:

• A list of all activities that need to be done to accomplish the plan.

- A description of who will do each activity.

- Starting and completion dates for each activity.

- The impact the plan has on others.

- Resources other than people needed to accomplish the plan.

Regardless of the planning chart system you use, you will find it useful to visually display the plan itself. This makes it easier to monitor progress toward the plan and to communicate the plan to others who might be involved.

4. Implement goals and objectives in your area.

While many departments use goals and objectives, some have vague goals or none at all. Planning is useless unless you know where you want to go, so setting good goals and objectives is a prerequisite. If your goals and objectives leave something to be desired, set up a system such as Management by Objectives (MBO) in your area. Set targets for the year, month, or week. Be very specific in stating the outcomes that you want to accomplish with each goal, and make sure you can measure goal accomplishment. Then draw up specific plans for accomplishing each goal.

5. Devote time each day to accomplishing plans.

A problem affecting many in the workplace is that day-to-day busywork gets in the way of accomplishing goals and work plans. Phone calls, visits, paperwork, and other busywork can get in the way of important goals. The solution is to block off some time **each day** to work on specific goals and plans. Schedule a block of time for work toward goals just as you would schedule a meeting. If interruptions are a problem, try to close the door to your office or go into a conference room. The important point is to continually make progress toward accomplishing the important goals and plans for your area.

6. Seek out projects or jobs with planning responsibilities.

While every job provides some opportunities for planning, some jobs offer more potential than others. For example, jobs with project responsibilities offer many chances for planning while assembly-line work may offer limited opportunities. If you are in a job with limited planning opportunities, volunteer for projects that might allow you to do more planning. This might occur when starting up new equipment or production methods, reorganizing the department, or beginning special projects. By getting a chance to plan, you can build skills in this area.

7. Involve others in your plans.

It is rare that a plan can be designed, implemented, and used on an ongoing basis by just one person. If nothing else, others may benefit by knowing what you accomplished with your plan and may be able to use it on their own. And of course, your plan may more directly impact the work of others. For example, planning a change in how the company pays bills will impact virtually every department. Think of how other employees—staff, peers, and others—might be impacted by your plan, and involve them in the process early on. Let them know what you are planning to do and ask for their suggestions. By using a teamwork approach your plan will be much more successful.

8. Draw up contingency plans.

It would be nice to think that every plan can come off without any problems. Yet there are many things going on in any organization that can affect your plans. The key is to not abandon planning because of this, but to anticipate these problems and develop contingency plans for handling them. For each activity listed in your plan, think of what might go wrong. Then list out how you can correct these potential problems should they occur. By anticipating problems, you will be better prepared to handle them if they occur, and ultimately accomplish your goal.

9. Determine how your area can accomplish larger organization goals.

Good planners establish plans that are linked to larger company goals. For example, the company might have a goal to increase quality or sales by a certain target, or open additional offices, or centralize/decentralize certain departments. Good planners think of how they can help the company achieve these larger goals. They think of what can their department or area can do to contribute to the overall goal. Try to use this perspective yourself. Draw up plans for those areas you have in mind and take them to others for their approval. By helping accomplish larger goals, you can help your organization attain greater success.

10. Evaluate how changes in technology and demographics impact your area.

Effective planners try to anticipate the future as much as possible. They try to assess how larger changes going on in the world affect their area. For example, employee demographics have changed dramatically in the past few years. Technology has virtually revamped most companies and will continue to do so. Try to evaluate changes that you see going on in the world with a particular eye toward your area of responsibility. Could new technology change the way you or your employees do their jobs? Would this make you more effective? Try to identify the changes impacting your area, and plan an effective transition to make your area more effective.

11. Regard plans as dynamic and changing.

Some people avoid planning because they think too many things will change between the time the plan is drawn up and implemented. Or they regard the current way of doing things as "cast in concrete" and refuse to change. Both sets of attitudes lead to problems. There is constant change in the workplace, and this should be seen as an opportunity for improving the current way of doing things. Good planners value change and reevaluate and change plans whenever needed. Rather than abandon planning because of change, they use change as a reason to do more planning. See if you can use this perspective as well. Have an open mind to change and design and modify plans to deal with it.

12. Consider the resources needed to accomplish a goal.

Some individuals are good at planning for themselves, but fail to consider how other resources are needed to accomplish a larger goal. For example, implementing some new software in your department might require the resources of the systems department. Effective planners think of all of the other resources that might be needed to accomplish their plan. These resources might include people, money, equipment, or supplies. Think of all the resources required to accomplish each of your goals, and obtain approval for them where needed.

13. Reward yourself for accomplishing your goals.

It is important to note the accomplishment of goals. Try to reward yourself in some way for accomplishing each of your goals. Larger goals, which might involve a number of people, might be celebrated with a luncheon, after-work refreshments, or a letter of thanks. By using rewards, you will help ensure the continuation of planning and goal setting in your work. Involving others in sharing some modest reward ensures that teamwork will continue in helping accomplish future goals and plans.

14. Write clear goals for each plan.

Establishing clear goals is essential for drawing up good plans. There are several characteristics that make for clear goals. These are as follows:

- The goal should be specific ("increase sales by 10%" versus "increase sales.")

- The goal must be measurable.

- Action verbs (e.g., complete, implement, change) are preferred over passive verbs.

- The goal should be achievable by someone who works hard and has the right skills.

- Use a deadline for accomplishing the goal wherever possible.

By keeping in mind these characteristics, clear goals can be established, and concrete plans put together to accomplish the goals. Develop clear goals whenever possible.

15. Use a "linking pin" concept for your goals.

Poor planners see themselves as isolated departments or work areas that do not relate to other areas. Effective planners see a link between what they do and what others do. This "linking pin" concept is frequently in their minds and communicated to others. The link can be in several directions. First, your goals can be linked to larger company goals. Second, your goals can be linked to those of your peers since they are likely affected by what you do. Last, for those who have a staff, your goals are a roll-up of your staff's goals added to your personal goals. Having a linking pin perspective aids in setting, communicating, and accomplishing goals.

16. Break larger projectes into smaller ones.

Some employees are hesitant to implement plans beyond daily plans. They are fearful of the magnitude of long-range plans. The solution to this is to simply break up large plans into a series of smaller plans. Then flush out the specific activities needed to accomplish each of the smaller plans. By breaking a large plan into several "bite-size" pieces will make it easier to set up the plan and ultimately accomplish it. Think of doing this with any of your plans that may seem intimidating.

17. Plan social events to gain experience at planning.

Those employees who are new to planning might find it difficult to create work plans. One way to gain experience at planning is to let the employee plan out company social events such as department outings or parties. This is an easy way to test out the employee's abilities in a (hopefully) non-critical situation. The knowledge gained from this type of planning can be carried over to other kinds of planning back on the job. Think of developing planning abilities through the use of social events wherever possible.

18. Plan events at home to gain experience at planning.

Those inexperienced or new to planning might find it useful to plan events at home to gain experience. The planning of a vacation, hobby project, or fund-raising campaign, can all help develop the necessary skills that can be applied back on the job. Employees should try to identify planning projects at home that take more than a few days to accomplish. By setting goals and using a charting system, the employee will learn how to apply this back at the workplace. Reviewing the plan with a manager can help improve the learning process.

19. Anticipate problems in advance.

Good planners anticipate problems in the workplace before they occur. It is a bit like a baseball team covering the outfield differently for different hitters. When problems occur, the good planners are ready to handle them because of the advance thinking that they did. Think of the operations in your area and what types of problems might develop. Maybe it is a piece of equipment breaking or someone quitting their job. List out various plans that could be put into action should these problems occur. While you may hope that you never have to put these contingency plans into action, assembling them in advance enables you to do your job more effectively.

20. Use a calendar to monitor progress on your plans.

Employees who are good at planning use calendars of some sort to monitor the progress of their plans. Key target dates for each plan are put on the calendar and reviewed periodically. Target dates for more than one plan are superimposed on the same calendar, and this makes it easier to figure out the work load across projects. Some computer software programs also enable you to calendar dates and generate printouts of progress toward plans. Some sort of visual calendar system will greatly help monitor progress toward the accomplishment of plans.

21. Develop a "where are we going" perspective.

Poor planners focus on the past or merely the present. Better planners focus on the future. They think about where their area should be going in the future and how to improve its effectiveness. Try to develop this perspective yourself. Become more future oriented and think about where you want the area to be. For many, day-to-day activities consume their time, and no time is spent thinking about the future. But the effective planners make sure they take the time, even if it is in the evening or weekends, to plan out where they are going in the future.

22. Review progress periodically.

Probably the worst thing that can happen is for someone to put together a wonderful plan, then have it gather dust for the next several months. Progress on plans should be reviewed periodically, the time period dependent upon how long the plan takes to implement. Even annual plans should generally be reviewed every week or two to ensure progress and make changes where needed. Staff meetings or other similar events provide an excellent forum for reviewing progress with plans. If you do not have such meetings on a regular basis, then schedule them with those who are involved in accomplishing your plan. If the plan is a solo effort of your own, then check your progress independently every week or so. Reviewing the progress periodically ensures that the plan is not forgotten with all of the other activities going on.

Recommended Readings

Abell, Derek F. *Defining the Business: The Starting Point of Strategic Planning*. Englewood Cliffs, NJ: Prentice-Hall, 1980.

Allen, L. *Making Managerial Planning More Effective*. New York: McGraw-Hill, 1982.

Argenti, J. *Practical Corporate Planning*. Winchester, MA: Allen & Unwin, 1980.

Brooks, Julie K., and Stevens, Barry A. *How to Write a Successful Business Plan*. New York: AMACOM, 1987.

Georgoff, David M., and Murdick, Robert G. Manager's Guide to Forecasting. *Harvard Business Review*, Jan-Feb, 1986, 64, p. 110-115.

Gray, H. Uses and Misuses of Strategic Planning. *Harvard Business Review*, Jan-Feb, 1986, 64, p. 89-97.

Hammermesh, Richard G. Making Planning Strategic. *Harvard Business Review*, July-Aug, 1986, 64, p. 115-118.

Handbook of Business Planning for Executives with Profit Responsibility. Edited by Thomas S. Dudick and Robert V. Gorski. New York: Van Nostrand Reinhold Company, 1983.

Hussey, David E. *Introducing Corporate Planning* (3rd ed.). Oxford: Pergamon Press, 1985.

Kaufman, Roger. *Strategic Planning: An Organizational Guide*. Glenview, IL: Scott Foresman, 1991.

Kravetz, Dennis J. *The Human Resources Revolution: Implementing Progressive Management Practices for Bottom-Line Success*. San Francisco: Jossey-Bass, 1988.

Lorange, P. *Corporate Planning: An Executive Viewpoint*. Englewood Cliffs, NJ: Prentice-Hall, 1980.

Makridakis, Spyros. *Forecasting, Planning and Strategy for the 21st Century*. New York: The Free Press, 1990.

Marrus, Stephanie K. *Building the Strategic Plan: Find, Analyze, and Present the Right Information*. New York: Wiley, 1984.

Naisbitt, John. *Megatrends: Ten Directions Transforming Our Lives*. New York: Warner Books, 1982.

Radford, K.J. *Strategic Planning*. Englewood Cliffs, NJ: Reston Publishing Company (Prentice-Hall), 1980.

Schilit, Keith W. How to Write a Winning Business Plan. *Business Horizons*, Sept-Oct, 1987, 30, p. 30-32.

Stoltenberg, John. How to Cut a Monster Project Down to Size. *Working Woman*, March, 1987, 12, p. 118-119.

6

Organizing

This chapter helps improve performance in the following areas:

- Organizing your desk, files, and work area.
- Being able to locate memos, reports, etc. more easily.
- Clarifying job responsibilities.
- Running a more efficient area.

Action Items for Organizing

1. Organize your desk into "ABC" files.

Perhaps one of the most common problems with poor organization is having a messy desk full of papers and not being able to locate anything. It happens to many people and gives an impression of not being organized. The solution is to organize every piece of paper on your desk into an "A, B, or C" file. Briefly, these files represent the following:

- "A" file—memos, letters, etc. that must be responded to relatively quickly and have a high priority.

- "B" file—material that must eventually be read and dealt with, but has a lower priority right now.

- "C" file—reading material of low priority (e.g., flyers from outside vendors) that will be looked at only if time permits. This file is normally kept in a lower desk drawer.

Each time a new piece of paper comes across your desk, classify it into the appropriate file, and rank-order it within the file. Material can change files, for example, going from "B" to "A." If the "C" file is not looked at within a week or two, simply discard it and start a new "C" file.

2. Set up a category system for everything you do.

Poorly organized people do not classify the things they do into categories. As a result they have a hard time locating materials and working efficiently. A motto for them to follow is "everything in its place." Try to categorize all of your projects, papers, etc. into categories. For example, there might be a category called "bills to be paid," another for "special accounting project," another for "performance appraisals," and so on. Production workers might put their tools and reference materials into categories in the same manner. As a result of doing this, you will be more able to locate the materials you need and work more efficiently. Keep using your category system as more memos, etc. are added in the area. Create new categories whenever they are needed. Ask for help in setting up you initial categories if you need assistance.

3. Place materials into appropriate file folders.

Probably every employee in an office environment, and many production employees, would benefit by keeping a box of empty manila file folders in their desk. As you start new projects, take out a manila file folder and label it. Place all of the related materials in this folder from the very beginning, and keep adding to it. Keep the folder handy, for example, in your desk drawer, if you are working on the project frequently. Move the file to another file cabinet or storage area when the project is complete. Getting into the habit of quickly creating file folders will ensure that you never get disorganized.

4. Try to use a personal computer if possible.

One nice thing about using a personal computer in your work is that it **forces** you to organize materials into categories. For example, after you write a memo on a PC you are forced to name the file and, in many systems, place the file into a directory you created. This forced filing makes it easier to keep track of written matter. And there is the important added benefit of not having to keep paper copies around to clutter up your desk. Since filing on a computer is electronic, you can create and store tremendous amounts of material without adding one piece of paper to your desk. Think of using a PC if at all possible in your work.

5. Clean off your desk each evening.

Poorly organized people keep accumulating more and more material on their desks each day. They may have buried under the clutter a file folder from a project they worked on weeks ago. More organized people clean off their desks each and every evening. They replace file folders or reference books where they belong. An ongoing project folder might be placed in the top desk drawer where it can be pulled out early the next morning. The only things remaining on the desk in the evening are desk accessories. Try to get in this habit yourself. Clean off your desk each evening to reduce the amount of clutter.

6. Improve the work flow in your area.

Take the time to analyze how the work flows into and out of your area. Are there things that can be done differently? Are there bottlenecks that slow down the flow of work? Managers should look at their own desks as well as those of their employees. If your work flow is not efficient, draw up another plan and discuss it with the appropriate employees. Chances are these other employees will appreciate any suggestions for improving work flow as well. Implement the changes that will improve the functioning of your area.

7. Model your area after those who are well organized.

If you are having trouble organizing your area, you might want to spend time with someone whose organization you admire. This might be a colleague in-house or someone at another organization who you know. Ask them for suggestions on how you can improve your organization and see how they run their area. List out the improvements you think will apply to your own area. Then implement the ideas which are effective ones. You can definitely learn from the experience of those who are well organized.

8. Clarify your job responsibilities.

A poorly organized area might stem from people not knowing exactly what to do. Is this true of your area? Are you clear on what your responsibilities are? Is it clear who does what between you and your peers? Are there any fuzzy areas which need clarifying? If the answer to any of these questions is yes, take the time to clarify your job responsibilities (and those of your staff if applicable). Meet with your boss and/or peers to list out more clearly who does what.

Try to keep the focus positive—you do not want a "turf" battle, but merely to work more effectively together. By clarifying who does what, the company will be better organized and more productive.

9. Improve your span of control.

This action item is applicable only for those who have other employees reporting to them. An area may be poorly organized if too many or too few employees report to a given manager. Too many reports may spread you too thin while too few may lead to over-managing. Take the time to look at your organization. Do you have too many or too few direct reports? Would the situation be improved by reorganizing in a different way? Try to put your ego aside when looking at the span of control and also avoid the tendency to think "this is the way we've always been organized." Look at other changes with an open mind. Implement those that make sense and help improve your organization.

10. Bring in new technology to improve your area.

Part of being well organized is making sure employees have the proper equipment to do their jobs effectively. Are there tasks being done manually now that can be better done by machine? Are you (or your employees) using equipment that is outdated? While new equipment such as computers will cost money, this equipment can also increase productivity. Present your recommendations for new equipment with this in mind. Show how the benefits in improved productivity outweigh the costs of the equipment itself.

11. Eliminate a duplication of tasks.

Poor organization might result from more than one person performing some of the same tasks. This most commonly occurs across departments but can also occur within departments. You should evaluate your position in terms of duplication. Is there anyone else who does some of the same tasks you do? Have either of you ever been confused on who does what? If so, try to clarify who should best do these duplicated tasks. You might not only be confused yourself, but others in the organization might be confused as well. Eliminate the duplicated tasks to improve organization and productivity.

12. Improve the physical layout of your work space.

Part of being well organized is physical organization. How is your work space laid out? Do you have easy access to files and other materials that you use often? Are you close to those people that you need to interact with often? Is it easy for information to be exchanged with you? Your answers to these questions might be helped by studying the pattern of movement throughout the day. How often do you get up during the course of the day? Where do you go most often go? Who typically visits you? By answering these questions, a new and improved design of the work space may become apparent. Implement those changes you feel are helpful.

13. Better organize who makes decisions.

Another source of poor organization is how decisions get made. For example, making certain decisions at too high of a level can use up the valuable time of executives and under-utilize the time of those lower in the organization. In other cases, it may not be clear as to who has the authority to make certain decisions. If any of these problems exist in your area, try to get them clarified. Decide who best should make the types of decisions that are necessary in your area. Clarify this with all applicable parties and implement immediately. It can greatly improve the organization of your area.

14. Clean out files at least once a year.

Every work area can suffer from building up too many files and reference materials. This unnecessary clutter can get in the way of more important work. It can be a particular problem if you tend to be the type of person who does not throw things away. Examine the last time you have cleaned out your personal files and those of your area. Production employees may want to examine the last time they cleaned out storage rooms and the like. If it has been longer than one year since your last cleaning, make this a project immediately. You might find it easiest to come in on a weekend and clean out the files and storage rooms. Those materials that have not been referred to or used in a year or more should be discarded unless there are legal or other reasons for keeping them. Periodically cleaning out your area is still another way to improve organization.

15. Organize the flow of information to and from your area.

How does information come to your area? How does it leave the area? Are you keeping others informed of what you are doing? Are they informing you? Organization frequently breaks down with information flow between peers. In many cases, a peer will not receive needed information from a co-worker which could help them do their job. Or materials such as articles and memos may sit in someone else's in-basket for long periods of time before getting to the right person.

Examine the information flow into and out of your area. Keep your peers informed of what you are doing and share out written information that would be helpful for them. Encourage them to do the same to you. Try to avoid having materials sit in your in-basket for long periods of time that could be used by others. Put in process any mail procedures that can speed the flow of information.

16. Compile a desk manual for your area of responsibility.

Many people have procedures, policies, and the way they do their job "in their minds" rather than written down. That may work well until the person goes on vacation, or is transferred, or terminates. Then the area may seem disorganized until the new person gets up to speed. To avoid this problem, develop a desk manual which details how you do your job. Include only the essential procedures and activities. Write this as a "cookbook" so someone else can use it in a step-by-step fashion. While it may take time to write a desk manual, it can be extremely useful in keeping your area organized in your absence.

17. Ask whether you do tasks that are better done by someone else.

Each of us may be doing certain tasks that are better done by another person. For example, a manager may spend time going through the incoming mail when that may be better done by a secretary. A secretary might spend a great deal of time typing memos that could be written on a PC by a professional employee. Review the tasks that you do on your job. Are there any that could be delegated to someone else? Are there tasks done by others that should be done by you? Look at this process as a two-way street—you may delegate away or take on other tasks that simply fit your job better. The important point is to organize the tasks in the most productive way.

18. Re-organize your area by centralizing or decentralizing where needed.

Another aspect of effective organization is the degree to which activities are centralized. Evaluate your area with this in mind. Are there activities that you do which might be more effectively done in a centralized headquarters? Are there activities that you do which are better decentralized to others? You should approach this area with an open mind. The key is to improve the productivity of the area, so try to avoid making centralization a turf issue. Oftentimes, centralizing and decentralizing works both ways, with some activities being decentralized out and others coming back to a more centralized environment.

19. Practice organizing skills at home or in volunteer activities.

Organizing things at home can build the skills which are needed in the workplace. Paper-oriented materials which can be organized include receipts, recipes, mail, magazines, records, and so on. You can organize physical things such as tools, basement or garage storage areas, and furniture. By applying some of the practices mentioned earlier in the home environment, you can practice organization skills in another setting. What you learn from your experience at home can be applied back on the job.

20. Survey others to assess better ways to organize your area.

Sometimes we are too close to a problem to be able to objectively assess it. This might apply to the way you are organized. Ask for the opinion of customers, peers, bosses, or those in other parts of the organization. If necessary, hire a consultant to review how to organize your area better. Take the feedback you get as constructive help. It may involve changing things that you set up yourself in the past. Yet if the new ideas can improve the organization of the area, it is in your best interest to use them.

Recommended Readings

Bain, D. *The Productivity Prescription: The Manager's Guide to Improving Productivity and Profits*. New York: McGraw-Hill, 1982.

Balderston, Jack. *Improving Office Operations*. New York: Van Nostrand Reinhold Company, 1985.

Bonoma, Thomas V., and Slevin, Dennis P. *Executive Survival Manual*. Belmont, CA: CBI Publishing Company, 1978.

The Dartnell Office Administration Handbook (6th ed.). Chicago: Dartnell Corporation, 1984.

Douglass, Merrill E., and Douglass, Donna N. *Manage Your Time, Manage Your Work, Manage Yourself*. New York: AMACOM, 1978.

End-of-the-Year Suggestions from the Desks of Three Creative Secretaries. *Creative Secretary's Letter* (Englewood Cliffs, NJ: Prentice-Hall), Nov 16, 1988, p. 95.

Here's How You Can Meet Your Deadlines—Set Up a Game Plan. *Creative Secretary's Letter* (Englewood Cliffs, NJ: Prentice-Hall), Nov 30, 1988, p. 104.

Januz, Lauren R., and Jones, Susan K. *Time Management for Executives*. New York: Charles Scribner's Sons, 1981.

Lakein, Alan. *How to Get Control of Your Time and Your Life*. New York: P.H. Wyden, 1973.

Miller, G. Make Better Use of Your Time. *Supervision*, Oct, 1987, 49, p. 9-10.

Prevent Missing Papers with One Quick Checklist. *Creative Secretary's Letter* (Englewood Cliffs, NJ: Prentice-Hall), Nov 30, 1988, p. 99.

Terry, George R., and Stallard, John J. *Office Management and Control* (8th ed.). Homewood, IL: R.D. Irwin, 1980.

Timpe, A. Dale. *The Management of Time*. New York: Kend Publishing, 1987.

Winston, Stephanie. *The Organized Executive: A Program for Productivity*. New York: Norton, 1983.

7

Setting Priorities and Managing Time

This chapter helps improve performance in the following areas:

- Working more efficiently.
- Making better use of time.
- Getting the most important activities done first.
- Setting priorities.
- Reducing the amount of down time.

Action Items for Setting Priorities and Managing Time

1. Touch a piece of paper only once.

A problem many employees have is to waste time by going back to the same work repeatedly. For example, you might receive a three-page memo from someone. At first you scan the memo to see what it is about. Then you put it aside thinking you will read it later when you have more time. Over the next week or two you run across the memo several times, briefly scanning it each time but never dispensing with it. All of this activity wastes time, and contributes to unnecessary clutter.

A good rule to keep in mind is to touch a piece of paper only once or twice. Do not scan things multiple times, then go back and read them later. Instead, read the material all the way through and dispense with it by filing it, forwarding it, etc. Or, place the memo in your "to-do" file and thoroughly read it later. The key is to avoid briefly scanning and touching the memo multiple times. By practicing this rule, you will use your time more efficiently.

2. Review the "ABC" files each day.

In the chapter on organization, we discussed setting up "ABC" files for classifying all of your work. These files reflect higher and lower priorities, with the materials in each file being rank-ordered when they are initially placed in the file. Once ABC files are established, you should review them each morning, and switch materials across files as needed. Then rank-order the materials within the "A" file so that the highest priority items are on top. This helps you review all of the things that need to be done and the relative priority of each.

3. Establish a tickler file.

For those not using an ABC file system, it is helpful to use a tickler file. The tickler file is simply a folder containing reminders of things that need to be done. These reminders might be memos that require a response, notes to yourself, or phone messages that require more research before you can reply. It is best to rank-order each morning the priority of the items in the tickler file. Then work through the items in the order in which they are ranked.

4. Compile daily lists of things that need to be done.

One method which is helpful in managing time and priorities is to compile a daily list of those things to accomplish that day (some may want to use a weekly list instead). This enables you to see on one sheet of paper all of the activities that need to be done. The list itself should be made up of those items you have in your tickler file or "A" file, depending upon which you are using. Most find it helpful to compile the daily list in the morning before interruptions have started. Others like to compile the list of the next day's activities before they leave for the evening. Use the system that you feel works best for you.

5. Manage interruptions more effectively.

One problem that many have in the workplace is that interruptions interfere with carrying out the priorities of the day. Reports, memos or other activities do not get done because of phone calls, personal requests, or memos that come across the desk during the course of the day. The solution to this problem is to not regard each interruption as the highest priority. Instead, rank order the interruptions which require action against the other items on your list (see Action Item 4 above). Insert the new items in the appropriate slot on the list and keep working through the items in the new order. This will ensure that the important things still get done first.

6. Block off time for project work.

Some individuals can never find time for project work. Day-to-day phone calls, visits from co-workers, administrative paperwork, and meetings consume most of the day. That special project never gets done because of time spent on other activities. Employees who are effective in managing time will block off periods for project work (or for writing memos, reports, etc.). The time blocked off is treated just like a meeting, with no other interruptions allowed to occur. If necessary, the employee might go to a conference room or someone else's office to concentrate on the project. Try using this approach to see if you can get more project work completed.

7. Use mornings for the most difficult work.

Normally, mornings are best for the most difficult work you have to do. At this time, most employees are relaxed, fresh, and have a higher energy level. Waiting till the end of the day may not prove effective since individuals are more likely to be tired at that time. Many employees schedule daily activities so they can coast downhill, with the most difficult activities coming first and the easiest (e.g., reading) coming at the end of the day. What is a difficult activity for you may be different than for others. Some people might find writing a long report or policy a difficult task. For others, having a long meeting might be the most difficult. Think of what is the most difficult for you to do, and schedule that activity early.

8. Check off and reward yourself for activities completed.

Many employees have found it psychologically helpful to check off items on their to-do list as they are completed. It is even more satisfying for many to crumble up that piece of paper with a completed activity listed on it. By eliminating the completed item from your desk, you can visually see that progress is being made and get some minor psychological satisfaction as well. When an activity is completed, reward yourself as well. Take a brief break after writing several memos. Take a day off after completing a major project. Using rewards and a check-off system will help you get through the items on your priority list.

9. Save reading for late in the day, or evenings or weekends.

The incoming mail can serve as a source of distraction for many people. By taking the time to read flyers or magazines, valuable company time can be wasted. Try to avoid reading general mail if you can during the middle of the day. Read it late in the day only if time permits. Otherwise take it home for evening or weekend reading, read it on the train or airplane, or simply discard it. If possible, have a secretary or assistant separate important from less important mail. The main point is to be certain that your prime working hours are not spent reading unimportant mail.

10. Reduce the amount of "down time" you have.

Employees in the workplace typically spend a brief amount of time in informal conversations with others, be it about the recent ball game, the weather, or whatever. Similarly, brief phone conversations with family or friends at home are very common at the office. Care must be taken as to how long these conversations go on, and with how many people they go on with each day. Some employees may never get to their more important responsibilities because of too much down time. Try to become more aware of how much down time you have—how long do your informal conversations go on? Eliminate or reduce the amount of time spent in unnecessary conversation with others (or shift it to after hours or at lunch).

11. Keep an activity log of how you spend your day.

Employees are sometimes surprised by the amount of time they spend in certain activities. For example, personal phone calls may seem just like a couple of minutes, but can actually be much longer. One way to get a handle on how you spend your day is to keep an activity log for a few days. On a blank sheet of paper write in the various hours that you are typically in. Then fill in entries for literally everything you do, such as personal phone calls, meetings, paperwork, etc. Leave room to write in a brief note on what type of meeting, phone call, or paperwork you just completed. Fill in the log for several days.

After completing this log, summarize what you found. How much time was spent in meetings? How much on the phone? Paperwork? Down time? Draw some conclusions. Are there things you are spending time on that are better done by someone else? Is there too much down time? Are important activities done at times when you are most productive, such as in the morning? Make changes that will enable you to be more productive and make a better use of your time.

12. Manage your away-from-work activities effectively.

The efficient use of time on the job can be increased by managing time away from the job effectively. It has been shown that people who are effective in using their time do so both on the job and away from work. They follow the same procedures described in this chapter for the management of time at home. Inventory your use of time at home. For example, do you find it difficult to find time to exercise or read, or pursue other activities of interest to you? If so, schedule a block of time for each of these activities just as you would schedule a meeting at the office. Inventory your use of time at home. How much time is spent listening to television or music? Is it more than it should be? You effective management of time at home will transfer back to the job, so use good practices.

13. Run meetings effectively.

Many employees feel there is too much time spent in meetings, and that this prevents them from getting other things done. What that usually means is that the meeting they attended was unproductive, or there was no need for them to be there. While you cannot control other people's meetings, you can run your own meetings effectively. Be sure to invite the right people—give those who may not need to be there the option of attending. Once the meeting is started, keep things on track. Do not let war stories or tangents go on for very long. Tactfully suggest getting back to the next point. Prepare and distribute an agenda so everyone knows what has to be covered and in what order. The effective running of meetings will help everyone manage their time better.

14. Calendar important due dates.

Part of managing time effectively is to know and anticipate when certain milestones are approaching. Be sure to calendar the key dates when various projects or other activities fall due. Go through you calendar each day to refresh your memory on what activities need to be done in the near future. Compare your calendar due dates against the items in your tickler or "A" file. Then determine which need to be done first and complete them in priority order.

15. Return phone calls early or late in the day.

For many, returning phone calls becomes a game of "telephone tag"—messages get traded back and forth without reaching the other party. The net result is that both parties waste time that could have been used more productively. One solution to the problem is to return phone calls when people are most likely to be available. More often than not that is very early in the day or very late in the day (the lunch hour is another possibility for some). Normally, employees do not schedule meetings at these times, so you are more likely to reach them. Try returning your calls early or late when you should have a better success rate. By doing so you will be able to better manage your time.

16. Spend some time each day on important goals and objectives.

A problem for many is that busywork and interruptions use up much of the day. Those important objectives that you have may not get worked on. To ensure that this does not happen, block off a portion of each day to concentrate on your important objectives for the year. Calendar the time just as you would for a meeting or luncheon. Try to work on the goals without interruption. If necessary, go to a conference room or other quiet location. By doing so each day, you will ensure that important, larger goals, such as increasing sales or developing a training manual, are accomplished.

17. Eliminate the feeling that "everything is a top priority."

Some employees lament that they have nothing put top priorities to work on all day. They may not see the difference between something that is truly urgent and something that is less urgent. If this is a problem for you, try to force a ranking of the choices that you have. Ask the following questions to assist in ranking the alternatives:

- What would happen if this activity were not done?

- How big of an impact does the activity have on the company/department?

- Can someone else do this activity in my place?

By answering such questions, you can prioritize your activities and think of other possible ways of getting them done. If you are still struggling with this, ask your boss for some advice. Managers, by being in a higher position, can help determine which activities are most important to do first. By knowing how your manager thinks will help you make these decisions on your own.

18. Reduce putting off activities.

It is tempting to delay that big, intimidating project by saying you will start it when you "have more time." Some people like to procrastinate, particularly when a large project is to be started. There is probably no better time than now to start that large project. If the entire project is too large, break it into smaller, easier-to-manage pieces. Then take on the smaller pieces individually. This will make it easier to manage your time and helps with progress toward completing the larger project.

19. Reduce the total number of activities you have.

Some individuals get involved in a very large number of activities. They are named to virtually every committee in the company, are very active in charitable work, professional associations, community activities, sports, etc. Eventually they reach the point of no return, where no matter how well they manage their time, there simply is not enough to go around. If you are in this situation, evaluate all of the activities you are involved in. Are some really needed? Should you "retire" from some of the activities that you have done for several years? By carefully selecting the number of activities you pursue, you can use your time more productively. Make the changes that are needed.

20. Increase the work hours you put in.

This sounds pretty obvious, but there are many people who complain about not having enough time, yet manage to arrive and leave work very promptly every day. Someone once said that the most productive hours are those hours after 5:00 (or before every one gets in). If you are having trouble doing all of the tasks that are required of you, take time to evaluate how many hours you actually put in. While there is no magic answer on how many hours to work, putting in the minimum required may not be enough to get everything done. You should try to increase your hours for work on those projects or activities that there is insufficient time for during the regular day.

Recommended Readings

Alessandra, T., and Catheart, J. A Guide for Managing Time. *Marketing Communication*, April, 1985, p. 74-75.

Ashkenas, Ronald N., and Schaffer, Robert H. Managers Can Avoid Wasting Time. *Harvard Business Review*, May-June, 1982, p. 98.

Bittel, Lester R. *Right on Time! The Complete Guide for Time-Pressured Managers*. New York: McGraw-Hill, 1991.

Blanchard, Kenneth H. *The One Minute Manager*. New York: Morrow, 1982.

Braid, R.W. Effective Use of Time. *Supervisory Management*, July, 1983, p. 9-14.

Cohen, William A., and Cohen, Nurit. *Top Executive Performance: 11 Keys to Success and Power*. New York: Wiley, 1984.

Fenney, E.J. Getting the Most Out of Your Time. *Management World*, Sept, 1985, p. 18.

Goodloe, Alfred; Bensahel, Jane; and Kelly, John. *Managing Yourself: How to Control Emotion, Stress, and Time*. New York: Franklin Watts, 1984.

Januz, Lauren R., and Jones, Susan K. *Time Management for Executives*. New York: Charles Scribner's Sons, 1981.

Klassen, M. How to Get the Most Use of Your Time (20 suggestions). *Supervision*, April, 1983, p. 9-10.

McConalogue, T. Developing the Skill of Time Management. *Management Decisions*, 1987, p. 5-8.

Oncken, W., Jr. *Managing Management Time: Who's Got the Monkey*. Englewood Cliffs, NJ: Prentice-Hall, 1984.

Scannell, Edward E. We've Got to Stop Meeting Like This. *Training and Development*, January, 1992, p. 70-71.

Schilit, W. K., and Schilit, H. M. Improving Your Time Management Skills. *Journal of Accountancy*, July, 1986, p. 116-117.

Time, Goods, and Well-being. Edited by F. Thomas Juster and Frank P. Stafford. Ann Arbor, MI: ISR Publishing, 1985.

Timpe, A. Dale. *The Management of Time*. New York, NY: Kend Publishing, 1987.

Tobia, Peter and Becker, Martin. Making the Most of Meeting Time. *Training and Development*, August, 1990, 34-38.

Winston, Stephanie. *The Organized Executive: A Program for Productivity*. New York: Norton, 1983.

8

Project Management

This chapter helps improve performance in the following areas:

- Designing and completing projects.
- Working as a project team member.
- Being a project team leader.
- Figuring out the necessary steps in projects.
- Ensure a smooth running project effort.

Action Items for Project Management

1. Draw up clear project goals.

The beginning point for having an effective project is to clearly define what the goals of the project are. Without knowing this, there is no telling where you will wind up. In many cases, the project goals are defined by those in higher levels. However, their definition may not be complete. Try to answer all of the following questions in clearly defining project goals:

- What outcome is to be achieved with this project?

- What deliverables (actual products) are expected?

- What sort of resources can be committed to the project?

- What is the targeted completion date?

- Who is to be the project team leader?

By answering questions such as these, you should be able to clearly define the project goals, and also understand some of the parameters you have to work with.

2. Determine the resources needed.

Some projects fail because the project leaders do not evaluate all of the resources that are needed. If a shortfall occurs, the project might have to be abandoned mid-way through completion. The solution to this is to clearly lay out all of the resources required before the project begins. Resources to consider include the following:

- Financial resources.

- Human resources.

- Equipment, supplies, and materials.

Once these resources are identified, get the approval of others, if needed, to ensure the resources are available. Approval will ensure a successful project. If approval for all resources is not obtained, determine the impact of this on the project itself and make the necessary adjustments.

3. Sell the project to key decision makers.

Many projects fail because they are not sold to others in the organization. For example, the accounting department may draw up a new expense account form that would make their accounting work easier. However, others in the organization might resist the new form, finding it too complicated or detailed. The better approach would have been to sell the idea of a new form in the first place. For any project you are working on, discuss the impact of it with others who are likely to be affected. Incorporate their thoughts and ideas into what you actually do. With their approval, the project can get off to a good start and not surprise people at the end. If the project goal is not to their liking, it is very helpful to know and resolve this before actually getting started.

4. Utilize an ongoing review committee.

Many projects benefit from the ongoing review of a committee. Their input and suggested changes can make for a more successful outcome. A review committee should be selected for larger, more important projects. Think of those who are impacted by, and interested in, the scope of the project. Try to get those with different viewpoints—stacking the committee with only avid supporters may prove costly in the end. Get the committee together to review various milestones in the project. The use of such a review committee can aid in the implementation of the project results. The results will be seen as "our" project, not "your" project.

5. Assign clear responsibilities to project team members.

Those on a project team sometimes suffer from poor leadership. Members may be confused on who does what and when. If you are a project team leader, give people clear assignments on what they are to do. These assignments can either be individual ones or done with another team member. Use whichever you feel is more effective. Think of each person's interests and abilities when giving out an assignment. State expectations for what each person is to do and what limits they have to work with. If you are a team member, but not project leader, make sure your own responsibilities are clear. Go to the project leader and discuss the expectations in more detail if necessary. You want to ensure that you are performing in the way expected, and this is more challenging with someone other than your boss giving direction.

6. List out all of the activities which must be done.

An important starting point for any project is to list out all activities that need to be done. It is best to do this in chronological order, thinking of every step from start to finish that is needed to complete the project. Assign each activity to an appropriate person, as discussed in the preceding action item. Also list out the resources needed for each activity, and ensure that they are adequate to get the job done.

7. Draw up completion dates for each activity.

Projects may fail due to unclear dates for the completion of each activity. Team members may work out of sync with one another or take too long to complete an individual activity. As a project leader, you should see to it that a clear date is set for completing each project activity. See this as a collaborative effort between you and the other members of the team—recognize that each team member has other job responsibilities that may conflict with the ideal target dates for the project. Try to negotiate acceptable dates for all. Gain the commitment and support of each member for working within the deadlines established.

8. Visually lay out the project plan.

A picture is often worth a thousand words, and this can help with project work as well. Draw a chart showing each activity step for the project, who is to do it, and targeted start and completion dates. You can use a Gantt chart or other similar format. Once drawn, share out the chart with all team members so they can get the "big picture" of how the pieces fit together. In some cases, you may want to visually display the chart in a project conference room so members can see it whenever entering the area.

9. Schedule periodic review meetings.

Some projects suffer from the lack of communication between members. Everyone is doing there own work without the knowledge of others. If you are a project leader, schedule periodic meetings with all of those on the project team. Keep these meetings focused and as brief as possible. Have each member provide an update of what they have been doing, if appropriate. You want to use these meetings to ensure that all members know what the others are doing. Also, openly discuss all problems which have come up or are anticipated. Get all team members involved in the solutions. It will make everyone feel like part of the team and lead to a higher quality solution.

10. Emphasize teamwork to all of those on the project team.

A project team can be a cohesive unit of people working together, or a collection of individuals working on their own. The cohesive teams are usually more successful than the group of individuals. As a project team leader, ensure that everyone on the project is an important member of the team. Mention that the entire team has a common goal to accomplish, and that each member has an important role in accomplishing that goal. Emphasize unity and working together rather than working individually. This can be enhanced even more by assigning individual activities to more than one person. Use a "we are all in this together" approach for all of your meetings and communications. Making the group of individuals into a team will not only result in more success, but be more satisfying as well.

11. Give out rewards to team members.

If you are a project team leader, remember to give out rewards to each member of the team. On many occasions, special projects are add-on responsibilities for team members—they may not get to project work until after normal hours or on weekends. Also, the regular managers of team members may not provide recognition for this project since they may be less aware of what the employee is doing. This increases the need for the team leader to provide recognition. Use praise for a job well done. Write letters of commendation to the managers of team members. Luncheons or small gifts may be appropriate after the completion of a major project. Try to make these rewards available whenever you lead a project team.

12. Be a conduit for information as team leader.

Project teams may suffer if information is not made available to all. It is more difficult to share out information with project teams since the team members may not be in the same department and not see each other often. This increases the importance of sharing out information to all. When you are the team leader, think of sharing each important piece of information as soon as you become aware of it. Make copies for distribution to all or share out verbal information at your review meetings. If you are not the team leader, keep others aware of what you are doing on the project even if not asked to do so. You can never over-communicate to others, but you can under-communicate.

13. Promote cooperation amongst those with different approaches.

Project teams can sometimes go astray when individual team members have different approaches to handing the project. With the absence of a clearly defined boss, some team members may be more independent and less cooperative. If you are a team leader or team member, do what you can to promote harmony within the group. Encourage cooperation and compromise. Try to discourage certain team members from being too dominant, talking with them in private if necessary. Emphasize negotiation, compromise, or tabling issues where there are wildly different opinions. Seek out a higher level manager to help steer the group if consensus cannot be reached within the group. Keep the group dynamics positive and helpful.

14. Develop contingency plans for each step of the project.

Project work may be dealt a great blow if an unexpected problem is encountered. The team may not only lose momentum, but may even cancel the project when this happens. To better prepare for such an event, develop a contingency plan for each project activity. Ask yourself what would happen if a team member were no longer available as a part of the team or certain equipment were not available. What can you do when this occurs? Are there other solutions (e.g., hiring a consultant to replace an internal team member) that would still allow the project to go forward after this loss? It is inevitable that every project will have some setbacks. The successful teams see these setbacks as merely a time to implement the contingency plan, with the project continuing onward.

15. Set up a climate of openness for the project team.

Some project leaders take their job too seriously. They feel they have to make all decisions by themselves on every project item. This can alienate other team members who might regard the project leader as a peer. The climate for the team can be one of keeping silent and doing as you are told. That sort of environment is not conducive for successfully completing a project. If you are the project team leader, try to set up an open, sharing climate amongst the team. Encourage them to express how they feel and resist making every decision on your own. Do not try to make a judgment or evaluation on each comment the members of the group make. It is highly likely that your project will require some readjusting as you go along, and that readjustment will work best if you have the helpful ideas of all.

16. Resolve time conflicts with team members.

Many times, project team members may be wearing more than one hat. They are working on a special project part of the time, and continuing on the regular job the rest of the time. Sometimes individual team members may defer on project work because of the demands of the regular job. How do you handle this as project leader if you see that project work is not being done by the team member? First, candidly discuss the situation with the team member. This person may be unaware of the importance of meeting deadlines to keep the project moving ahead. You may be unaware of some of the demands on their time. See if some sort of compromise can be worked out.

If this does not produce a solution, tell the employee that either you or he/she needs to speak with their manager. Approach the manager in a positive way. You are not there to criticize the employee or the employee's manager, but see if some option can be worked out so the project is not delayed. Perhaps the manager can assign someone else the employee's responsibilities, or assign someone else to the project team. Whatever the solution, it is important for you to take some sort of action, for the failure to act could mean the failure of the project.

17. Resolve performance issues with team members.

On occasion, the team project leader may have performance problems with one or more of the team members. If this problem does not improve, some sort of action is necessary. First, meet with the individual team member in private. Use the guidelines and steps provided in the Introduction to this book. Describe the problem in a candid and positive way. Work for a solution, and give the team member a chance to improve. Be sure to reward changes in performance if you see them.

If the problem still persists after your coaching, and you feel it is hurting the success of the project, then meet with the employee's manager (or have your manager meet with the employee's manager). Perhaps someone with the wrong skills was assigned to the project, or the individual could not handle the project demands. Be thankful and appreciative for the work which was done, but see if the manager can assign someone else. This might be best for both the project and the employee.

18. Let all team members lead in their area of expertise.

Project team leaders who have limited experience in a leadership role can sometimes go too far with their new responsibilities. They may assert control so strongly in becoming the "boss" that other team members resent this. This can be particularly true of peers on the project team. The best leadership role is a "participative" one— let others lead those aspects of the project where they are the experts. They know their areas best, so let them recommend and lead for those portions of the project. Resist the temptation to be an autocrat and give too-frequent orders which others may resist. Instead be more of a catalyst who makes things happen by letting others do what they do best.

19. Team leaders should be coaches and coordinators rather than bosses.

As project team leader, set a leadership style that is more of a coach and coordinator rather than a boss. Recognize that you may be leading a very diverse group of people without the implied or actual power that a boss has over an employee. See your role as helping coordinate the entire project so that it gets completed on time.

Try to coach and work with others as peers rather than as a boss. Help motivate them, reward them, and candidly discuss performance or other problems which might occur. While the role of project team leader can be very fulfilling, it must also be handled very carefully.

20. Schedule project work in blocks if necessary.

As a project team member or leader you, like all others on the team, may have to juggle project responsibilities with other job activities. To make this as easy as possible, think of scheduling your project work in blocks of time rather than do it throughout the day. Block off amounts of time just as you would block off time for a meeting. This will help you get more done through improved concentration. If necessary, go to a conference room or other private location where you can work undisturbed.

Recommended Readings

Aaker, David A. *Developing Business Strategies*. New York: Wiley, 1984.

Aptman, Leonard H. Project Management: Setting Controls. *Managing Solutions*, Nov, 1986, p. 31-33.

Brooks, Julie K., and Stevens, Barry A. *How to Write a Successful Business Plan*. New York: AMACOM, 1987.

Georgoff, David M., and Murdick, Robert G. Manager's Guide to Forecasting. *Harvard Business Review*, Jan-Feb, 1986, p. 110-115.

Gray, H. Uses and Misuses of Strategic Planning. *Harvard Business Review*, Jan-Feb, 1986, p. 89-97.

Handbook of Business Planning for Executives with Profit Responsibility. Edited by Thomas S. Dudick and Robert V. Gorski. New York: Van Nostrand Reinhold, 1983.

Hardaker, Maurice, and Ward, Bryan K. How to Make a Team Work. *Harvard Business Review*, Nov-Dec, 1987, 65, p. 112-117.

Haynes, Marion E. *Project Management: From Idea to Implementation*. Los Altos, CA: Crisp Publications, 1989.

Hussey, David E. *Introducing Corporate Planning* (3rd ed.). Oxford: Pergamon Press, 1985.

Meidan, Arthur. Methods and Approaches to Corporate Planning. *Management Decisions*, 1986, p. 44-54.

Meidan, Arthur. Organising for Corporate Planning. *Management Decisions*, 1986, 24, p. 55-66.

O'Connor, Rochelle. *Tracking the Strategic Plan*. New York: Conference Board, 1983.

Rosenau Jr., Milton D. Software Can Help You Manage R & D Projects. *Research & Development*, Nov, 1985, 27, p. 86-88.

9

Work Quality

This chapter helps improve performance in the following areas:

- Improving work quality.
- Setting higher personal standards.
- Becoming more vigilant at work.
- Implementing quality improvement programs.

Action Items For Improving Work Quality

1. Proofread written materials before they are sent out.

Quality is shown to others in many different ways. If you are sent a letter, memo, or report with typographical errors, you immediately notice the poor quality. This leads you to believe that the writer, and the writer's company, have poor quality. Whenever you send out written materials to others, take the time to carefully proofread the materials for errors. It makes no difference if the material is being sent to in-house or outside individuals—they will make judgments about you based upon what they see. If it is helpful, have a second person also read the material before it goes out. They may notice errors that got by you the first time.

2. Increase your personal standards.

Part of doing high quality work is to set internal standards of your own. Some individuals do not set standards for themselves, and if you are like this, begin by setting standards now. Think of your job and the work that you do. What are the key ways that someone can evaluate the quality of your work? How can you increase the quality in different ways? List out the ideas you come up with and use these as your own internal standards. Even if others do not give you quality goals to achieve, work toward reaching your own personal goals. The quality will be noticed regardless of the type of work that you do. That will have a lot to do with your performance appraisals, career advancement, and personal pride in doing your job.

3. Double-check the accuracy of each task you complete.

The quality of work is enhanced greatly if everyone takes the time to double-check the tasks that they do. It makes no difference if you are filling out a form, assembling a piece of equipment, or setting up an agenda for a meeting. Take the time to briefly go over what you have just completed to make sure it is accurate. This simple habit can do wonders to increase the quality of someone's work. Ask yourself if you currently double-check the work that you do. If not, try to implement this as soon as possible.

4. Repeat the verbal messages or requests of others.

The quality of conversations with others is enhanced if you repeat the message someone has just given you. For example, if a customer calls with a complaint, repeating what you think the complaint was will ensure better communications and better service. By repeating the phone number of someone leaving a phone message will ensure that you have recorded the number accurately. Use this technique of verbally repeating part of the conversation to ensure a high quality of communications with others.

5. Make quality inspections and tests of your work.

Work quality is enhanced by periodically auditing the quality of the work. You can do this on your own by occasionally auditing yourself—inspect for accuracy and quality the products you assemble, the written materials you prepare, or other work you do. If you identify problems, work at correcting them. Those who are managers should do periodic audits of not only their own work, but the work of staff as well. Make everyone aware of the importance of quality and the need to check the work itself. If your employees primarily do verbal work, try to listen in on sample conversations with their knowledge and check on quality in this way.

6. Make quality improvements in steps.

It can be very frustrating for an employee to try to go from quality performance which is average or below average to perfect. Employees in this situation may give up after making a single error, and not try to improve beyond their prior performance. While being perfect is the ultimate goal, it is best to get there in steps rather than all at once. Set up a series of stepping stones to improve your quality.

When you reach a certain plateau, start working toward a higher level, and keep repeating the process. Managers should think of using a similar strategy when helping their employees move to higher levels of quality performance.

7. Proofread written materials both forwards and backwards.

Expert proofreaders have found that it is best to proofread written materials in two directions—once forwards and once backwards. Proofreading in the forward direction helps to spot many typographical errors and errors in sentence construction (e.g., left out words). However, when reading forward our eyes jump from phrase to phrase, leaving out certain words which could be misspelled. By reading backwards, we focus on each and every word, since the sentence has no meaning when read backwards. Try out this technique when proofreading your own written materials, particularly if you find that certain errors are going by you.

8. Link work quality to higher level goals.

Work quality has a more important meaning for employees when it is linked to higher level goals that the department or company has. For example, the company might have a goal to increase quality by 10% or improve profits by 10% by reducing the number of re-jected products. Communicating this goal to all employees helps ensure that everyone sees his/her job activities as relating to larger, more important goals. This increases motivation to work harder at quality. As a manager, you should try to link quality to higher goals wherever you can. As an individual employee, you should try and understand how your work relates to larger company goals and is not merely an end in itself.

9. Attend problem solving training.

Part of improving work quality is being able to diagnose and correct what is causing quality problems. For this you need skills at diagnosis and problem solving. Specific training is available in this area through commercial training firms, professional associations, and some continuing education programs at colleges. You should try to take advantage of these programs to build additional knowledge at improving work quality. In addition, read the chapter in this book which deals with problem solving and decision making.

10. Visually chart work quality results.

Progress at improving work quality is aided by visually seeing the trends. Department or team results are particularly enhanced by charting them on a wall where all can see. This visual reminder keeps quality in the minds of all and clearly shows the progress being made. Managers should see that such charts are posted or circulated to others, depending on which is most appropriate. If your quality goals are individual rather than team oriented, chart your own progress on a piece of graph paper. Keep track of your error rates or related statistics and keep trying to improve. That charting will help you see at a glance how you are doing.

11. Seek out work quality ideas from others.

Employees sometimes fail to improve work quality because they are uncertain of how to improve. They try to solve the problem alone and get stumped. If this applies to you, seek out the advice of an "expert" in the area. This person might be a co-worker, boss, or person in another part of the company who might have some ideas. Tell them what you are trying to improve upon and see if they have any suggestions. Look at their advice with an open mind—criticizing their ideas will discourage them from offering more. Go back and evaluate the ideas you collected and implement those that will help you improve work quality.

12. Concentrate on one task at a time.

For many, work quality suffers by constantly going from one activity to another without completing any of the activities. This fragments your concentration and makes it difficult to do a high quality job on any of the activities. If you have a tendency to shift your attention from task to task throughout the day, try to work in a different way. Focus your attention on just one task until it is completed, then work on another task until it is completed, and so on. By doing this, you will have a more intense focus on the quality of your work and find it easier to do a high quality job.

13. Point out quality problems of others in your area.

Employees often have to work as part of a team in a department or other work area. Work quality is in many cases a matter for the whole team rather than just certain individuals. If one member is not working up to standard, the team's performance can suffer. Co-workers can often help each other out more easily than a manager can since they do the same work and interact often. If you notice a co-worker who is having some problems, take the opportunity to help the other person out.

During a break or lunch together, ask if they are having any problems in doing the job. If they do not mention any, share out what you have observed. Be careful to do this in a helpful, constructive way—you do not want to hurt the other person's feelings but instead help them to learn and improve. After stating what you have observed, quickly offer out any suggestions you might have. Offer out your expertise and what works for you. Tell them they can observe you or talk to you more about it whenever they like. By doing so, you help quality improve and build a better team.

14. Take the time to work out solutions to repetitive quality problems.

You may notice that a certain quality problem comes up more than once in your work. You may be told this by someone else or notice it yourself. If you see any pattern, set aside some time to figure out why this is happening. Consider a number of alternatives—initially you just want to list out as many possibilities as you can. Then do some homework and check out each possibility to see which may be causing the problem. Implement the solution on your own if you can. If you cannot, then see your manager or someone else about additional training, equipment, or supplies that will help you correct the problem.

15. Use the latest quality technology.

Doing high quality work can be aided by using the latest technology. Some may resist learning new things with changes in technology and this can hurt their work quality. As a simple example of technology improving work quality, consider personal computers. Most word processing packages for personal computers include a thesaurus for coming up with other words, and a spelling checker for identifying spelling errors. This new technology puts someone using it at a great advantage over someone who writes using a typewriter (or a note pad).

Identify any new technology that can help you improve the quality of your work, be it computers, fax machines, production equipment, test equipment, and so on. Try to get your manager to buy this equipment and put it to use immediately. If the company provides the equipment on its own, be eager to learn it and use it. It will help you do a better quality job.

16. Tie in rewards for high quality performance.

High quality performance will be sustained and increase if there are appropriate rewards for it. If you are a manager do all that you can to offer rewards for high quality work. Make sure that quality is an item on the employee's performance appraisal, and hopefully this ties in with salary increases. You might also link individual or group quality performance to some sort of rewards, such as a profit-sharing bonus if certain targets are met. If these financial rewards are not available, use praise, commendation letters, or the ''employee of the month'' concept to provide rewards.

If you are not a manager, it is still important for you to receive rewards for high quality work. If your organization does not make any rewards available for quality work (fortunately, nearly all do), you will need to reward yourself. Treat yourself in some way if you attain an important quality goal. Let your manager know what you have accomplished, and feel a sense of personal pride in what you have done. That will likely encourage you to do more of the same in the future.

17. Set aspirations to be the best.

Quality work is accomplished by first having aspirations to do high quality work. If you tell yourself that you want to be the best at whatever you do, you are well on the way to being a high quality performer. It makes no difference what your job is or where you work—simply set out to be the best at doing that job. This type of internal standard will continue to motivate a person on and on toward higher achievements. But it all starts with that simple desire to be the best. Aspire to this yourself if you are not currently doing so.

18. Join a professional association in the quality area.

Quality work performance can be enhanced by joining a professional association in the quality area. There are organizations such as the American Society for Quality Control which are dedicated to the quality area. They have newsletters, books, and seminars that can help employees in the quality area. While some of the programs or publications of associations are highly technical, there are many that can benefit any employee who wants to increase their work quality. Consider joining an association such as this and trading notes with employees in other companies in improving your work quality.

19. Increase the quality of outside resources.

Employees sometimes lament that the quality of a product is not high because an outside resource did poor work. The new brochure may not look good because "the printer did sloppy work" or phone messages are inaccurate because "the temporary agency employee is not very good." If you use outside resources in your area, you need to ensure that these people do high quality work. It makes no difference if they are printers, temporaries, consultants, contractors, or other outside resources. Give them high quality standards to attain and hold them accountable for attaining those results. In this way, your work and the work of your area will be high quality as well.

20. Set goals and standards for quality performance.

Quality work is greatly enhanced by the use of quality goals and standards. Managers should ensure that goals and standards are set for their area and each employee. Avoid using vague goals such as "improve product quality" since this may mean different things to different people. Set specific numerical targets wherever possible, and target a date for achieving the goal. If you are not a manager, suggest the use of goals and standards to your manager. Or set targets on your own in the quality area. It will be much easier to monitor and reward your progress in the quality area if you have specific goals and standards in use.

The remaining action items in this chapter are for managers only.

21. Build quality consciousness into everyone's job.

Companies with high quality products make quality an important part of everyone's job. Regardless of what the employee does, doing the job in a quality way is linked to the success of the product and the company. Review whether you build quality consciousness into the minds of all of your employees. If not, start by doing this right now. Ways to raise quality consciousness include the following:

- When new employees are hired, emphasize the importance of quality.

- Set quality goals and standards for everyone's job.

- Review quality performance at staff meetings.

- Post charts or circulate tables showing the latest quality performance.

- Have meetings dedicated to improving quality.

- Reward high quality performance.

By implementing ideas such as this, you will raise the quality consciousness of your employees, and the quality of your products and services.

22. Implement quality improvement teams.

Another way to increase quality is to assemble formal teams to deal with quality issues. These might be called quality circles, quality improvement teams, participation teams, or any one of several other names. The key is not the name, but the mission of the group, which is to improve the quality of the company's products and services (or the quality of worklife at the company). While less popular now than several years ago, to be effective these teams must be given the training to solve quality problems and the authority to implement actions.

Earlier quality circle efforts failed in many cases when managers resisted implementing the ideas the teams came up with. Ensure that management support is available before setting up such teams. If you are doing many of the other activities suggested in this chapter, such as making quality a part of everyone's job, these formal quality improvement teams may not be needed except for special projects.

23. Use a participative management style.

If quality teams or individuals are asked to improve quality, managers must be willing to listen and implement. An autocratic manager may resent the ideas that employees come up with, feeling it is his/her job to improve quality and make all decisions. That style has given way to a more participative style. Participative managers delegate to the lowest level and do not feel threatened when employees come up with ideas to improve work quality. The employees are allowed not only to generate ideas, but implement those ideas within limits. Evaluate how participative your management style is, and change it if you need to. By being more participative, you will set up a climate that encourages and supports high quality work.

24. Schedule periodic brainstorming sessions.

Managers can improve the work quality of their area by scheduling periodic brainstorming sessions. These sessions are dedicated exclusively to improving the quality of work. After giving some general directions, ask the employees to brainstorm ideas for improving quality. Do not criticize or evaluate any of these ideas—you merely want to generate as many as you can. Then go back and evaluate the ideas you generated, and identify those that look the most promising. Discuss what can be done to implement these ideas. Have one or more individuals assigned the task of implementing an idea. Have them report to the rest of the group, and extend the idea to all if appropriate. Using periodic brainstorming sessions like this can be fulfilling to employees and help improve quality.

25. Increase the visibility of quality efforts.

Work quality can benefit from making your efforts visible to all. Circulate to your employees articles or success stories from your company or other companies. Write up in a newsletter quality examples that everyone could benefit from. Post banners or charts which are visible reminders of the need for quality. Give out coffee mugs or pens with "Quality No. 1" ideas embossed on them. Institute an employee of the month concept for high quality work. These and many other ways can be used to increase the visibility of quality efforts at your company.

26. Implement statistical quality control.

Many departments can benefit from instituting formal quality control programs such as statistical quality control. This is particularly true of production departments where clear, quality measures are easily available. There are several different statistical quality control programs which can be set up. Interested managers should read more on the different techniques available and select one for implementation. Formal training and monitoring systems can be obtained from consulting firms offering assistance in this area. It is still yet another way to increase the quality of your department's work.

Recommended Readings

Barry, Thomas F. *Quality Circles: Proceed With Caution*. Milwaukee, WI: American Society for Quality Control, 1988.

Brocka, Bruce and Brocka, Suzanne. *Quality Management*. Homewood, IL: Business One Irwin, 1992.

Burck, C. G. What Happens When Workers Manage Themselves. *Fortune*, 1981, 104, 2, 62-69.

Cox, Allan. *The Making of the Achiever*. New York: Dodd, Mead & Company, 1985.

Crosby, Philip B. *Quality is Free*. New York: Mentor American Library, 1979.

DeMare, George. *101 Ways to Protect Your Job*. New York: McGraw-Hill, 1984.

Galagan, Patricia. Work Teams That Work. *Training & Development*, Nov, 1986, p. 33-35.

Harrington, H. James. *The Improvement Process: How America's Leading Companies Improve Quality*. Milwaukee, WI: ASQC Press, 1986.

Imai, Masaaki. *Kaizen: the Key to Japan's Competitive Success*. New York: Random House, 1986.

Implementing Total Quality Management: An Overview. San Diego: Pieffer and Company, 1992.

Johnson, Gary and Dumas, Roland. How to Improve Quality If You're Not in Manufacturing. *Training*, November, 1992, 35-38.

Leibfried, Kathleen H.J. and McNair, C.J. *Benchmarking: A Tool for Continuous Improvement*. New York: Harper Business, 1993.

Manz, Charles. *The Art of Self Leadership: Strategies for Personnel Effectiveness in Your Life and Work*. Englewood Cliffs, NJ: Prentice-Hall, 1983.

Mroczkowski, Thomasz. Quality Circles Fine—What Next? *The Personnel Administrator*, June, 1984, 173-184.

Peters, T. J., and Austin, N. *A Passion for Excellence*. New York: Random House, 1985.

Peters, T. J., and Waterman, R. H. *In Search of Excellence: Lessons from Americas Best Run Companies*. New York: Harper & Row, 1982.

Revzan, Henry A. Quality Control in White Collar Settings. *Management Review*, Oct, 1986, 75, p. 48-50.

Rodgers, Buck. *Getting the Best Out of Yourself and Others*. New York: Harper & Row, 1987.

Solving Quality and Productivity Problems: Goodmeasure's Guide to Corrective Action. Written by the Staff of Goodmeasure. Milwaukee, WI: ASQC Quality Press, 1988.

Zeithaml, Valerie; Parasuraman, A.; and Berry, Leonard. *Delivering Quality Service*. New York, Free Press, 1990.

10

Work Quantity

This chapter helps improve performance in the following areas:

- Volume of work done.
- Work efficiency.
- Reducing "down time."
- Attaining more goals.

Action Items for Work Quantity

1. Establish clear goals and targets.

The beginning point for increasing work quantity is to set up clear goals and targets. Some employees come to work each day without any specific targets in mind. For them, it is easy to see why a high quantity of work does not get done. As a manager, ensure that each of your employees has goals and targets to shoot for. This is particularly true of professional and office jobs where the pace of work is more under the employee's control. If you are a non-manager and your manager has not set targets for you to accomplish, set goals for yourself. Think of the key things you need to get done each day and write these out. Work through the day trying to make sure you accomplish what is most important to do.

2. Clarify priorities with your manager.

An employee's work volume may be of concern to a manager despite the fact that the employee appears to be working hard. What is often the problem is that the employee is working on low priority items while disregarding the high priority items the manager is monitoring. This focus on the wrong priorities may lead to a problem from the manager's perspective. If this might be a problem in your case, discuss the situation with your manager. Clarify those areas where there may be a different perspective on priorities. Discuss ways the lower priority work can be handled. The key is to ensure that your work volume as an employee corresponds with the areas your manager is most interested in.

3. Target gradual increases in work volume.

Increasing work volume is most easily done by gradual steps. Trying to make dramatic increases may frustrate employees and cause them to give up. A better practice is to use stepping stones for getting to the eventual target. Both manager and employee should reach agreement to what the eventual target is and the steps to get there. Progress should be monitored, and reinforcement given when the various steps are achieved. Use a series of stepping stones to build your work volume.

4. Keep a log or diary of your progress.

It is helpful to keep a log or diary when trying to increase work volume. At the end of each day, record all of the things you have done. Try to quantify wherever you can (e.g., number of pages typed, number of products assembled), and look for trends. Those days where there is not much to be recorded might be reviewed more carefully to see what went wrong. By keeping a daily log or diary you can pinpoint when you are most productive and what causes you to be less productive. By learning from this, you can take more specific actions to increase work volume.

5. Use time more efficiently.

Work quantity is affected greatly by the use made of time. Review how productive your use of time is. Is most of your time spent accomplishing the key activities in your job? Or less important administrative work or down time? Analyze how are you spending your time and how you can make changes. For more specific guidance on the effective use of time, see the chapter on time management.

6. Extend the number of hours worked.

It sounds very simple, but there is a simple correlation between how many hours employees work and how much they get done. Review the amount of time you spend on the job. Do you leave at a certain time because it is customary, or because you have finished all you need to do on that day? Many employees cannot get to their more important project work until late in the day (or early in the morning) when things are more quiet. It may be necessary to extend the number of hours you work to complete everything that needs to be done. Let your work volume determine the hours you work rather than the clock determining how much work you do.

7. Visually chart out your work volume.

Increasing the quantity of work done can be enhanced by visually seeing your progress. If your job lends itself to daily or weekly volumes of work done, take the time to chart your production on a graph. Plot a point for each day's or week's volume and compare that with where you were in the last time period. By seeing the trends, you may be able to identify problems. For example, you may be less productive on Monday than on other days. By seeing your progress and correcting obstacles, you can improve upon the quantity of your work.

8. Give out rewards for hitting volume targets.

Rewards have a way of sustaining human performance. Very simply, humans are more likely to repeat something if they are rewarded for it. If you are a manager working with an employee who needs to improve work volume, be certain to reward them in some way for improving their work volume. Use praise if no other rewards are available or appropriate. If you are a non-manager employee who is trying to increase your work quantity, reward yourself in some way for reaching your targets. Give yourself a treat or buy some small item like a record, book, or piece of clothing when you reach a volume target. Tell yourself that the reward is for hitting the target. This will help sustain you to do more of the same in the future.

9. Use the latest technology to help increase work volume.

Some employees hold themselves back by refusing to use the latest technology. A secretary refusing to use a personal computer for typing will find it takes a great deal more time to do this work with a typewriter. The same is true for most other jobs. Evaluate how you currently do your job. Is there any new equipment or procedures that you can be using to improve your work volume? If so, go to your manager and see if the equipment can be purchased—sell the idea on the fact that it will increase productivity and pay for itself. When your manager or other person comes to you with suggested improvements in equipment or procedures, look at these with an open mind. You do not want to hold yourself back from accomplishing more.

10. Plan out each day carefully with a checklist.

Some employees do not get a lot done because they have no plan for the day. They simply start working on whatever is in front of them and let interruptions take them in many directions. A better way is to begin each day by planning out what is most important to do. Then draw up a list of the key things you want to accomplish and check off each of these activities as you complete them. This way you can visually see the progress you are making and remind yourself of how many things you need to do that day. Gradually increase the number of items on your daily list so you build your work volume.

11. Set aside time for special projects.

Special project work might be difficult to accomplish if calls, visits, and other interruptions prevent concentrated effort. As a result, work quantity may not be what it could be for the employee. If this is a problem for you or one of your employees, try to set aside specific time for project work. Treat the time to be spent on a project just like a meeting or other scheduled activity. Literally write it on your calendar and block off an appropriate amount of time. Try to hold phone calls. Close the door to your office or go to a conference room so you can work interrupted for the necessary amount of time. By setting aside specific time for project work, you will help attain overall work quantity goals.

12. Reduce the amount of "down time."

Work quantity can seriously be impacted by too much down time. Many employees do not realize the amount of time they spend in non-productive activities. Take the time to see how much down time you have each day. Review how many personal phone calls to family and friends you have each day, and how long these calls last. How many breaks and visits do you have from co-workers where the talk is not business related? How many periods do you have where you may not be doing anything in particular but perhaps watching others? While some down time is unavoidable and even desirable, the key is to keep it within reason. By doing so you can attain higher work quantity levels.

13. Concentrate on one task at a time.

Work volume may be impacted negatively from too much switching from task to task before completing anything. Review whether your day goes like this, and whether it has an impact on the quantity of your work. Do you stop doing what you are doing to open and read the mail as it is delivered, or shift gears to deal with someone's phone request even if it is not urgent? If so, try to work on only one task at a time. If other requests come your way while you are working on one task, then add these new requests to your list for the day. Slot them according to their priority versus other items on the list. By concentrating on one task at a time, you can increase your work volume.

14. Set aspirations to do more volume than others.

Employees with little or no aspiration to get a lot done will not likely achieve very much. It is important to have high aspirations to generate a high quantity of work and get more done. If you suffer from low aspirations, set goals to outperform your former self (or outperform others). Appeal to your sense of pride, to your being as good as, or better than, others. While we actually compete with ourselves more so than with others, some competitive inspiration may get people started on the track of doing more. Once there, they can look to improve upon what they have done in the past.

15. Reduce down time at home.

Making more productive use of time at home can also help you get more done at the workplace. First of all, scheduling blocks of time for home activities can build skills that can be used back on the job. Second, if you use your time more productively at home, you might find some additional time for work activities. And in this way increase the volume of your work. While some down time for relaxation is needed by all of us, there can be too much time wasted on nothing of particular value. Evaluate how much time you spend watching television or doing other leisure activities that could be reduced a bit. By using your personal time more effectively, you can open up more opportunities for improving work volume.

16. Keep verbal and written communications focused.

Some employees may spend too much time in non-essential communication with others, and this can reduce the volume of their work. Such employees may make too many personal phone calls or let conversations go on for too long with co-workers. On the written side, some may write very lengthy memos or reports which take a great deal of time to prepare. If you have any of these problems, try to sharpen the focus of your communications with others. Keep a cap on the number and length of personal conversations with others. Keep your written communications more brief and to the point. By practicing these suggestions, you will be able to accomplish a larger work volume.

17. Audit how you spend your time.

Work quantity can be improved by knowing how you spend your time and making changes where needed. Use a day calendar or sheet of paper with times written in fifteen minute increments. After you complete each activity, be it a phone call, memo, break, or whatever, log in the amount of time spent on that activity. Do this for one week, then go back and analyze how you spent your time. When were you most productive? Was there too much down time? Could some of the things you did be better done by someone else? Did you work on your key goals as much as you should have? By auditing how you spend your time and making changes, you can increase the efficiency of your work. This, in turn, can help you increase the amount of work you get done.

18. Reduce or eliminate low priority items.

Some employees may spend too much time on low priority items, such as reading unimportant flyers or articles of little use. Evaluate if you spend your time on tasks like these or unessential administrative chores. Perhaps you can reduce the amount of time you spend on them or eliminate doing them altogether. By doing this, more time is freed up for work on more important tasks that others feel are important for you to do. This can help your performance from a volume standpoint.

19. Break up large tasks into smaller pieces.

Work volume can be adversely affected by having huge projects. For example, a systems analyst may have a goal to create a new piece of software which will take over one year to develop. Or a sales representative may have a yearly quota of $500,000 in new sales. Employees in these situations may be hesitant to even start such a project without a large block of free time, or they may procrastinate getting started because of the enormity of the job. If you are affected by this, make the situation easier by breaking up that large task into several smaller pieces. By doing so you will find it easier to start the project, and you will feel a sense of accomplishment as you finish each piece. It is still another activity that help increase work volume.

20. Visualize rewards at the end of the day.

Jobs that have a great deal of repetition may make it difficult to get through the day. If you have a job like this, try to visualize something that you value that you will get if you hit your target and get the day's work done. Perhaps that reward that you value is a favorite meal, or the ability to play sports or watch a favorite program after work. Try to keep this in mind and see it as your "reward" for completing the daily work. By successfully doing this, you will find the day more enjoyable and be able to attain a higher volume of work.

21. Get ideas from co-workers on increasing work quantity.

If you are perplexed about how to increase the quantity of your work, try talking to some of your co-workers. They probably have watched you work and may have noticed things that you cannot see in yourself. They also may have discovered certain short-cuts that they may share with you if you ask them. Encourage them to be very candid about anything that they feel could help. Listen to what they have to say with an open mind—you want to learn from the experience, not get defensive. Perhaps you could watch them work more closely. Incorporate their useful suggestions in the way you handle your job. It could very well help you improve the amount you get done.

Recommended Readings

Calano, Jimmy, and Salzman, Jeff. *Career Tracking: 26 Successful Short-cuts to the Top*. New York: Simon and Schuster, 1988.

Cox, Allan. *The Making of the Achiever*. New York: Dodd, Mead & Company, 1985.

Kriegel, Robert J. and Patler, Louis. *If It Ain't Broke, Break It*. New York: Warner, 1991.

LeBoeuf, Michael. *Working Smart: How to Accomplish More in Half the Time*. New York: McGraw-Hill, 1979.

Levoy, Robert P. *The Successful Professional Practice*. Englewood Cliffs, NJ: Prentice-Hall, 1970.

Manz, Charles. *The Art of Self Leadership: Strategies for Personnel Effectiveness in Your Life and Work*. Englewood Cliffs, NJ: Prentice-Hall, 1983.

Norris, Kenneth E. *Winning at Work*. Blue Ridge Summit, PA: Tab Books, 1987.

Rosen, Betty. *How to Set and Achieve Goals: The Key to Successful Management*. Englewood Cliffs, NJ: Prentice-Hall, 1981.

Stuart-Kotze, Robin, and Roskin, Rick. *Success Guide to Managerial Achievement*. Reston, VA: Reston Publishing Company, 1983.

Timpe, A. Dale. *The Management of Time*. New York, NY: Kend Publishing, 1987.

Turla, Peter, and Hawkins, Kathleen. *Time Management Made Easy*. New York: E.P. Dutton, 1983.

11

Work Habits

This chapter helps improve performance in the following areas:

- Poor attendance.
- Tardiness.
- Poor job attitude.
- Business ethics.

Action Items for Work Habits

1. Improve attendance on the job.

Poor attendance on the job is a source of discomfort for many managers since it is difficult to provide coverage for the absent employee. Too many days off also raise questions about reliability and trust. Some employees treat ill days as vacation days, feeling that they should take their full quota each year even when they are not sick. Studies have shown that the average person is too ill to work only 2-3 days per year. Unless the employee is under treatment for a serious illness or injury, days taken beyond 2-3 may reflect time taken off for personal reasons or minor illness such as a cold.

As an employee, you should review how many days you miss per year. Are you taking off sick days for minor illness or injury when you could really been working? Have you used sick days for personal matters? If so, what does this say about your reliability and trust? Would you promote and give extra responsibility to someone you could not rely upon? Cut down on the days taken off sick. Use them only when you are too ill to come to work.

2. Arrive early for work each day.

Some employees have a habit of arriving late for work much of the time. If they make every stop light and traffic is normal they arrive exactly on time. If conditions are not so favorable, they are late. Evaluate if you are guilty of this. Do you try to cut it too close in the morning? Would you promote or give additional responsibility to someone who is not reliable to come in on time every morning? If arriving late is one of your problems, do not try to cut things so close. Set the alarm fifteen minutes earlier each day and regard your starting time as the latest you can be there, not the **earliest.** Arriving on time will help you develop a good image throughout your career.

3. Establish high personal ethics.

A common concern for many in the workplace is the work ethics of certain employees. Such employees may be more interested in looking out for themselves than the company, and are willing to violate laws, policies or practices to get there. Evaluate your personal business conduct and make changes where needed. Your ultimate career future can depend on how ethical you are, not to mention saving your job and legal action. Sometimes even hinting of compromised ethics can erode your credibility, such as could happen if a manager jokingly asks a vendor, "What's in it for me if I do business with you?"

Refrain from taking any actions that compromise your business ethics. Avoid doing anything which would violate laws or company policies. Do not accept gifts of any kind which have a monetary value. Do not throw hints of impropriety around others, even your trusted co-workers. Avoid making statements about people in general that indicate they cannot be trusted—eventually co-workers will come to believe that you are projecting feelings about yourself. Report practices to superiors that violate laws or policies. In short, stick to a very solid set of personal ethics in everything you do.

4. Avoid calling in sick to take a personal day.

Employees occasionally need personal days off to take care of home matters or personal business. Some, instead of candidly describing the situation to the manager, will simply call in sick. That erodes trust, particularly if the "too ill to work" employee seems perfectly fine the next day. Try to take care of personal matters (dentist appointments, parking tickets, etc.) on your personal time whenever possible. If you must use company time, candidly explain the situation to your manager and ask for the time off. Doing so will preserve your integrity and ethics with your manager.

5. Show a more positive attitude to others.

Some employees show a negative attitude to others—they always seem to be complaining or criticizing things. By doing so they are really saying to others that **they** are negative on life, and having personal problems. Evaluate your degree of complaining or criticizing. Doing some of this is unavoidable, but when it becomes a habit, you are a loser in the eyes of others. Keep a log each day of how many times you complained about things or criticized others. Try to cut down as much as you can by catching yourself when you start to say something negative. Work on coming up with positive things to say or say nothing at all. By monitoring your progress, you will be able to improve in this area, and find that people are more likely to want to interact with you.

6. Take more pride in your job.

Some employees, even those in low-paying jobs, take a great deal of pride in what they do. They try to be the best they can and feel good about being an expert in their work. Other employees seem to always be in the doldrums about their job. They find it boring and are quick to express the negatives. Evaluate whether you are guilty of being negative about your job. How much pride do you show when others ask you about the job?

If you are not excited about the job, then try to change the job by looking more at the positive side, and adding projects that make the job more interesting. Speak favorably of your work when others ask you about it. As a last resort, think of changing into a more challenging job if you really think this is your problem. However, recognize that your lack of pride and enthusiasm may carry over to the new job as well. It may well be **you,** rather than the **job,** which is in need of change. Start being more positive and showing more pride.

7. Increase your work hours.

Managers and co-workers read a great deal into someone's dedication and work ethic based upon how many hours they put in. The employee who is quick to leave at the end of the day when an important meeting is still going on will not convince others that they are hard working and dedicated. Part of the problem is that employees may get into habits, albeit unnecessary habits, about commuting. We leave at a certain time to catch a certain train or because we always leave at that time.

A better approach is to let the work flow determine your hours, not a train schedule. Put in the time required to get the job done, unless there are unusual circumstances that require you to leave early. If staying late is a problem, then think of coming in early. The important point is to employ work hours that show others that you are dedicated and will do what is required to get the job done.

8. Avoid saying "can't" in the workplace.

Some employees use the word "can't" too often in the workplace. Examples include "I can't help you with that," or "it can't be done that way." When overusing the word "can't," it leads others to believe you are negative or not willing to go out of your way to help others. Take the time to think of how often you use can't or its equivalent ("it's not my job") in carrying out your responsibilities. Try to cut back on this and instead be more helpful and positive. That is a more positive work habit to use in the workplace.

9. Avoid conflicts of interest.

Most organizations have clear-cut policies which prohibit a conflict of interest in carrying out job responsibilities. For example, employees could not share out information to a competitor or enter into a business relationship with a competing firm. While these are obvious cases of a conflict of interest, there are many which are more subtle. As an employee you should avoid any actions which even **hint** of a possible conflict of interest. For example, do not recommend that the company use a certain printer who is a relative of yours. Or, do not push an internal or external job candidate who happens to be a friend of yours. By doing things such as these, even if they are not technically prohibited, you will become known as someone who is political, plays favorites, etc. and that is not a good image to have. The better approach is to simply stay out of any situations where a conflict of interest might occur.

10. Show more initiative in carrying out the job.

Some employees do the minimum that is required to carry out the job. They simply do what they are asked to do, and nothing more. That type of work habit does not lend itself to high performance ratings, salary increases, or promotions. Ask yourself whether you take on extra assignments above and beyond what is required. If not, try to change your behavior. Think of ways to improve the job or ways of saving the company money. Do small, add-on projects that are not required, but very helpful. Present the results of your efforts to your manager or others. Make doing something extra a regular work habit of yours.

11. Listen to inspirational audiotapes.

Sometimes people get into a rut with regards to their work habits and outlook toward their lives and jobs. There needs to be some special event which breaks the person out of that rut and onto a new path. There are many inspirational and motivation audiotapes that can help accomplish this. Relatively inexpensive, such tapes can serve a useful purpose in getting people to change their attitudes and outlook toward their job. Use them yourself or recommend them to someone you think might benefit from them.

12. Have an objective outlook on decisions in the workplace.

Many employees make decisions in the workplace based upon what is best for the organization. Others think of themselves, and what they will get out of the situation. If you tend to make decisions based upon what is in it for you, change your style. Otherwise, co-workers and others could turn against you since they think you are only interested in yourself. Try to consider all sides of an issue, and take your position based upon what is best for the organization. Occasionally, champion the ideas of others and support decisions that benefit others rather than yourself. You will have the support and backing from them if this becomes one of your work habits.

13. Model yourself after someone who has excellent work habits.

It can be useful to apply some of the work habits that you have observed in others. Perhaps you know of a manager who is at work early every day, or always takes a fair, objective approach in making decisions that benefit the company. Take the time to note what you admire in this person and what they do or say that makes you feel that way. Then, try to do more of the same yourself. Use them as a model in improving upon your own work habits.

14. Decrease defensiveness when suggestions are brought to your attention.

Some employees have a negative work habit of becoming defensive when others suggest that they change things. Such people take suggestions as a personal attack, instead of how they were intended. After hearing the suggestion, they may be quick to write it off, argue with the person suggesting it, or not pay any attention. How do you respond when others suggest ways for you to improve upon your work habits? Do you look upon their ideas with an open mind or are you quick to get defensive and attack the person? If necessary, change your style to be more receptive to ideas. See them as opportunities to learn and get better at what you do. That attitude can only help in the long run, not hurt.

15. Eliminate substance abuse.

Professional counseling organizations feel that perhaps 10% of the workforce has problems with substance abuse—be it drugs, alcohol, or the abuse of prescribed medications. Substance abuse hurts job performance in many ways. For example, it is the leading cause of absenteeism, particularly the Monday/Friday variety. It can hurt job performance by making people depressed or unable to carry out their jobs. Substance abusers are also several times more likely than the general population to have health-related problems; this being due to the negative long-term affects of drugs or alcohol.

If these were not reason enough, most companies have explicit or implicit policies prohibiting substance abuse on the job (or arriving at work under the influence). Evaluate your use of any substances such as drugs or alcohol. Are you unable to stop at any time? Is your usage daily rather than occasional? If yes, see a counselor now to get professional assistance before the problem costs you your job and self-esteem.

16. Greet others in a friendly manner.

Some employees have a cheerful disposition; they are quick to greet others and smile. Others never look to say hello and seem more crabby. This is a day-in day-out work habit that can make a big difference in how others see you. Even if you have a positive attitude inside, you need to show that on the outside by how you interact with others. Review you work habits in terms of friendliness and greeting others. It does not take much time to smile, say hello, and make with some limited small talk. Yet that can make a big difference in the how others perceive you and the attitude your show.

17. Carry out the activities you said you would.

One poor work habit that some employees have is to not deliver what they said they would. They might promise to complete a report by a certain time, or help someone out but then fail to deliver because they were "too busy" or some other reason. That erodes the trust and respect you have for the person, and may make you want to avoid them. Review how often you deliver on promises you made to others. Try to deliver on every single occasion, or do not promise to do so in the first place. If you forget to carry out what you said, develop a better system for keeping track of the activities you need to do. Coming through for others as you said you would is a very important work habit to practice.

18. Go out of your way to assist others.

Some employees go out of their way to assist others. Perhaps it involves giving clear directions to a visitor, taking the time to listen to someone's problem, or transferring calls to the correct person. This extra assistance not only helps the other party, but creates a positive impression of the employee. Such an employee is seen as someone who is helpful, good with people, etc. Make this your style as well. Take the initiative to assist others when not necessarily required.

19. Complete activities on time.

We all have had to deal with people who do not complete projects on time. In some cases, we are inconvenienced when the party does not deliver when expected (e.g., repairs on your car not done on time). For some employees, there is a greater than normal trend to be late in getting things done on time. When this happens, questions are raised about the person's reliability and trust. Avoid this type of problem yourself. Promise completion dates that are realistic, not best-case possibilities. If the unexpected comes up and causes a delay, call the other person and explain the situation. This will avoid surprises and help maintain trust.

20. Show new employees "the ropes."

Some employees have the nice work habit of showing new employees the ropes. They go out of their way to point out where things are located, how the company does things, etc. This add-on activity is a good way to befriend others and get a working relationship off to a good start. You will also establish yourself as someone who is easy to talk to and get along with. Try adding this action item to your other effective work habits.

21. Allow extra commuting time for days when the weather is bad.

Some employees are always late when the weather is bad. Their excuse: the bad weather. Others somehow manage to always get there on time. Evaluate your style. Are you often late on bad-weather days? If so, pay more attention to the weather reports. If you know the weather is expected to be bad, get up earlier than normal. Take an alternative way of commuting which might be more reliable. By arriving on time on even bad-weather days, you will establish yourself as more reliable employee with good work habits.

22. Keep lunch hours and breaks reasonable.

Nearly everyone takes time for lunch and breaks—some just take much longer than others. While no manager likes to bring up this problem, it is easy to notice when employees are not around. Review your practices regarding lunch and breaks. Do you always take the maximum or go beyond the maximum? Have you ever skipped a break or had lunch at your desk in just a few minutes? Avoid the actions that show you are not as serious about working as others you work with. Put in practice those actions that are good work habits.

23. Keep expense account items minimal.

A poor work habit of some is to take advantage of expense account charges, even if they fall within the company's guidelines. For example, an employee on travel status might go to a better than average restaurant for lunch because "the company is paying for it." Or they might add on extra auto mileage or tips that were not really incurred. Managers often have a way of knowing when expense accounts are being padded. Someone who does this runs the risk of losing the trust and respect of their manager, not to mention company action against more serious violations.

Keep your expense account charges as low as you can. Think of it as spending your own money, not the company's money. What type of hotels would you stay in and how much would you pay for a lunch if you were doing it on your own. Look to save where you can and save your employer the extra money. That is a positive work habit to have and one that will be noticed by your manager.

24. Arrive on time for meetings.

Another poor work habit is to arrive late for meetings. While this is almost fashionable in some companies, it makes it very difficult to conduct business. For how can you start a meeting if the participants are not there? How long should you wait? Try to have a positive work habit in this area. Arrive on time for your meetings. If you really have to be late because of another commitment, call in advance to explain your delay and expected arrival time. This will help others in the company, and increase your image as a reliable employee.

Recommended Readings

Blanchard, Kenneth and Peale, Norman Vincent. *The Power of Ethical Management*. New York: William Morrow, 1988.

Brown, Marvin T. *Working Ethics: Strategies for Decision Making and Organizational Responsibility*. San Francisco: Jossey-Bass, 1990.

Calano, Jimmy, and Salzman, Jeff. *Career Tracking: 26 Successful Short-cuts to the Top*. New York: Simon and Schuster, 1988.

Cameron, Charles, and Elisorr, Suzanne. *Thank God it's Monday: Making Your Work Fulfilling and Finding Fulfilling Work*. New York: St. Martin's Press, 1986.

Cox, Allan. *The Making of the Achiever*. New York: Dodd, Mead & Company, 1985.

Covey, Stephen R. *The Seven Habits of Highly Effective People*. New York: Simon & Schuster, 1989.

DeMare, George. *101 Ways to Protect Your Job*. New York: McGraw-Hill, 1984.

Edwards, Alan. Just Down or Out? Helping Troubled Employees. *Supervisory Management*, June, 1984, 29, p. 10-12.

Farrant, A.W. Block that Absenteeism. *Supervision*, Aug., 1985, 47, p. 14-16.

Grasing, R. Back to Basics: A Refresher Course on Managing Attendance Problems. *Supervision*, Oct, 1987, 49, p. 3-5.

Griffith, T.J. Want Job Improvement? Try Counseling (Dealing with Personal Problems and Improving Performance). *Management Solutions*, Sept, 1987, 32, p. 13-19.

Hill, Napoleon, and Stone, W. Clement. *Success Through a Positive Mental Attitude*. New York: Prentice-Hall, 1987.

Johnston, Sally A. Dealing with a Grieving Employee. *Management Solutions*, July, 1987, 32, p. 18-26.

Kennedy, Dennis. A Counseling Approach for Chronic Tardiness. *Supervisory Management*, Nov, 1984, 29, p. 25-29.

Kite, P. Preventing Employee Tardiness. *Supervision*, July, 1984, 46, p. 14-15.

Kravetz, Dennis J. *Getting Noticed: A Manager's Success Kit*. New York: Wiley, 1985.

Lampert, Adrienne. Supervising an Employee in Therapy. *Supervisory Management*, Feb, 1985, 30, p. 33-36.

Loehr, James E., and McLaughlin, Peter J. *Mentally Tough*. New York: M. Evans and Company, 1986.

Manz, Charles. *The Art of Self Leadership: Strategies for Personal Effectiveness in Your Life and Work*. Englewood Cliffs, NJ: Prentice-Hall, 1983.

Nelson, Andre. I Won't Be Able to Come to Work Today . . . *Supervisory Management*, May, 1985, 30, p. 34-36.

Oldfield, Kenneth, and Ayers, Nancy. Pay the New Job Dues, Avoid the New Job Blues (Advice to the Newly Hired Employees). *Personnel Journal*, Aug, 1986, p. 48-56.

Pryor, Mildred G., and Golden, Mitchell K. The Depressed Employee. *Supervisory Management*, Oct, 1984, 29, p. 14-16.

Schwartz, A.E. Counseling the Marginal Performer. *Management Solutions*, 1988, 33, p. 30-35.

Waitley, Denis, and Witt, Reni L. *The Joy of Working*. New York: Ballantine Books, 1985.

Ward, Richard H., and Hirsch, Nancy A. Reducing Employee Absenteeism: A Program that Works. *Personnel*, June, 1985, 62, p. 50-54.

12

Gathering and Analyzing Information

This chapter helps improve performance in the following areas:

- Collecting all needed information.
- Analyzing information.
- Making better decisions.
- Keeping track of information.

Action Items For Gathering and Analyzing Information

1. List out all information needed for making decisions.

A useful starting point prior to collecting information is to list out all of the information that you need. Items on the list could include, for example:

- The opinions of others.

- Reference material (books, articles, manuals).

- Survey information.

- Observations of people or machines.

- Test-runs.

Brainstorm all sources of information that are needed to make a decision or solve a problem. Once this list is developed, divide it up amongst different people with clear directions as to who will do what. Begin collecting the information as early as possible so you will not face a deadline crunch.

2. Use interviews and discussions to collect information.

Some technical employees may forget the "people side" when collecting information. They may gather facts and figures, but eliminate talking to others. When a final decision is made, some may feel left out or resistant to the decision. A better approach is to get the ideas and thoughts of others as well as facts and figures. Not only can employees provide you with important information, but their involvement ensures that they buy into the final decision. Think of all of those who might have knowledge or be impacted by your decision. Set up a time with them to tap their feelings. Group meetings may be useful if you have a fair number of people impacted by your decision.

3. Use written surveys for collecting information with a large number of people.

If there are a large number of people impacted by your decision, it may be impractical to interview them, even in groups. Think of drawing up survey questions so that you can get the opinions of a larger number of people. Keep the survey multiple-choice if at all possible. This makes it easy to analyze the results, be it by hand or by computer. Fill-in questions are much more difficult to draw conclusions from, and are much more time consuming to process. Provide summary feedback to all participants if possible so they will know how the results came out.

4. Use open-ended questions when interviewing others.

Unlike surveys for large numbers of people, interviews give you the chance to ask follow-up questions and probe feelings in much more depth. You can do this best by using open-ended questions. Open-ended questions are those that cannot be asked with a "yes" or "no." Examples of open-ended questions are as follows:

- "Tell me your feelings about the new changes."
- "What is your opinion about changing our production schedule."
- "Can you say more about why you like the equipment from Company X."

Answers to open-ended questions like these will shed more light on what someone's feelings are. They also suggest good follow-up questions to get yet more information. Closed-ended questions are used primarily to confirm information that you already have. Make use of open-ended questions in any one-on-one or small group interviewing sessions that you might have.

5. Avoid drawing conclusions too quickly.

Some employees make the mistake of drawing conclusions when they really should be gathering information. Such employees may feel that they have heard the answer before, or simply jump too quickly to the wrong conclusion. Resist the temptation to do this in your information gathering. Ask your open-ended question, and sit back and let the other person answer until they are through. Try not to interrupt unless you are dealing with someone who rambles a great deal. After your interview is complete, then go back and draw conclusions about what you heard. This is an effective way to gather information and make better decisions.

6. Keep an open mind when information gathering.

Some individuals find it hard to keep an open mind when interviewing others, particularly if the other person says something they disagree with. They tend to jump in with their feelings and debate the matter. This discourages the other person from saying anything further. They may also feel their time is being wasted, and that they are not being listened to. If your primary purpose is to gather information, look at whatever you collect with an open mind. Do not challenge the ideas at this point. Draw the other person out and encourage them to say exactly what they feel.

7. Use an effective note-taking system for interviews.

The results of information-gathering interviews should be recorded in some way. It is very dangerous to "keep it all in your mind," particularly if you go back and try to quote or restate what someone said. Be certain to take notes (or have another person do so) whenever you interview others as part of information gathering. You might also tape record conversations in person or over the phone, but be certain to tell the person in advance that you are doing this and see if they mind. Having good notes to work from ensures that your information is accurate.

8. Mentally or verbally restate what the speaker is saying.

Some individuals are quick to forget what the speaker said. Their retention of even key points does not last very long. Note-taking can certainly help this, but so can restating what the speaker has said at various points in the conversation. One way to do this is to simply restate to yourself what the person's key points are. By doing this all of the time throughout the conversation, you are more likely to retain what was said. Another technique is to verbally restate what you thought you heard someone say. Say something like, "If I understand you correctly, you feel. . ." By mentally or verbally restating what someone else has said, both retention and accuracy of information gathering will be improved.

9. Question and listen more than you speak.

An employee will never be good at information gathering if they spend more time speaking than listening. Talkative people or those with strong feelings may have to suppress the urge to talk during an information-gathering conversation. Assess how much time you spend talking in an interview to gather information. If it is more than fifty percent, try to cut back. Limit your talking to perhaps 25% of the conversation. Share out your purpose, ask questions, paraphrase, and give out enough information to make the speaker comfortable. The remaining time should be spent in listening and note-taking.

10. Read the body language of the speaker.

People communicate not only by the words that they say, but by the way they say them. If you want to be the best at gathering information, notice the body language of the speaker as well. For example, someone might say, "I'm not mad" when their body language is telling you otherwise. Know how to recognize when someone is uncomfortable, relaxed, not telling the truth, or bored. Adapt what you say or do based upon what you have read. Use more than just the words to interpret the information you are collecting.

11. Let ideas "pop into your mind" at all times.

When gathering and analyzing information, there may be times when ideas simply pop into your mind—often when you least expect it and are not trying to think of an answer. These ideas might be things to do, or explanations for why something occurred. Some individuals cut off such thinking when they are at home. They feel they do not want to deal with work away from the workplace. More successful employees will keep a note pad handy wherever they go and jot down the ideas as soon as they can. This includes when relaxing at home, driving in the car, or at other locations. Going back to these ideas later can often provide leads that would never be thought of in the workplace. Try to take advantage of ideas that pop into your mind.

12. Tap the ideas of staff, peers, and others.

Some managers and employees make the mistake of trying to do it all on their own. When gathering information for a project, they rely exclusively on their own ideas, and perhaps what is written up about the subject of interest. However, each of us is but one person, and has but one set of ideas. By using the ideas of others you can greatly increase the quality of information gathering. Managers should use a "participative" style of management with their staff— get their ideas to add to your own. Recognize that employees are sometimes closer to a problem than the manager and have valuable insights.

Employees who are not managers should obtain the ideas of their peers and those in other parts of the company. Seek out those people who may have ideas of use to you on your project. Take the best of their ideas and combine them with your own. The quality of your information will be much better than doing it on your own.

13. Use observations and test runs in your information gathering.

When collecting information, it is always useful to see things with your own eyes. For example, understanding the sales process at a company is helped by making sales calls with a sales representative and seeing what the person does. Try to spend time observing people whenever it helps you in making a decision. Get their permission in advance so the individuals will not feel that they are being watched. Make detailed notes and work these in with the rest of the information you have gathered.

Similarly, the use of test runs can be helpful in evaluating information. Before concluding that a certain piece of equipment or a certain process works best, try a test run. Experiment and try out the equipment and process and see what the results show. The information you get from the test run can save you the embarrassment of implementing something and then finding out that it does not work as planned. Test runs are an important part of evaluating information.

14. Network with colleagues to gain more information.

The employees at any given company will have a limited perspective on any subject due to their unique operating practices. Your perspective can be broadened by talking with others outside the company. Their knowledge and experience may add much more to what you already know. For example, if you are an accountant and want to purchase new software for accounting applications, talking with those at other companies could be very valuable. They may have experience with the very software you are thinking of buying. Call on colleagues in other companies. In many cases they will be willing to share out information to help a fellow professional, or steer you to someone who has the information. Networking with others can be a valuable addition to your information gathering process.

15. Practice effective listening when meeting with others.

An employee can rapidly bring an end to an information-gathering meeting by not practicing good listening. By not paying attention or looking distracted, the speaker may soon end the conversation. When you are gathering information from others, be sure to practice good listening skills (see the chapter on listening if necessary). Briefly, these good listening practices are:

• Maintain good eye contact.

• Show empathy by saying "I know" or "I understand" at various points in the conversation.

• Avoid interrupting others.

• Make notes or otherwise show you are paying attention.

• Vary your facial expressions throughout the conversation.

• Have a relaxed body posture.

• Nod your head to indicate understanding where appropriate.

16. Utilize professional associations and references in collecting information.

Regardless of what field you are in, there is likely a professional association dedicated to employees in that field. Many of these associations publish books and journals for those who are interested. They may also have libraries of information available for any who care to use them, and perhaps sources of people to contact for free information on any subject. Utilize these professional sources in your information gathering. They make an excellent starting point. People at the association offices may have much better sources available than you could ever develop on your own.

17. Use a file system for collected information.

When starting to collect information on any project, develop a filing system in the very beginning. Place the information you collect in these files as it becomes available. This will ensure that written matter is easier to keep track of as you go forward. You might have, for example, a file for interview notes, one for relevant articles, one for notes you made observing someone else's equipment, and

another for product brochures. Develop whatever categories are appropriate for your project and clearly label a file folder for each one. Good organization from the beginning will make it easier to draw conclusions at the end.

18. Summarize your key findings.

At the conclusion of your information gathering, force yourself to summarize what you have found out. Write up a brief summary and include a chart or table of key facts or results. Keep the write-up brief; eliminate all of the details which will detract from the rest of the report. It is especially useful to present alternative scenarios in your summary and the advantages and disadvantages of each. For example, you might contrast the purchase of a product from three different vendors with the related advantages of each, or three possible ways of implementing a new production system with the advantages of each. By summarizing your findings and making specific recommendations, your reader will be able to draw conclusions easily.

19. Chart out the results of your information gathering.

Charts or tables make it easy to draw conclusions from the information you gather. For example, you may have evaluated three consulting firms for designing a new training course. You might construct a chart showing the name, cost, time frame, and products each firm would develop. Someone seeing this chart could clearly understand what the pluses and minuses are of each firm. They will be better able to conclude what to do than by reading a text or hearing your describe the situation verbally. Use charts or tables whenever possible to summarize the results of your work.

20. View the ideas of others from their perspective.

When collecting information, try to view the ideas of others by "walking a mile in their shoes." This type of perspective will eliminate any bias in your information gathering—bias others may be able to detect. Try to view the situation from the perspective of the person who is sharing their ideas. This will not only enable you to understand better, but help you ask better follow-up questions. You do not have to agree with the person, but merely understand why they feel the way they do. By showing empathy with another's ideas, and looking at the situation from their perspective, will make you better at information gathering.

21. Practice information gathering at home.

If you want to improve your information gathering skills, practice them at home. You might, for example, try out these skills by evaluating which type of new car to buy. Even if you are not interested in buying a car, collect all the information you can. Talk to dealers and individual consumers, gather brochures and articles, and test drive the cars yourself. Summarize your conclusions and chart out the findings. By practicing these skills at home, you will develop them more, and be able to apply them on the job. This can not only help your job performance, but help you in your home life as well.

Recommended Readings

Albrecht, Karl. *Brain Power: Learn to Improve Your Thinking Skills*. Englewood Cliffs, NJ: Prentice-Hill, 1987.

Belson, William A. *The Design and Understanding of Survey Questions*. Lexington, Mass: D.C. Heath, Lexington Books, 1981.

Bradley, John. How to Interview for Information. *Training and Development Journal*, April, 1983, p. 59-62.

Huber, George P. *Managerial Decision Making*. Glenview, IL: Scott, Foresman and Company, 1980.

Jackson, K.F. *The Art of Solving Problems*. New York: St. Martin's Press, 1975.

Marrus, Stephanie K. *Building the Strategic Plan: Find, Analyze, and Present the Right Information*. New York: Wiley, 1984.

Nadler, Gerald, and Hibino, Shozo. *Breakthrough Thinking: Why We Must Change the Way We Solve Problems and the Seven Principles to Achieve This*. Rocklin, CA: Prima Publishing, 1990.

Sudman, Seymour, and Bradburn, Norman. *Asking Questions: A Practical Guide to Questionnaire Design*. San Francisco: Jossey-Bass, 1982.

13

Problem Solving and Decision Making

This chapter helps improve performance in the following areas:

- Solving job-related problems.
- Making higher quality decisions.
- Being more decisive.
- Anticipating problems before they become problems.
- Getting others to accept decisions.

Action Items for Problem Solving and Decision Making

1. Clearly define the problem you are trying to solve.

An important starting point for problem solving is to first define the problem you want to solve. For someone cannot expect to find a solution if the problem is not first defined. The problem itself should be written out and communicated to all involved in coming up with the solution. Care should be taken to break down (or enlarge) a problem to ensure it is on target. For example, different results will be obtained if the problem of "reducing turnover" is studied versus "reducing turnover in new hires." Slight wording changes will result in looking for, and implementing, different kinds of solutions. Take the time to clearly define the problem up front.

2. Brainstorm as many problem solutions as possible.

Some employees make the mistake of forcing a decision right after the problem has been defined. They either consider no alternatives, or make a quick choice amongst a couple of alternatives. That might be acceptable for unimportant decisions, but for larger decisions, more time should be spent in considering alternatives. Consider getting a group together for those larger decisions which have a major impact. Or spend more time alone brainstorming possible solutions.

Since a group can come up with more ideas than any individual in a group, get together those employees who can help with your problem. When brainstorming alternatives, set a climate that is open and friendly. Encourage people to think of as many ideas as they can, even if the ideas seem crazy. Do not evaluate any idea or let anyone else make comments at this stage—you merely want to get as many ideas as possible.

3. See problems as "opportunities in disguise."

Many people have a negative attitude about solving problems. They feel that problems take up time which they would rather use doing something else. With that type of attitude, problems will not be worked on in advance, resulting in still more problems. Effective employees see problem solving as a challenge that tests a person's creativity and intelligence. For them, problems are merely opportunities to improve the workplace. Try to have that attitude as you run across problems in the workplace. Taking the time to properly solve a problem will improve operations and make you more successful in your career.

4. Consider all four sides of a problem.

When trying to solve a problem, look at it from different sides to generate possible solutions. Generally speaking, there are four sides to any problem. These sides are as follows:

- Human (e.g., not enough employees, wrong kind of employees, lack of training).

- Methods/procedures—have improper procedures or none at all.

- Equipment—improper or no equipment where needed.

- Financial—limited resources causing the problem.

When stumped at generating solutions, shift the focus to one of the other sides and continue. Do not stop generating solutions until all sides have been considered. It will result in a better solution being identified.

5. Use a group of people to brainstorm solutions.

Some employees (some managers in particular) make the mistake of trying to solve all problems on their own. When you stop to consider it, each of us has but one set of ideas that we can come up with. Groups, on the other hand, can always generate more ideas than any one person in the group. Use a group of employees whenever appropriate for problem solving. Choose people that have knowledge about, or are impacted by, the problem you are trying to solve. The group process will guarantee a wide variety of ideas and a higher quality solution.

6. Suppress the urge to "shoot from the hip."

Important decisions should not be made on the spur of the moment. Some employees, by nature, try to make decisions quickly. They go by a gut feeling, regardless of what type of decision has to be made. That can be costly when the decision has a major impact on the area. If you have a "shoot from the hip" tendency, try to force yourself to take more time in decision making. List out possible solutions and evaluate the impact of each. If time permits, sleep on the decision overnight and see if you feel the same way the following day. Force yourself to fully evaluate options to improve your decision making quality.

7. Evaluate each solution on the basis of several factors.

When trying to decide amongst the possible solutions, evaluate each on several criteria. This will ensure that each solution is judged objectively. Possible criteria to evaluate solutions against include the following:

- The **time** to implement.
- The **cost** to implement.
- The **human resources** necessary.
- The **training** needed to implement the solution.
- The **equipment or supplies** needed to implement.
- The **impact on other parts of the business** this decision has.
- The fit of company **culture** with the decision.

By evaluating each solution on criteria such as these, the final decision will be more accurate. Use a process such as this with important decisions that you have to make.

8. Use participative decision making.

Management style has changed a great deal in the past few years with the growth of participative management. Part of the participative management process involves the role of others in decision making. When decisions need to be made, think of delegating to others where you can. Where you cannot delegate, let others have a say in the final decision. Use a collaborative process, letting everyone have their say. Not only will this help with the decision quality, but make the implementation of the decision more easy. This is due to the fact that employees buy into and accept decisions more readily when they have had an opportunity to be involved in the decision.

Participative decision making is particularly important to use when you are making decisions that affect someone else's job. To not involve the affected employees in the process could lead them to resist the decision or only half-heartedly give it a chance. Involve others in decision making wherever you can to increase acceptance.

9. Chart out the positives and negatives of each solution.

It can be quite complicated to try and pick from several possible solutions, particularly when each solution is evaluated on several criteria. To make the process easier, it is helpful to chart out the positives and negatives of each solution. On a flip chart or piece of paper, list out each solution down the rows. List the criterria (such as those suggested in No. 7 above) across the columns. Then use a ranking or rating system (e.g., high, medium, low) to fill in the cells on the chart. Some sort of scoring system might prove helpful as well. By visually seeing all of the solutions at once, along with their positives and negatives, you can make the final decision easier. Use charting to help with your decision making.

10. Let ideas "pop into your mind."

It is difficult at times to think of solutions to problems when the workplace is very busy and full of interruptions. Sometimes the best ideas come to mind when not trying to think of them, for example, when relaxing at home. Some employees try to totally disregard work when at home, and thereby lose their best ideas. If you have this tendency, try to at least jot down the ideas when you think of them. This takes but a few seconds to do and can be immensely helpful. Keep note pads in several locations in the home so you can jot ideas down without interrupting other activities. Think the idea through more thoroughly if not busy at the time.

11. Do not force decisions.

Employees sometimes force decisions due to pressure from others, job demands, time constraints, or self-imposed deadlines. If you are not comfortable in making the decision now, delay the decision until you are more comfortable in making it. While the circumstances may vary, it is usually the case that delaying a decision for a couple of days is less costly than making a poor decision quickly. If faced with a decision due to time pressures, ask what is the worst thing that can happen if you wait another couple of days. Tell others pressuring you that you want the decision to be the correct one and simply need more time. The key is to not force yourself into a poor decision.

12. Note trends in problems in your area.

The best solution to a problem is to avoid the problem in the first place. Due to day-to-day pressures, it may be difficult to sit back and analyze problems that come up repeatedly. You may need to block off time to review what sort of problems are coming up in your area. Do this on an occasional basis. Think of the last several problems you have had to deal with in your area. Do you see any patterns? Now think of what might be causing those problem. After doing this, come up with solutions and implement them. This may prevent the problem from ever occurring again.

13. Make decisions in an objective way.

While gut feelings always enter into decision making, sound decisions are usually those based upon objective facts. When emotions guide decisions, there is always a chance that feelings will change, producing regret at a later time. For example, making a key decision when upset or pressured may not lead to the right choice. To avoid this problem, make your decisions when you are more relaxed and able to think things through. Review your decision making process to ensure you were objective. Use charts or facts to guide your decision, as described in other parts of this chapter.

14. Be willing to change decisions as information changes.

Some employees make the mistake of sticking with their original decision even when circumstances change. That can be very costly inhuman and financial terms. If new and different information becomes available to you, be willing to go back and re-evaluate your original decision. Change the decision if necessary. It is much better to make a change and do things correctly than persist in doing it the original way. Have an attitude reflecting that events are in a constant state of change, and the right decision today may not be the right decision tomorrow. Recognize that eventually you may have to change every one of the decisions you have made in the workplace.

15. Delegate routine decisions to others.

This action item applies mainly to those who manage other employees. Some managers can become over-burdened with trying to make every decision in their department, even trivial ones. This prevents the person from getting to other activities that require attention. Review how many decisions you make on your own. How many decisions do you allow others to make in your behalf? If you do not delegate routine decisions to others now, start doing more of this. Think of who best can take over some of the decision making you now do. Explain to them their new responsibilities, and trust them to carry out these decisions. This will enable you to be more effective in using your time and making decisions you absolutely need to make.

16. Speed decision making by not researching unlikely solutions.

Some employees may take too long to make a decision. In part, this can be do to researching and evaluating every possible solution in great depth. The result is a very slow process that hurts the department's effectiveness. Evaluate whether you use this type of decision making style. Do others tell you that you take too long to make decisions? Do you spend time thinking through solutions or minor issues that are unlikely to change the outcome? If so, try to speed your decision making process. Go through all of the possible solutions and evaluate how many will likely impact the final decision and need to be pursued. Research only those solutions that are likely choices. Gather supplemental information only if it is needed to reach the proper conclusions. This will save time and improve your decisiveness in the eyes of others.

17. Escalate not only problems to others, but solutions as well.

Some employees have the habit of dumping problems in their manager's laps. The employee is good at identifying and escalating problems, but always leaves it to someone else to solve them. Evaluate whether or not you have a tendency to do this. How often do you go to your manager with a problem to be solved? Do you go in with a recommended solution or just the problem itself? If you use a "dump and run" technique, you need to change your practices.

The solution in this area is to solve as many problems on your own as you can. If you must escalate a problem to your manager, think through likely solutions beforehand. Then go to the manager with not only the problem, but your recommendation on how to solve the problem. This will show more responsibility on your part, and lead to better performance.

18. Brainstorm solutions to problems when you are most relaxed.

It can be difficult to brainstorm solutions to problems when you are distracted with busywork at the workplace. If you have this problem, try to block off some time when you are able to work uninterrupted and when you are more relaxed. This might be early in the morning or late in the afternoon. Perhaps you will want to do your brainstorming at home in the evenings or weekends. Whatever the case, choosing a relaxing and unhurried setting will likely lead to better results. Modify your brainstorming time and place if you are having problems in this area.

19. Reduce procrastination by using a cutoff system.

Some employees like to procrastinate with decisions—for them, there is never a good time to decide or never enough information on a subject. If you tend to procrastinate on making decisions, utilize a cutoff system to be more decisive. Decide in advance how much information needs to be gathered to make the decision, and resist the temptation to keep gathering more and more minor details. Set a deadline for making the decision once all of the needed information is in. Force yourself to meet the deadline if you have the tendency to keep extending it. By doing this you will be seen as more decisive and in charge by those who work with you, and ensure that you are not delaying key decisions for unimportant reasons.

20. Implement preventative problem solving.

Problems can often be avoided by correctly anticipating them. As you look at your goals and your job, try to anticipate what might go wrong. What would happen to your area if employees leave, or equipment breaks down, or financial resources are cut back? By anticipating problems such as these, you will be better equipped to handle them should they occur. For each potential problem, come up with contingency solutions that would help solve the problem. You might want to write these down and circulate them to others for their benefit. Preventative problem solving can go a long way in preventing problems or nipping them in the bud.

21. Solve as many problems on your own as you can.

Some employees do not try to solve problems on their own. When they become aware of a problem, they immediately go to others with it. While their speed in escalating the problem would be appreciated by managers, it would be even more appreciated if the employee would try to solve some of the problems. Try to review what your reaction would be if a problem would develop in your area right now. Would you first try to solve it on your own? Go to others right away?

If you have a tendency to avoid solving problems, take more initiative on your own. If necessary, meet with your manager to clarify your job responsibilities and what kinds of problems you can solve on your own. Then work on your own solutions as problems occur, escalating only those that are too difficult to solve or beyond your scope of authority.

22. Test out your decisions before implementing.

There are ways to minimize the risk of making a wrong decision. The most important way is to make a test run of the decision before implementing it for good. Think of some way to test out your initial decision—perhaps you can try it out on a sample production run or use it in only one department. By doing this, you can evaluate the correctness of the decision before using it on a large-scale basis. Use test runs whenever you can for critical decisions.

23. Increase your risk-taking in decision making.

Some individuals are reluctant to make decisions because of a fear that they might be wrong. For them, it is better to do nothing than suffer the consequences of being wrong. While that may seem safe, few jobs can be done well if the employee is not willing to accept responsibility for making decisions. This tendency is hard to self-evaluate, but perhaps you have noticed it in yourself or others may have mentioned it to you. The avoidance of risk-taking in making decisions usually takes the form of continually postponing decisions or trying to get others to make your decisions.

If you avoid decisions because of a fear that you may be wrong, change your thinking in this area. You can do this by recognizing the following:

- You know your area better than anyone else and are the best person to decide what needs to be done.

- Ask what is the worst that can happen if the decision is wrong. Usually the fear is much greater than the actual outcome.

- Focus on the positives from implementing your choice rather than the negatives. Every choice has both positives and negatives, but some people avoid decisions by focusing exclusively on the negatives.

- Be willing to accept the risks with your decision. Actually, everything we do has a calculated risk, and there is nothing unique about that decision you are fretting over.

24. Use cost/benefit analysis to help make decisions.

Not every decision can be made on a cost/benefit basis, but many can be analyzed in this way. If appropriate to your decision, take the time to first calculate the costs of each possible solution. Think not only of direct financial costs, but indirect costs such as employees, training, equipment, supplies, overhead, and other items. Next, estimate the potential benefit from each solution. What will it gain in terms of increased sales, reduced staff time, or savings in outside expenditures? Last, subtract the difference between the costs and benefits to help guide your decision. The use of cost/benefit analysis keeps decisions objective and focused on the bottom line.

Recommended Readings

Ackoff, Russell L. *The Art of Problem Solving—Accompanied By Ackoff's Fables*. New York: Wiley, 1978.

Albert, K.J. *Handbook for Business Problem Solving*. New York: McGraw-Hill, 1980.

Albrecht, Karl. *Brain Power: Learn to Improve Your Thinking Skills*. Englewood Cliffs, NJ: Prentice-Hall, 1987.

Blai, B. Jr. Eight Steps to Successful Problem Solving. *Supervisory Management*, Jan, 1986, 31, p. 7-9.

Brookfield, Stephen D. *Developing Critical Thinkers: Challenging Adults to Explore Alternative Ways of Thinking and Acting*. San Francisco: Jossey-Bass, 1987.

Cohen, William A., and Cohen, Nurit. *Top Executive Performance: 11 Keys to Success and Power*. New York: Wiley, 1984.

Drucker, Peter F. The Effective Decision. *Harvard Business Review*, Jan-Feb, 1967, 45, p. 92-94.

Easton, A. *Decision Making: A Short Course for Professionals*. New York: Wiley, 1976.

Georgoff, David M., and Murdick, Robert G. Manager's Guide to Forecasting. *Harvard Business Review*, Jan-Feb, 1986, 64, p. 110-114.

Heyel, C. *The VNR Guide to Management Decision Making*. New York: Van Nostrand Reinhold, 1980.

Huber, George P. *Managerial Decision Making*. Glenview, IL: Scott, Foresman and Company, 1980.

Kaufman, Roger. *Identifying and Solving Problems (A Systems Approach)* 3rd ed. San Diego, Calif: University Associates, Inc, 1982.

Kindler, Herbert S. Decisions, Decisions: Which Approach to Take? *Personnel*, Jan, 1985, 62, p. 47-51.

Nadler, Gerald and Hibino, Shozo. *Breakthrough Thinking: Why We Must Change the Way We Solve Problems, and the Seven Principles to Achieve This.* Rocklin, CA: Prima Publishing, 1990.

Using Logical Techniques for Making Better Decisions. Edited by Douglas N. Dickson. New York: Wiley, 1983.

Segall, Lynda, and Meyers, Carol. Taking Aim at Problems. *Management Solutions*, Feb, 1988, 33, p. 5-8.

14

Financial and Numerical Skills

This chapter helps improve performance in the following areas:

- Being more adept with budgets and costs.
- Skill in working with numbers.
- Familiarity and use of financial terms.
- Developing a better "bottom-line" orientation.
- Being more analytical and numbers oriented.

Action Items For Financial and Numerical Skills

1. Monitor the department's budget and expenses.

One way to improve upon financial and numerical skills is to seek out and review information of this nature. Department expenses and budgets are excellent sources of information that are readily available in most companies. If you typically do not have access to the department budget, seek out your manager. Tell your manager that you would like to build better financial skills, and offer to double-check expenses to verify accuracy. Normally, expense information is summarized once each month and, for many companies, computer generated. Review this information each month, and go an extra step by pointing out areas over budget and making projections to year end.

2. Project the cost savings of changing department activities.

When changes to the department are contemplated (e.g., new equipment, new procedures), project the cost savings of these changes. Evaluate how the change might save the company money. For example, buying a new computer might save significant staff time (and salary) by reducing the amount of manual work which is done. Similarly, changing the work flow of an area might improve the speed of production, saving money. By thinking of the cost savings related to suggested changes, you will likely save the company money, be seen as more of a manager, and build your financial and numerical skills. Calculate the related cost impact of contemplated department changes.

3. Read the company's annual report.

Employees with limited financial background may avoid exactly those publications that can help build financial knowledge. One such publication is the company annual review. If you are looking to build better financial and numerical skills, take the time to thoroughly read through the company annual review and quarterly supplements. Try to develop an understanding of many of the basic financial items such as profits, profit margins, return on equity, and so on. If uncertain of what these items mean, seek out someone at your company in the finance area or obtain a reference book which explains the terms. By understanding and referring to the annual report, your financial skills will increase as well as your understanding of the business.

4. Use graphs and tables to present your ideas.

Some employees like to make their points by verbally stressing why certain actions should be taken. Others like to show the numerical side of why something should be done. Both approaches contribute to getting ideas across. Evaluate your style when trying to sell ideas to others. If you rely exclusively on the verbal side, build more variety by presenting numbers in your presentations. These numbers might be costs, savings, production figures, quality figures, and the like.

Whenever presenting financial or numerical information, it is best to use graphs or tables. This makes it easier for others to understand results of this nature—a picture can be "worth a thousand words" when it comes to showing numerical trends and projections. Use graphs and tables as visual aids to get your points across with numerical or financial information that is detailed. Keep it simple, but present the information which is necessary to get across your key points.

5. Read the financial and business sections of the newspaper.

Financial knowledge and skills can be improved by reading the financial and business sections of the newspaper. Turn to this section every day and read it thoroughly. If you run across terms that you are not familiar with, look them up or ask others who are familiar with them. Try to relate the information you read about with other information you have available. For example, relate information about a company's sales and profit margins to the same results at your company. By reading the financial and business sections of the newspaper every day, you will develop better financial skills and acumen.

6. Draw up budgets for special projects.

Financial skills can be built by drawing up and monitoring budget progress. The next time a project comes up in your area which involves expenditures, volunteer to draw up the budget for the project. Your manager might even let you do this for projects which are not a part of your responsibilities. Think of all of the costs, direct and indirect, related to the project. Monitor actual expenditures on the project versus the expected ones. By doing this for multiple projects, you will develop skills at budgeting, forecasting, and evaluating the costs of various projects.

7. Evaluate different investment opportunities.

Skill in finance can be increased by evaluating investment opportunities. Even if you do not have the money to invest, you can build skills by practicing as if you had the money. Pretend you have $10,000 to invest, and come up with a list of possible investment choices. For example, pick a couple of stocks you might buy, a couple of bonds, a certificate of deposit, or other choices. Track the performance of each investment over six months and evaluate how much profit you would have made. Draw conclusions from this, and repeat the exercise. After doing this several times, invest your own money in the choices you feel will work out best.

8. Ask for cost and financial information from others.

If your co-workers propose ideas, ask them if they have evaluated the financial impact of what they are suggesting. If not, suggest that they go back and work up some numbers. Help them do this if you can, then review what they come up with. By doing so, you will increase your financial and numerical skills.

When reports or memos come across your desk with financial or other numbers in them, call the person who prepared the figures. Ask them how they came up with the numbers that they did. By doing so, you will learn more about financial and statistical techniques. If appropriate, offer your ideas on other ways to calculate the figures.

9. Take college courses in accounting, finance, business, statistics or math.

Learning more about finance and numbers can be greatly enhanced by pursuing college courses in this area. Many colleges and universities offer programs in the area as part of continuing education or degree programs. Sign up for the courses of your choice. In particular, you might look for courses in accounting, finance, economics, business, statistics, or math. Select those courses which relate best to the business world. If you are concerned about tests and grades, simply audit the courses (no grades or course credits). Try to apply the knowledge you have gained back on the job.

10. Double check figures in reports that come across your desk.

Skill with numbers can be increased by double checking and verifying the work of others. When a report with numbers in it comes across your desk, take out your calculator and double check the figures. Add the appropriate columns and rows to see if you come up with the same totals. If not, call the writer of the report to inform him/her of what you found out. By double checking the numerical work of others and asking questions about discrepancies, you will become better with numbers yourself.

11. Solve numerical problems, puzzles, or games.

An away-from-work way to build numerical skills is to practice with recreational learning. Buy workbooks or puzzles which require number skills to solve. Work through these in the evenings on your own. Practice adding numbers in your head, such as keeping track of estimated grocery costs when shopping. Play games such as Monopoly which involve finance and numerical skills. By practicing with these recreational activities, you can build better numerical and financial skills of your own. These skills can then be transferred back to the job and used in many different ways.

12. Do cost/benefit analyzes of planned changes.

If you or others in your area are thinking about changing you equipment, work methods, or hiring other people, do a cost/benefit analysis. Evaluate the cost of implementing these changes in terms of new employee salaries, training, equipment, supplies, and the like. Then evaluate the likely benefits gained from implementing the change. The benefits might be more sales, reducing expenses, quicker processing time (which is a savings), or many other possibilities. Then compare the differences between the costs and benefits to determine if the change seems justified. Cost/benefit analyses help built financial and numerical skills and give you a stronger business orientation.

13. Develop a better understanding of the economy.

While the national economy is difficult for even experts to fully understand, all of us gain more knowledge by trying to understand the basics. You can do this by paying more attention to the news when the nation's economy is being discussed. And by reading articles in the newspaper and in magazines. Try to understand what is meant by a balanced budget, the trade deficit, the value of the dollar, and related concepts. By understanding these concepts better, you can build your understanding of finance and skill at working with numbers. This can help you in becoming better at finance and numbers on the job.

14. Read business magazines and journals.

Better financial and numerical skills can be built by buying magazines and journals in the area. Examples of these include Forbes, Fortune, The Wall Street Journal, Business Week, and related publications. Try to pick these up at the newsstand and read them. Look up the financial terms that you are not familiar with. Relate the financial news in these publications to what is going on at your own company. By building more financial knowledge from outside publications, you will increase your financial skills within the company.

15. Have a "bottom-line" orientation.

Some employees fail to consider the bottom-line impact of changes they recommend. They argue for adding staff or buying equipment without having a sensitivity to the cost of these suggestions, and the impact on bottom-line profits. If you have this type of orientation, try to become more sensitive to the financial impact of what you or others are suggesting. Look at changes not only from the benefit side, but from the cost side as well. Perhaps the suggestions are still worth making, but by focusing on the bottom-line, you will have a deeper perspective on the impact of the suggestion. Calculate the costs and benefits of the changes, even if you have to use estimates. When listening to others present their ideas, ask them to assess the impact on the bottom-line as well. This perspective will help improve your financial and numerical skills.

16. Spend time with employees in finance and accounting.

One way to increase your knowledge of finance is to spend time with experts in the area. Schedule some time with the employees in finance and accounting at your company. Ask them what they do and how they track financial performance. In all likelihood they will be able to demonstrate the use of computers in their work. You might also ask them for other sources of information in their area—

such as company reports, outside publications, and professional associations. Pursue these if you feel they will help you without getting too technical.

17. Maintain home expense records.

Financial and numerical skills can be effectively practiced at home. One of the best ways of doing this is to track your expenses from month to month. Develop categories for expenses such as food, electricity, rent/mortgage, clothing, and gas. Save your receipts, and each month log in the amounts spent in each category. Total the expenses for each month and note trends across the months and from year to year. Trace back where your net income went in any given month. You might also develop a budget for each month and try to live within it. The experience you get from managing a budget at home can be directly translated to managing a budget at the workplace.

18. Use a personal computer with spreadsheet capabilities.

Personal computers can be an excellent way to learn more about finance and working with numbers. Computer spreadsheet software makes it easy to enter and track financial information and write programs to do calculations. Some software programs have tutorials that teach not only how to use the software, but some of the basics on finance and accounting. You should make an effort to use a personal computer either in the office or at home. In the office, you can use it to track department expenses and maintain a budget. At home, you can use the computer to track your monthly personal expenses.

19. Try to fill out as much of your taxes as you can.

Still yet another way to build financial and numerical skills is by filling out your taxes. While many tax returns require professional assistance, individuals can gain skills by doing as much on their own as they can. At the very least, you should sum your earnings, expenses and contributions for the year, putting the expenses into categories such as electricity, phone, etc. Read through the tax form guide published by the government and go as far as you can in figuring your taxes. If you use professional help, ask your accountant how he/she calculated various items on the return and try to learn from this. By understanding more on taxes, you can improve financial and numerical skills back on the job.

20. Come up with ways to save money at the company.

Financial people often think about ways to save the company money since they track and project expenses. You might do the same to improve your financial perspective and skills. Evaluate the practices of your department right now. Are there different ways of doing the work that would save money and not hurt quality? Is there equipment that can be bought which would save money over the current way of doing the work? Would training or job redesign save money? Could work be brought internally that is done on the outside to save money (or work done in-house farmed out to the outside)? By thinking through the answers to these questions, you should be able to come up with cost savings ideas. Come up with a dollar amount for each and present them to your manager.

21. Evaluate your net worth.

Another good exercise for practicing financial and numerical skills is to calculate your net worth. To do this, calculate the estimated value of your possessions and investments—essentially everything you own. Think of your home, car, bank accounts, stocks, collections, major appliances, and other items. Sum the estimated value of these to a total dollar amount. Next, calculate your debts, for example, the amount owed on a home mortgage, car, credit card payments, and other bills and debts. Sum these debts to get a single number. Last, subtract the debts from the value of all your possessions to come up with your net worth. Not only is this exercise enlightening, it helps build financial and numerical skills that can be used back on the job.

22. Try making future financial projections.

Another technique for building financial and numerical skills is to make financial projections. The purpose of the projection is to anticipate what future levels of expenses, sales, or budgets will be. Changes can then be made based upon what the projection shows. In the workplace, try making projections with categories of expense items (e.g., salaries, and office supplies). You might also try it with production volume, quality measures, sales volume, and other areas. Look at the trends of the past as an aid in projecting the future. You can also do this with home expenses such as phone bills and electricity bills. Try to forecast what they will be a year from now and budget accordingly. Financial projections are made easier by graphing trends in the past year or two, then extending the trend line out into the future.

23. Watch business television shows.

There has been a growth in television shows dealing with business and finance. Most of these shows are on public television—some being specials and others being regular series. Try to watch some of these shows to learn more about finance and the world of business. In particular, watch those shows that might pertain to increasing profits, accounting, finance, or reports on company growth and success. Relate what you hear to other information at your own company or what you have read or heard elsewhere. Watching these shows can help you learn more about finance and business, and apply the materials back on the job.

Recommended Readings

Clark, John J., and Clark, Margaret T. *A Statistical Primer for Managers*. New York: The Free Press, 1983.

Davidson, Sidney; Stickney, Clyde F.; and Weil, Roman L. *Accounting: The Language of Business* (6th ed.). Sun Lakes, AZ: T. Horton; Englewood Cliffs, NJ: Prentice-Hall, 1984.

Droms, William G. *Finance and Accounting for Nonfinancial Managers*. Reading, MA: Addison-Wesley, 1990.

Evans, Frank C. How to Read Your Company's Financial Report. *Management Solutions*, Dec, 1986, 31, p. 23-33.

Freund, John E., and Perles, Benjamin M. *Business Statistics*. Englewood Cliffs, NJ: Prentice-Hall, 1974.

Gallagher, Charles A., and Watson, Hugh J. *Quantitative Methods for Business Decisions*. New York: McGraw-Hill, 1980.

Helfert, Erich A. *Techniques of Financial Analysis*. Homewood, IL: Dow-Jones-Irwin, 1986.

Hitchcock, Earl B. *The Secretary's Deskbook of Practical Business Math*. Englewood Cliffs, NJ: Prentice-Hall, 1986.

Kaufman, Henry. *Interest Rates, the Markets, and the New Financial World*. New York: Times Books, 1986.

Peterson, D. *Mathematics for Business Decisions*. New York: McGraw-Hill, 1983.

Spurga, Ronald C. *Balance Sheet Basics: Financial Management for Non-financial Managers*. New York: Mentor Executive Library, 1986.

Thomsett, Michael C. *The Little Black Book of Business Math*. New York: AMACOM, 1988.

Valentine, Jerome L., and Mennis, Edmund A. *Quantitative Techniques for Financial Analyses* (Rev. ed.). Homewood, IL: R.D. Irwin, 1980.

Wood, Merle; Hendricks, Thomas; and Muller, Susan. *Basic Mathematics Skills and Applications*. New York: McGraw-Hill, 1983.

15

Creativity and Innovation

This chapter helps improve performance in the following areas:

- Coming up with ideas to improve the workplace.
- Being more innovative and resourceful.
- Brainstorming improvements.
- Doing more than just carrying out job tasks.
- Being more flexible and open-minded.

Actions Items for Creativity and Innovation

1. Do not be content with only doing assigned job tasks.

Some employees never take the time to think creatively. For them, merely carrying out the assigned tasks is all that is required. If they are not told to innovate or create, they will not attempt to do this. The more effective employee regards the job as more than just doing the assigned job tasks. This person sees part of the job as creating— taking that extra step to make things better and more effective. Such employees see innovating as an ongoing responsibility, whether or not they are assigned this activity. Make this your outlook as well. This first hurdle to being creative and innovative is to see creativity as a part of your job responsibilities.

2. Be willing to experiment with new ideas before judging them.

Some employees are quick to evaluate and judge ideas. Before giving an idea a fair chance, these individuals have already concluded that the idea will not work. In some cases that can be costly—a new, innovative idea which could improve productivity may never see the light of day. Try to suppress your tendency to quickly judge a new idea. Give it a realistic chance. Talk the idea out with others and, if possible, experiment with it before drawing conclusions. That non-judgmental attitude will cause more ideas to flow your way, and give you the opportunity to innovate more.

3. See problems as "opportunities in disguise."

Problems cause some individuals to fret and worry. They never take the time to step back and proactively manage their way out of problems. As a result, they spend most of their time putting out fires, and complaining about having to do so. More effective individuals see problems as opportunities. They look at problems as opportunities to learn, to improve upon, and to innovate in their area. Problems can stimulate new procedures or even new businesses if the problems are looked at from a "big picture" standpoint. Try having a positive, open-minded perspective on problems. Look upon them like someone tapping you on the shoulder and saying, "Here's a chance to improve the way you run your area." Then take the time to create and innovate from that tap on the shoulder.

4. Block off time for creativity.

The pace at many workplaces can limit creativity. It is difficult to innovate when there are many meetings and day-to-day interruptions. If this is a problem for you, block off specific time for creative, innovative work. Schedule the time just as you would schedule time for a meeting. The best time might be very early in the morning, late in the day, or on the weekends. If necessary, find some quiet space to do creative work. Go to a conference room or other area where it is likely to be quiet and you can work undisturbed. The key is to make time for creative efforts if you cannot find time for them during your regular workday.

5. List out a dozen ways to improve your area.

A good starting point for practicing creativity is your immediate work area. Since you know your job and your work area well, you should have no problem with coming up with improvements. Take a blank sheet of paper and list out a dozen or more ways to improve your area. Think of methods, procedures, policies, job responsibilities, equipment, supplies, physical layout, and anything else that could stand improving. Be specific on what can be done to improve the area, and how this could be accomplished. Once your list is complete, do not let it go to waste. Implement the changes within your authority, and present the other suggestions to someone else who can act on them.

6. Use group brainstorming techniques on an ongoing basis.

Creativity and innovation are greatly improved upon by using group brainstorming techniques. These usually work best with a group of six to ten individuals who each have potential ideas to contribute in the area. Brainstorming involves getting a group together to solve a particular problem or brainstorm general ways to make the area more effective. One person serves as the note-taker, ideally writing the ideas on a flip chart or wall board so all can see. Creative thinking should be encouraged—you are there to generate as many ideas as possible, not evaluate them. With this type of open structure the group will come up with a large number of ideas. Ideas should be evaluated for their usefulness at a later time. Use group brainstorming techniques to help you improve the effectiveness of your area.

7. Constantly be on the lookout for newer, better ways of doing things.

Less successful employees are content with things the way they are—they do not try to improve upon them. More successful individuals assume that there is probably a better way to do everything than it is done today. They are constantly looking for ways to improve their area. They seek out the ideas of others, no matter how crazy the idea might sound. They read articles and other information that might have some application. They take suggestions from peers or staff not as criticism, but useful ways to make the department more effective. This type of outlook is a healthy one. Try to be on the constant lookout yourself for ways to improve your area.

8. Consider new equipment that can improve your area.

Technology has changed the workplace very dramatically in the past few years. Computers and "smart machines" have had an effect on nearly everyone's job. You should examine your area in light of the latest technology. Is there equipment of any sort that can improve productivity or increase quality? Take the time to creatively think through how your area can be improved with the latest equipment.

If this equipment is not available "off-the-shelf" perhaps something could be designed or modified to fit your needs. Talk to in-house or outside experts to see what can be done. The key is to brainstorm the types of equipment that might be beneficial for your area.

9. Take your innovative ideas to others.

Some employees may come up with good, creative ideas, yet never present those ideas to others. As a result, nothing happens with the idea. Be certain that you are not guilty of this. If you have good, creative ideas on how to run your area more effectively, take time to write the ideas down. Do your homework by figuring out costs and time to implement the idea as well as the benefits that would be gained. Present the idea to your manager or other individuals at the company who you think will be interested. Do not let the idea die by itself. Let others know of your thoughts and suggestions.

10. Improve the work methods and procedures that need updating.

Some employees get into a rut with the performance of their job. Since it has "always been done that way" they continue to do it that way, even when the methods and procedures need updating. Just as new equipment can help an area, so too can new work methods and procedures. Do some creative thinking about the way you do your job. Are there other, more effective ways to do it? Are some of your procedures and policies out of date? If so, take the time to update and improve upon the way the job is done. If necessary, present your suggestions to others for approval.

11. Stay with your creative ideas until they are implemented.

It can be tragic for someone to come up with good ideas, have them approved, and then fail to implement. Yet that is exactly the case for some employees. Due to a fear of making changes, or the lack of time, their excellent ideas never become implemented. Review whether you have ever been guilty of this. If you have, draw up a game plan for putting your ideas into practice. Figure out exactly what needs to be done, who will do it, and when it will be done. By setting a concrete goal and deadline, you are more likely to implement your ideas. Then carry out each step, and do not give up until all are done and the idea is fully implemented.

12. Let your imagination run wild on occasion.

Creativity is enhanced by not restricting your thought process. On occasion, you should let your imagination run wild. Pretend you had all the time and resources you could imagine. How would you improve your department? What would the perfect department look like? How would it operate? By listing out these ideas, and where you stand right now, you are on the right track to improving your effectiveness. You may find that those "wild ideas" are not so far-fetched after all. With planning and execution, many of the ideas can actually be implemented. Open up your thinking periodically and see where it will lead you.

13. Do not criticize the brainstorming ideas of others.

Whenever you hear brainstorming ideas from your staff, peers, or your boss, look at these ideas openly. If you are quick to criticize the ideas of others, people will not give you any more of their ideas. The effectiveness of the department will suffer since no one will feel comfortable with suggesting improvements. On the other hand, if you give an idea some consideration, it is likely that employees will offer more suggestions. This does not mean that you have to use the ideas, only **consider** them. Reflect over the ideas as you hear them, and resist the temptation to shoot down the idea too quickly. If need be, go back to the person later to explain why the idea cannot be used. However, thank them for the idea and encourage them to offer out more.

14. Take up creative hobbies.

You can stimulate creative thinking by taking up hobbies that require creativity. For example, hobbies such as art, crafts, writing, and music require creativity to carry them out. By pursuing such hobbies, as well as others, you will be learning how to do creative thinking in general. You can then apply your creative thinking back on the job by turning your mind loose on improvements in the workplace. Away-from-work hobbies can help your on-the-job creativity.

15. Seek out ideas from those with different perspectives.

Creativity and innovation can be helped by getting ideas from others with a different perspective than your own. You undoubtedly know co-workers who have different perspectives because of their jobs, background, or prior experience. Seek out these employees and ask for their ideas for improving your area. Tell them you would value their suggestions, and avoid criticizing their ideas should you disagree. By combining the ideas of others with your own, you can come up with more creative improvements than you could by yourself. Seek out those with different perspectives whenever you can.

16. Avoid using the first idea that comes into your mind.

Some employees think creatively, but make the mistake of using the first idea that comes into their minds. This can restrict the quality of ideas since the first idea is not always the best one. Evaluate whether you use the first idea offered out of habit or a lack of time. If so, force yourself (and others who might be with you) to think of more ideas before deciding on a final course of action. The additional time can be well spent in producing valuable ideas to implement.

17. Set up a file for improvements.

You may find that creative efforts are enhanced by keeping one or more files for creative ideas. First, you might jot down on a slip of paper those creative ideas that cannot be fully developed at that time. Place these in your file marked "Improvements." Add to this file additional ideas, articles, mail, etc. that might help you run your area more effectively. When you have more time to pursue creative ideas, go back to this folder and more fully develop those initial thoughts that came into your mind. By having all related materials in one folder ensures that your ideas, and those of others, do not get misplaced with all of the other paperwork in your area. Your improvement file should be cleaned out periodically as certain ideas are abandoned.

18. Let creative thoughts pop into your mind.

Some employees hamper their own creativity by restricting the time for creative thoughts. For example, if an excellent idea comes to mind while at home in the evening, they will not take the time to write the idea down and think about it more. That can hamper the creative process since ideas may come to a person at any time. If you have this tendency, allow ideas to be developed at any time, be it at the workplace, at home, while driving, etc. As soon as is convenient, make a note of the idea. If you cannot think about it more at that time, then let the note remind you to more fully develop the idea later. The important point is to not let the clock on the wall restrict your development of creative ideas.

19. Use reference sources to stimulate creative ideas.

References can help stimulate creative ideas. If stumped on how to improve in a certain area, seek out other sources at the library or through professional associations. Examine books, articles, and the ideas of others in the field. Even if you cannot use these ideas directly, they might be utilized in a modified form. Look at the materials with an eye towards use at your company. Ask yourself,

"Will this idea work for me? Could I change it somewhat and still use it?" By using publications to stimulate your ideas, your own creativity can reach higher levels.

20. Do not give up on creative suggestions because others do not use them.

Some employees find it very frustrating when others do not use their ideas. They might think, "What's the use of making suggestions if no one ever uses them." While it is easy to understand the frustration, it is unrealistic to think every idea will be used. When we stop to think about it, do we always use the ideas of friends, co-workers, or others in our lives? Sometimes we use the ideas and sometimes we do not. The same will be true with **your** ideas at the workplace. Some of the ideas may be good ones, but cannot be used because of costs, time, or conflicts with other activities. Do not cut off your creativity because of occasional frustration. Recognize that is normal for some ideas to be used and for others to be discarded. Do not become discouraged by this but keep thinking of other ideas which might be used.

21. Eliminate any restrictive thinking.

Some employees tend to think negatively about any ideas that come their way. They are quick to reject ideas before giving them sufficient thought. Their restrictive thinking involves making statements such as the following:

- "It will never work."

- "That's not the way we do things around here."

- "We thought of that a long time ago."

- "We've never done it that way before."

- "Management will never buy the idea."

If you have ever used statements like these, try and eliminate them. What you are actually saying is "I don't want to improve or get better." And you will not by making these statements and thinking this way. Not only will good ideas fail to be implemented, but people will be hesitant to give you suggestions knowing your reaction. Be more positive and receptive in your thinking.

22. Brainstorm when you are relaxed.

Brainstorming activity can be hampered when you are pressured, tired, or busy. To get the most out of brainstorming activity, you should try to do it when you are relaxed. Seek out a comfortable location that is quiet and free of interruptions. Try to do your brainstorming there whenever possible. Personal relaxation techniques can be helpful if you are tense or pressured. Breathing deeply and slowly can help relax you, as can physical exercise or a whirlpool. Such activities may make it easier to think creatively at home or on the job. Use them as well as a good environment if you have difficulty in thinking creatively.

23. Create by adding to or modifying what already exists.

Many employees incorrectly assume that creating and innovating is a difficult process. They think of it as starting from point zero and coming up with something new. Actually, many creative ideas are extensions of what has already been done. Someone takes an existing idea and goes a step further with it to turn it into a unique creative application. See creativity as this way yourself. Do some advance homework to see what others have done in the area. Using this as a starting point, try to brainstorm modifications to these ideas that fit your unique circumstances. Once these ideas are out on the table, other ideas may come to mind which are completely different from the original ones.

24. Read about future trends to stimulate ideas.

Many articles are being written about cutting-edge trends in the workplace and new innovations. These trends include new work methods, new management techniques, changes in technology, and changes in employee demographics. Reading articles such as these can help stimulate new ideas on your own for innovating your department. Try to pick up magazines and books that deal with the future and the latest trends in your field. Read these regularly and go the extra step of thinking whether the idea has any possible application at your company. If it does, put together a plan for making the appropriate changes.

25. Develop a vision for your area.

Creative change for your area can be enhanced by developing a vision for the area. The term "vision" means knowing where you want your area to be in the future, what goals must be accomplished, and what improvements need to be made. By writing out this vision, and comparing it to your current situation, changes for your area will become apparent. You can then brainstorm ideas to make these needed changes. Think of developing a vision for your area of responsibility as a means for stimulating creativity.

26. Be more creative by relating together unrelated facts.

Another way to stimulate creative thoughts is to try to relate together facts which are not normally related. Examples of this might be as follows:

- You might read that demographers are predicting an aging of the work force and an aging of the population. You relate this to the products your company sells and employee staffing at the company.

- You read that technology is changing jobs faster than ever before. You relate this to the need for more training at your company.

There are many other examples as well. The point is that an item in the news stimulates some thinking about your company and your department. As a result, you take some actions to run a more effective area. Try to look for more links between news that you read and the running of your department. It will help you be more creative.

27. Practice openness and looking for newer ways to do things.

Some employees get many creative ideas because they are always looking for new ideas. They encourage peers and staff to suggest new, different ways of running the department. They are open and receptive to new ideas and implement those that are worthwhile. That sort of attitude will draw creative ideas from others on an ongoing basis. Review how often you seek out improvement ideas from others. Are you willing to listen and give thought to each suggestion without criticizing the idea? Take on a style which tells others you are interested in suggestions to make your area more effective.

28. Look at ideas from a different perspective.

Creativity is enhanced by looking at ideas from a different perspective. Sometimes all it takes is to twist an idea slightly and new, helpful ideas come into focus. For example, a printer tried to advertise his business to only **individuals** and found the business grew up to a point, then stopped. When he shifted the same advertising to **companies,** he found his business grew by leaps and bounds. That minor change in perspective caused the creative ideas that lead to success. And it is that way with many other fields of endeavor.

Try to look at your own ideas from a different perspective if you can. If you can only go so far by yourself, then get others involved who might have a different perspective. The combining together of many different ideas will likely generate more creative responses than having just one perspective. Use a change in perspective whenever you can.

29. Generate more than just one or two creative ideas.

Creativity works best when a large number of creative ideas are generated, then narrowed down to just a few. The chosen idea is just as likely to be the first idea as the last idea. Some employees generate only one or two quick ideas, then try to make a decision on what to do next. While that may work fine on deciding where to go for lunch, more complex issues require much more time and thought. If you stop your creative thinking at one or two ideas, force yourself to consider more than that. For important issues, do not stop until you have generated a substantial number of ideas. Obviously, getting other employees involved can increase the number of ideas generated. But at first you must recognize the need to have a comprehensive list of ideas.

30. Play games and work puzzles that require creativity.

Creativity and innovation can be enhanced by activities done at home. One way is to play games or work puzzles that require creativity. Some of these "brain teasers" require a good deal of thought and concentration. Examples of brain teasers are solving mazes or putting together a plastic, three-dimensional puzzle.

Games such as Scrabble require you to continually create new words. Crossword puzzles or math puzzles may also require creativity to be solved. Buying and playing some of these games and puzzles may help stimulate creativity on your part and help you with on-the-job creativity.

Recommended Readings

Blake, Robert R., and Mouton, Jane Srygley. Don't Let Group Norms Stifle Creativity. *Personnel,* Aug, 1985, 62, p. 25-33.

Caroselli, Marlene. *Breakthrough Creativity*. White Plains, NY: Quality Resources Press, 1994.

Higgins, James M. Creating Creativity, *Training and Development*, November, 1994, p. 11-15.

Kravetz, Dennis J. *Getting Noticed: A Manager's Success Kit*. New York: Wiley, 1985.

LeBoeuf, M. *Imagineering: How to Think and Act Creatively*. New York: McGraw-Hill, 1980.

Michalko, Michael. Bright Ideas. *Training and Development*, June, 1994, 44-47.

Raudsepp, Eugene. *How to Create New Ideas for Corporate Profit and Personal Success*. Englewood Cliffs, NJ: Prentice-Hall, 1982.

Raudsepp, Eugene. How to Increase your C.Q. (creativity quotient). *Business Marketing*, July, 1983, 68, p. 80-82.

Raudsepp, Eugene. How Creative Are You? *Nation's Business*, June, 1985, 73, p. 25-26.

Rawlinson, J. Goffrey. *Creative Thinking and Brainstorming*. New York: Wiley, 1981.

Ray, M.L. Strategies for Stimulating Personal Creativity. *Human Resource Planning*, 1987, 10, p. 185-93.

Ray, Michael, and Myers, Rochelle. *Creativity in Business*. Garden City, NY: Doubleday, 1987.

Sonnenberg, Frank K. and Goldberg, Beverly. Tapping Creativity in Others. *Training and Development*, March, 1992, 65-68.

Von Oech, Roger. *A Whack on the Side of the Head*. New York: Warner Books, 1990.

Waitley, Denis E., and Tucker, Robert B. *Winning the Innovation Game*. Old Tappan, NJ: Fleming H. Revell, 1986.

16

Flexibility and Handling Change

This chapter helps improve performance in the following areas:

- Being more open to change.
- Being less rigid and more flexible.
- Having an open mind.
- Having a broader perspective.

Action Items
For Flexibility and Handling Change

1. Look at change as inevitable.

Change is regarded by some employees as an unnecessary event. They would rather have the workplace continue as it has in the past, with no change whatsoever. The fact is, change is always occurring, and companies that fail to change will no longer be competitive with other firms. The pace of technology simply does not let anyone to stand still for very long. If you regard change as an intrusion, your attitude will prevent you from handling change well and being successful. Instead think of change as a normal, beneficial event that needs to occur for companies to be successful. With that sort of attitude, change will not concern you.

2. Manage change rather than have it manage you.

If change is inevitable, then it is going to affect our lives one way or the other. The choice we have is to have change forced upon us, or to actively manage the process. Try to handle change in a pro-active way. Look to manage the process from beginning to end. Start out by anticipating the changes which might occur in your department. Then do all that you can to make the change happen by being actively involved in the process from as early on as possible. In this way you will be in control of change and on top of it, rather than having change force you into certain actions that you are unprepared to take.

3. Abandon policies, procedures, and work methods when they no longer work.

Some employees cling to established ways of doing things for too long. For them, the old policy or work method is used even when it is out of date. More flexible employees continually assess whether the old way of doing things is still correct. When the current system needs to be updated, they take those actions to improve the area. See this as a way to increase your effectiveness and have a more productive area. Make a list of any policies, procedures, or work methods you are using that are out of date. Abandon those practices that are not effective any more, and work proactively to bring in more useful policies, procedures, and work methods.

4. Avoid the tendency to make quick judgments.

Inflexible employees tend to make very quick judgments. They decide very quickly on someone's ideas by merely relating the idea to their existing feelings. As a result, ideas are not looked at with an open mind and this can frustrate the other person. Examine how quickly you judge the ideas of others. Do you give them an opinion before they are even finished speaking? Do you ask follow up questions to fully draw out someone's thoughts? Try to delay your quick judgments. Ask more questions to fully understand the other person, and if appropriate, think about the idea for awhile before making your decision.

5. Break up rigid, inflexible habits.

Some employees get into an established pattern that they find difficult to break. They might arrive and leave work at exactly the same time each day, and have a certain work routine that they follow to the letter each day. Such employees may have very strong habits at home as well. They might eat a particular food on a certain evening of the week, have a routine for hobbies, exercising, etc.

While habits and schedules are useful up to a point, people who over-rely on them might find it difficult to give up the routine. When change at the workplace must be made, rigid people will find it very difficult to adapt. If you tend to have rigid habits and work patterns, try breaking out of the mold occasionally. Shift out of your routine with work and home activities. Vary your schedule, work habits, and evening activities. By doing so, you will better handle change when it is necessary.

6. React to change objectively rather than emotionally.

Employees who have a difficult time handling change might let their emotions get the best of them. When hearing about change, they become so emotionally upset or anxious that they do not listen or pay attention to what is going to happen. Try to assess how you react when you first hear about a change, such as new job responsibilities or new technology being introduced.

If you first reaction is emotional, try to look upon change more objectively. Ask questions and gather information to lessen your anxieties and concerns. Once your have more information, you will probably realize that the change is not so bad after all. Then shift your focus to what you can do to adapt and make the change easier for all.

7. Communicate change to others as soon as possible.

If you make changes as a manager or team leader, be certain to communicate those changes as soon as possible. Anxiety over change is greatest when there is limited information. At those times, the rumor mill starts to operate and employees begin to expect the worst. The way to lessen the anxiety is to keep others informed as much as possible. You can never over-communicate planned changes, but can always not communicate enough. Think through each step of your planned changes, and ask yourself what affected employees would want to know about it. Get the information out there as soon as possible and be willing to provide more if requested.

8. Anticipate and plan for handling change.

The best way to handle change is to prepare for it in advance. If you anticipate change forthcoming, then prepare yourself by planning specific actions. Being ahead of the game will help you cope with the change when it occurs. Areas of possible change in companies include the following:

- New manager.

- Company merged or acquired.

- Computers being introduced or modified.

- Changes in policies or procedures.

- Movement into a new job.

- Reorganization.

- More automated equipment.

How would you prepare for changes in the above areas? If you even think a change in any of these areas is likely, begin by planning now. Plan out your actions in a positive and proactive way.

9. Let your first reaction to change be positive rather than negative.

Some employees get off to a bad start from the very moment they hear about a change. The first words out of their mouths are negative. Examples include comments like "that will never work," or "that's not the way we do things around here." When someone's initial reaction is negative, they tend to build on that as time goes along—thinking about all of the negatives rather than the positives. Assess your first reaction when you hear about change. Do you express concern or do you give the idea a fair chance? If you tend to be negative, change your first reaction. Force yourself to list out or verbally express the positive things that might result from the change. Later, you can balance your feelings with some of the negatives if need be.

10. Show an understanding of another person's position.

Inflexible people who are resistant to change tend to look at an issue from only their viewpoint. If someone else's position is different from their own, they are quick to reject the idea. If you ever do this, try to develop a better understanding of the other person's feelings, **particularly** when those feelings are different from your own.

Ask open-ended questions to fully understand why someone feels the way that they do. Show empathy for the other person by saying things like the following:

- "I can understand why you feel the way you do."

- "I know how you feel. It must be upsetting for you."

- "If I understand you correctly, you feel we should . . ."

Showing empathy does not mean you have to agree with the other person, but that you understand their feelings. By developing a better understanding of others, you can increase your flexibility on issues.

11. Seek out more information or training if you are unclear about changes.

Many employees feel they are not given enough information about upcoming changes. Rather than try to change the situation, they fret about the unknown. If you are ever in a position of feeling unclear about changes, seek out others who can help. Ask your manager or other people to give out more details than they have in the past. Recognize that on some occasions they may not have all of the answers themselves. If you are uncomfortable with new equipment or work methods, seek out more training. Ask your manager or someone with expertise in the area to spend more time with you until you are comfortable. The key is to take actions which result in more information or training to help you handle the new change.

12. Set realistic goals for implementing change.

Large changes, such as introducing new equipment or a new organization structure, can seem overwhelming at first. So much change occurs that to get back to normal seems impossible. The way to ease the pain is to set realistic goals for implementing the change. Do not expect to be performing at the same level as before in a short period of time. Instead, get to the targeted performance level by a series of steps which reflect growth. Also, break up the ultimate goal into bits and pieces, each of which is easy to accomplish. For example, the first goal in converting to new equipment might be to design a training program for building needed skills and knowledge. By breaking apart a major change into a series of realistic and accomplishable goals, implementing change will be much easier.

13. Lessen your tendency to be critical of others.

Some employees have a tendency to criticize others frequently. They seem to enjoy finding out what is wrong with people or ideas, and emphasizing this over any positive areas. Being critical of others goes hand in hand with coming across as inflexible and resistant to change. If you have a tendency to be too critical of others, try to reduce this. Look for and mention the positive things about others. If you must mention negative feelings, at least balance this with positive feelings. This more balanced and positive approach will help you be more flexible and able to handle change.

14. Do preparation work in advance of changes.

An excellent way to lessen the anxiety of change is to do preparation work in advance. For example, say that you know you will be moving into a new job. Before starting the job, do some homework to ease the transition into the job. Find out more about the job responsibilities, procedures in the area, equipment used, and so forth. When assuming the new job, you will already feel comfortable with what you will be doing and have a base of knowledge to build upon.

You can prepare for any type of change by doing some homework. Talk to people who have been through the change before at your company or other companies. Read articles or books that might help you handle the change. Seek out the advice that professional associations might have to offer. All of these activities will help you handle change more effectively.

15. See change as an opportunity to improve.

Some employees view change in a negative way—that it makes the job more difficult rather than easy. That sort of attitude makes them resistant to change and less able to adapt when changes are eventually implemented. Assess your outlook toward change. If you have a negative attitude toward change, alter your viewpoint. See change as an opportunity to improve the productivity of the area. See it as the chance to learn new skills and knowledge that can be applied not only on the current job but elsewhere as well. After the change is implemented, you will likely be a more valuable employee to not only your current employer but other companies as well. By having this type of attitude you will find it easy to deal with change and master new techniques.

16. Identify those areas where you are inflexible.

To become a more flexible person, it helps to understand those areas where you are inflexible. Try to list out as many of these areas on your own as you can. Also seek out the help of a trusted friend, your spouse, or co-worker. Perhaps you are most inflexible on the way you do your job, company policies, your viewpoints on certain employees, or your feelings about certain products. Most people who know you well should have no difficulty in helping you develop a list of those areas where you are most opinionated.

Once your list is developed, imagine that some new, reliable information became available that was different from your opinion. How would you react to this? What would the first words out of your mouth be? More flexible people would be willing to listen and get more information. If appropriate, they would change their opinion. Try to use that approach yourself.

17. Constantly be on the lookout for newer, better ways.

Flexible people are continually seeking out new information, and they use that information wisely. If the information does not agree with their previous viewpoint, they gather more facts and information. Then they are willing to alter their viewpoint if needed. You should have that outlook as well. Constantly be thinking about newer, better ways to do your job. Recognize that what worked best yesterday may not be the best for tomorrow. Be willing to adapt and change as new information becomes available. And instead of avoiding this type of information, seek it out. Be willing to deal with new information that might conflict with your viewpoint. By constantly adding new information to your knowledge base, you will become a more successful employee.

18. Restate the ideas of other people.

Inflexible people often do not try to understand the viewpoints of others who disagree with them. They try to brush over the ideas of others and merely restate their own. This can make others feel frustrated and not want to deal with the inflexible person. When listening to others express their viewpoint, try to restate their feelings from time to time. Make statements like, "you feel we should. . ." or "if I understand you, you think. . ." By restating the ideas of others, you will show more understanding and flexibility. Even if you do not change your own thinking to match that of the other person, the fact that you restate their ideas will make you seem more flexible and easy to deal with. Try using this as much as you can.

19. Experiment with new ideas.

If you are not convinced of the correctness of a new change, at least be willing to try it out. Experiment with the new procedure, policy, or equipment. Look at the situation objectively and collect information to see how it works. Recognize that it may take a while to learn the new change, but evaluate its long-term potential based on what you found out in the trial run. Then make a final decision as to whether or not the new change is better. By experimenting with a new process, you will be more objective in evaluating it. Use trial runs to increase you flexibility and handling of change.

20. Get started with change as soon as possible.

Some individuals delay implementing a new change as long as they can. They dread the new change and figure it might be easier to implement with the passing of time. Actually, the situation is frequently made worse by waiting. The employee's anxiety can increase over time—the build-up is largely a fear of the unknown. People have a tendency to imagine the worst, and this does not go away until they start implementing the new change.

Rather than delay implementing change, get started as soon as possible. Gather all of the information you can about the change. That information gathering will itself help lessen the anxiety about change. When you have enough information to get started, begin implementing right away. Use trial runs if you cannot implement the change all at once. Implementing change in a timely way will help you with the adjustment.

21. Volunteer to be on a "change committee."

Waiting for change to occur can be difficult for many, particularly if it will take months to make the new changes. One way to make this more bearable is to get involved yourself. Volunteer to be on a committee which is responsible for making a planned change. Convince others that you would like to be involved and have something valuable to contribute. By being a part of the change team, you will likely know as much information about the change as anyone else. This will help you feel more comfortable and able to implement the changes when your work is through. Remember also to keep others informed who are not on the committee since they will want to know what is forthcoming as well.

22. Avoid arguing when hearing a different idea.

Inflexible employees are seen as quick to argue and dig in their heels when they hear an idea different from their own. Everyone is entitled to have an opinion— the difference is that inflexible people tend to resist change and go to great lengths to defend their own feelings. You should evaluate how quick you are to argue or defend your ideas when your hear thoughts different from your own. Do you dig in your heels and go back and forth with others if the discussion goes on? If so, you should avoid the arguing and defensiveness. Listen to others openly and state your own feelings, but stop short of turning the conversation into an debate.

23. Broaden your perspective by seeking out others.

When thinking about making changes in your area, seek out others with a different perspective. For example, if you are making changes in a production area, you might get ideas from people in finance or human resources. Their different perspectives might give you new ideas on evaluating the cost of your changes, or help you think through the training of people after the change is implemented. Those different perspectives, when added to your own, will lead to a better change effort. Think of seeking out others with different perspectives whenever you are planning a significant change in your area.

24. List out what needs to be changed in your area.

If you are not aggressive in changing things in your area, you can alter that immediately. Start now by making out a list of those areas which need updating. Think of policies, procedures, work methods, equipment, job responsibilities, and work flow. Write out specifically what could be done more effectively, using both your ideas as well as those of other people you work with. Draw up plans to put the changes in place. See the plans through to completion so that changes are made wherever needed.

Recommended Readings

Beckhard, Richard, and Harris, Reuben T. *Organizational Transitions: Managing Complex Change* (2nd ed.). Reading, MA: Addison-Wesley, 1987.

Berry, Waldron. Overcoming Resistance to Change. *Supervisory Management*, Feb, 1983, 28, p. 26-30.

Binsted, Don. Learning to Cope with Change. *Management Decisions*, 1986, 24, p. 32-36.

Black, H.S. Riding with Change. *Management World*, Dec, 1985, 14, p. 12-14.

Brown, Arnold, and Weiner, Edith. How to Make Your Ability to Cope with Change an Effective Tool for Survival. *Management Review*, April, 1984, 73, p. 8-15.

Brown, Arnold, and Weiner, Edith. *Supermanaging*. New York: McGraw-Hill, 1984.

Dalziel, Murray M., and Schoonover, Stephen. *Changing Ways: A Practical Tool for Implementing Change Within Organizations*. New York: AMACOM, 1988.

Lawrence, Paul R. How to Deal With Resistance to Change. *Harvard Business Review*, Mar-Ap, 1986, 64, p. 178.

Lippert, F.G. Forestalling Resistance to Change. *Supervision*, Feb, 1984, 46, p. 16-17.

Mainiero, Lisa A., and DeMichiell, Robert L. Minimizing Employee Resistance to Technological Change. *Personnel*, July, 1986, 63, p. 32-37.

Martel, Leon. *Mastering Change: The Key to Business Success*. New York: Simon and Schuster, 1986.

Michael, Stephen R.; Luthans, Fred; Odiorne, George S.; Burke, Warner; and Hayden, Spencer. *Techniques of Organizational Change*. New York: McGraw-Hill, 1981.

Miller, D.E. Coping with Changes: Blending the Old with the New. *Supervisory Management*, June, 1983, 28, p. 36-39.

Odiorne, George S. *The Change Resistors*. Englewood Cliffs, NJ: Prentice-Hall, 1981.

Oromaner, D.S. Winning Employee Cooperation for Change. *Supervisory Management*, Dec, 1985, 30, p. 18-23.

Peters, Tom. *Thriving on Chaos: A Handbook for a Management Revolution*. New York: Alfred A. Knopf, 1987.

Scott, Cynthia D., and Jaffe, Dennis T. Survive and Thrive in Times of Change. *Training and Development*, April, 1988, p. 25-27.

Stanislao, J., and Stanislao, B.L. Dealing with Resistance to Change. *Business Horizons*, Jul-Aug, 1983, 26, p. 74-78.

17

Personal Motivation

This chapter helps improve performance in the following areas:

- Getting ahead.
- Increasing motivation on the job.
- Career planning and development.
- Increasing personal standards and goals.
- Being more successful.

Action Items For Personal Motivation

1. Make career plans.

It is sad to say, but many employees spend more time planning their vacations than they do planning their careers. If you do not believe this, just ask someone about to go on a one week vacation what they plan to do. The person will likely have very detailed plans. Then ask them what career plans they have for the next five years and you will get a vague answer, if any, about earning more money or getting ahead. If they do not know where they are going, how can they expect to get there?

Make career planning a specific activity for you. Write out where you want to be one year, three years, five years down the road. What job do you want to be in? What additional skills or responsibilities do you want to have? Where do you want to be working and who for? By answering these questions and others, you can put together a specific career plan for attaining your goals. That will greatly increase the chances you have of attaining those goals.

2. Identify specific jobs which match your interests and abilities.

You can help attain career goals by identifying specific jobs you want to pursue. When a specific job is identified, it is easier to put together a career plan and build skills and knowledge for attaining that job. To identify a specific job, first think of your interests, skills, abilities, education, and job knowledge. Then think of jobs that match your unique profile. These jobs could be at your company or at another company. The job may not even exist right now but may be a dream job. Seek out more information about the jobs which are of interest to you. For example, do they require certain skills or knowledge that you lack? Once these jobs are targeted, you can focus your career development efforts.

3. Expand your current job.

Some employees get into a rut with their current job. They have done it for so long that the challenge is missing, and their motivation deteriorates. If this is happening to you, work to change the situation. Expand your current job by adding tasks or responsibilities that will make it more exciting and interesting. Think of both permanent changes as well as one-time projects for expansion. If necessary, get the approval of your manager for this expansion. Sell the benefits of taking on the extra responsibility. The key is to change the job on an ongoing basis to build in more learning, growth, and personal motivation.

4. Increase your work hours.

For some employees, work hours consist of putting in the minimum number of hours, and never any more. That type of motivation is not likely to lead to promotions or other career success. Would you promote someone who did not seem like they wanted to make an extra effort? Take inventory of how many hours you work per week. Can you do more to increase your hours occasionally? Try a schedule variation that works best for you. That might be coming in a bit earlier, staying later, or putting in a few hours on Saturday. Whatever the case, do not limit your career potential due to lack of effort.

5. Learn new job skills.

You can increase your motivation by taking the initiative to learn new job skills. By broadening out a bit more, you will increase your value to the company, and open up career opportunities. Think of broadening into areas outside of your immediate area of responsibility. For example, production workers might try how to learn to use a personal computer; accountants might learn more "people" skills; and human resources professionals might add skills in finance. Try to add skills that can be used at your company and relate to other jobs you have your eye on. By adding new skills, you can keep growing and improve your chance for success.

6. Increase your personal goals and standards.

Some employees are content to do an adequate job. They hold themselves back because they do not aspire to higher goals. It is no surprise that they fail to advance or achieve a great deal on their current job. Be certain that your personal goals and standards do not hold you back. Set tough goals and standards for yourself in how you do your job. Do not accept errors or being average. Be a tough critic of yourself and aspire to do higher quality and quantity of work than you have in the past. These types of personal standards will help you achieve more and lead to greater career success.

7. Enroll in college courses.

You can increase your personal motivation and career success by enrolling in college courses. Most companies provide tuition reimbursement so this should not be a cost issue. If you are not interested in getting a degree, simply take a course or two that will help broaden you out. You can even audit the course and not have to worry about grades. There are many colleges to choose from, as well as adult education courses at many high schools.

While the most likely courses to pursue are those related to your job, think of broadening into other areas as well. Take a course on computers if you do not use them now, or take a course on business or finance that can help you down the road. Such courses can enable you to learn new knowledge and skills that can improve your career success.

8. Expand your reading into new areas.

Many employees get into a rut by reading only technical publications in their field. Personal motivation and career development can be enhanced by reading materials in other areas as well. For example, a production employee who is interested in management might want to pick up some books and articles in the management area. An accountant might want to read books and articles on presentation skills or sales skills. By expanding your reading into new areas, you will develop new insights and ideas that can be used on your current and future jobs. The new learning will also be stimulating and motivating.

9. Thoroughly self-assess your strengths and weaknesses.

Some employees fail to advance by not understanding themselves well. If someone else gets promoted, it was due to "the company" or "management." In reality, the employee may not have been as qualified as someone else but not willing to deal with that. Take an inventory of your personal strengths and weaknesses. Write out on a piece of paper the skills, abilities, and knowledge that you have. Also list out those skills, abilities, and knowledge that you lack for a particular job that you are interested in. By developing this inventory, you can pinpoint areas for improvement and work on them. This will help your career advancement as well as improve performance on the current job.

10. Cut down on non-productive activity.

Some individuals fail to use non-work time to help them develop their careers. Most hours away from work are spent in leisure or recreation, be it watching television or other pastimes. As a result, their career development may stand still, since at least some of the after-work hours are needed to learn skills and knowledge.

While everyone needs to have some leisure time, take an inventory of how you spend your hours at home. Try to change if you spend virtually no time on career development after work. Cut back on the time watching television or other pastimes and substitute career development activity. Find an hour or two a week to read a book or article on management, take a college course, or listen to some audiotapes. By doing so, you will help yourself get ahead and advance your career.

11. Seek out the opinion of others about yourself.

Another excellent way to develop and get ahead is to seek out the advice of others. Go to people who know you well. This could be your boss, co-worker, friend, or family member. Ask them for a candid assessment of your strengths and weaknesses. Go to great lengths to make them feel comfortable in sharing out how they feel. Tell them you simply want to learn and develop by knowing how others see you.

Take the information they give you with an open mind. Even if you do not think it is accurate, you must deal with the fact that others see you that way. What can you do to change that impression? What sorts of skills and abilities can you work on to be more effective? By using the opinion of others, you can grow and become a more effective person.

12. Reward yourself for reaching milestones.

To sustain motivation and career development, it is important to reward yourself periodically. If you reached a personal productivity goal on the job, reward yourself with some minor gift, such as a record, book, or clothing item. Also, enjoy the inner feeling of pride and satisfaction with attaining an important goal. Do the same with career development goals, such as completing college courses and developing new skills. Use larger rewards for long-term goals that you have attained such as getting promoted. By rewarding yourself, you will sustain your motivation over the length of your career.

13. Brainstorm ways to increase earnings.

There are many ways to challenge yourself and get ahead at your current place of employment. However, you can also look to grow and get ahead outside your primary place of employment as well. Start out by brainstorming ways that you can increase your earnings. Perhaps this is through a hobby, such as buying and selling antiques or coins that you now collect. Perhaps you can turn a hobby such as crafts, woodworking, or photography into a part-time job.

You might also invest in real estate such as a rental home or apartment building. By coming up with ways to increase earnings, you can grow, learn, and develop another source of motivation.

14. Set specific targets with deadlines.

One problem for many in personal development is the lack of concrete targets. Someone might conclude, for example, that they want to learn how to use a personal computer, but not have a specific target in mind. You will be much more successful by setting specific goals and deadlines. Figure out first what activities have to be done to accomplish the goal. Then set a deadline for accomplishing each activity. For example, for learning to use a computer you might have, "Take the Computer Basics Course at XYZ College by June 30." In addition, "Learn how to use word processing software by completing tutorial by September 30."

Post your targets so you will see them periodically. Place dates in a calendar as well. Using clear targets with deadlines will greatly help in motivating you and help you attain your developmental goals.

15. Envision yourself being successful.

Many successful people envision themselves in the future attaining greater success. They imagine themselves in a higher level job, or living in a bigger home, or owning their own business. These are not idle daydreams, but conscious attempts to visualize the attainment of goals. Try using this technique yourself. Spend a couple of minutes each day (before turning in is best) envisioning yourself in the future. Imagine yourself attaining whatever goal it is that you have. Think of the of how good it will feel to attain the goal. Practicing this each day will help motivate you to attain your goal.

16. Monitor your progress toward personal goals.

It can be very useful to monitor your progress toward attaining personal career goals. Periodically review where you are at in reaching your goals. Keep a file, log book, or diary to help you monitor progress. Review samples of your work to track quality. Make note of the volume of work you have accomplished on a daily, weekly, or monthly basis. By tracking your performance, you can note trends and ensure that you continually make progress toward your goals.

17. Break down larger career goals into smaller pieces.

Some employees become intimidated by larger goals and end up doing nothing. For example, getting a Master's degree or writing a book may seem too difficult to take on. It helps to break down large career goals into smaller bits and pieces that are more manageable. For example, completing a single college course and writing one chapter in a book are not very intimidating. Yet by repeating these smaller achievements, the longer-term goal is reached. Try using this approach for your larger career goals. Make them more manageable and achievable by breaking them down into easily attained segments.

18. Recognize that you are never too old for career development.

Some employees lament that they are too old for new challenges and career progression. It is interesting to note that many company CEO's do not attain their positions until into their fifties or beyond. Ray Kroc did not buy his first McDonald's hamburger stand until he was in his fifties, and Colonel Harlan Sanders did not start the Kentucky Fried Chicken franchise until he was in his sixties. The point is that people are never too old to start new careers or learn new skills in their current career. Be certain that you do not limit yourself by your own attitude toward your age and ability to learn.

19. Make "value-added" your philosophy.

Some employees do the minimum that is required and that is all. Others consistently go above and beyond the call of duty by providing something value-added. That value-added may be by working longer than others when not asked, taking on additional projects when not asked, providing better customer service, or countless other ways. Review your job behavior. Are you carrying out the minimum required and nothing more? If so, think of the value-added services you can provide in your job. Go out of your way to do more and make this an ongoing style rather than a one-time-only effort. It can greatly enhance your career advancement.

20. Be willing to take risks.

Personal success often requires taking risks. Moving into a new job, learning new skills, and starting a new business all require initial risks. Even suggesting a new product or new procedure involves taking some risk. Some people may fear the risk-taking and decide to play it safe by not changing at all. For example, someone may turn down a management position, fearing the new responsibilities. As such, these people limit their own success by not trying to forge ahead. Often the fear of the risk is more of a barrier than the actual risk itself.

Evaluate whether you have ever held back your own career by fear of changing and taking a new risk. If so, try to gradually increase your risk-taking. Be willing to suggest ideas on your current job that are new and different. Be willing to change equipment and procedures when the need arises. We are not suggesting foolish risk-taking, but limited risk-taking. You can gradually broaden your risk-taking to your career in general.

21. Ask for the assistance of others.

Personal motivation and career development can be helped by the assistance of others. Identify someone who might help you in your career. This might be a former boss, a manager you know, or even a co-worker. Pick someone you admire who can give you advice and counsel. Ask them if they can help you in your career by being a mentor. If so, ask this person to be very candid with you in your career development. Have them advise you on the "tricks of the trade" and what you need to do differently. Try to implement the advice that you get, and reward your mentor by buying them lunch or some other small gift periodically.

22. Do an annual audit of your career progress.

It is helpful to periodically assess the progress you are making in your career. An annual audit, just like an annual physical, is the best way to approach it. We recommend that you formally write out the progress you are making. Questions you might ask yourself include:

- What skills and abilities have I improved or acquired in the last year?

- What new job knowledge have I learned?

- Have I improved upon any personality traits in the past year?

- Have I broadened out and made myself a more valuable employee?

- Am I on the right track in progressing in my career goals?

- What do I need to change or do in the coming year?

Draw up concrete targets and dates, as discussed earlier, for those areas that are in need of improvement. Reward yourself for the excellent progress made. The use of an annual audit such as this ensures that you can look at the "big picture" in your own development and keep on track.

23. Go out of your way to suggest how the company can make or save money.

Some employees do not look beyond carrying out their immediate job responsibilities. The day-to-day activities become overwhelming and they do not think of additional ways to help the company. One way you can break out of this mold is to suggest additional

ways that the company can make or save money. Brainstorm a list
of ideas and narrow the list down to those that seem most promising. Write up a brief summary and present it to your manager or
someone else in the company. Do not become discouraged if some
ideas are not used—many things have to be considered in the final
decision. The important point is to go beyond merely carrying out
your job tasks.

24. Aspire to become the best in your area.

Many employees want to become highly expert in their area. Rather
than broaden out to become a "generalist," they want to be the best
specialist there is in their particular field. You should take on similar
aspirations as well if you do not want to be a generalist. Ask yourself
how you can acquire more knowledge and skill in your area. It might
be through books and articles, professional associations, networking with other people in the field, or working with experts. Aggressively acquire the additional knowledge and skills. Always be
on the lookout for new information to help you become better at
whatever you do. This type of attitude will motivate you toward
greater career success.

25. Broaden out to become a "generalist."

Some employees have exactly the opposite goal of those mentioned
in the above action item. Rather than become the best specialist in
a particular area, they want to become a broader based "generalist."
For them, growth and learning is constantly stretching into new
fields and new endeavors. If you are one of these people, broaden
out by first listing out areas that relate in some way to your current
field. For example, an accountant might want to branch out into
other areas of finance where the accounting field serves as a good
stepping stone. Then go out and learn as much about the new field
as you can through publications and personal contacts. By continually trying to stretch your development, you will attain greater
career success.

26. Inform others that you want growth and learning.

Some employees keep it a secret when they want more growth and learning on the job. As a result, they may not get the needed assistance of a manager or other employee. If you feel you are becoming stale in your current job, discuss this with your manager. Do not present it as a complaint, but rather a desire to broaden out and learn more. Though there are many things you can do on your own, your manager can help you as well. For example, the manager may be able to give you a special project, or rotate some of your job responsibilities with another employee. Inform others of your desires and goals.

27. Start new away-from-work activities.

Think of beginning new away-from-work activities as a source of motivation. These might be activities that relate to your job, for example, a sales person helping out a community organization with a fund-raising project. Or taking up a new hobby that you would find enjoyable. Not only will you develop skills and knowledge, but meet new people as well. The away-from-work activities can be an excellent motivator and means to broaden out. Look at newspapers and other sources for requests for volunteers. Take the initiative to get involved where appropriate.

28. Buy motivational tapes.

There are many motivational audiotapes available. Many of these are inspirational and help people motivate themselves. Try some of these to see if they help you. You might pick up new ideas on setting goals, increasing your aspirations, or leading others. The tapes can be listened to at home or played in your car. Many libraries have these tapes as well, should you want to avoid purchasing them.

29. Place goal reminders where you will see them.

In order to ensure that you continually make progress on your career goals, you need to place reminders where you will see them. The best place is in a calendar where you will frequently see the reminder. Other places might be in tickler files or taped to the wall or furniture in your work area. By using a reminder system, you will be more likely to take the actions to help you in your career. Use this system if you are not currently doing so.

30. Volunteer for committee work.

All companies have committees of some sort. They range from coordinating social events to project committees that develop new solutions. If you do not participate in these committees, volunteer to be a part. Contact the committee chairperson and ask if they could use someone else. Or meet with your manager and explain that you would like to be a part of committee work. Either way, you are bound to be chosen for some committee activity in the future. This work might put some spark and motivation in your career by injecting new variety and giving you a chance to work with other people.

31. Be receptive to performance appraisal feedback.

Some employees react negatively to performance appraisal feedback. They see the feedback as criticism, judging, or unfair evaluation. Rather than learn from the process, they walk away feeling angry and bitter. As a result, they learn nothing and do not change their performance. While managers vary in performance appraisal skills, it is important to see the process as one of learning, growing, and developing.

Outstanding employees actually seek out feedback on their performance all of the time. They are constantly on the look for better ways of doing things, and as a result, they continually learn and get better. Try to make that your approach as well. Do not become defensive at performance feedback by seeing it as criticism or a threat. Instead see it as an opportunity to learn and grow and improve in your career development.

Recommended Readings

Bolles, Richard. *What Color Is Your Parachute?* Berkeley, CA: Ten Speed Press, 1990.

Cassedy, Ellen, and Nussbaum, Karen. *9 to 5: The Working Woman's Guide to Office Survival.* New York: Penguin Books, 1983.

Catalyst Staff. *Making the Most of Your First Job.* New York: G.P. Putnam's Sons, 1981.

Connor, Tim. Your Ten-year Plan: Pointers for Inner Success. *Management World*, July-Aug, 1986, p. 1-3.

Cox, Allan. *The Making of the Achiever.* New York: Dodd, Mead & Company, 1985.

Cuming, Pamela. *The Power Handbook: A Strategic Guide to Organizational and Personal Effectiveness.* New York, NY: Van Nostrand Reinhold Company, 1981.

Gallup, George H.; Gallup, Alec M.; and Proctor, William. What Successful People Have in Common. *Readers Digest*, June, 1987, 130, p. 110-112.

Garfield, Charles A. Peak Performance in Business. *Training and Development*, April, 1987, 41, p. 54-59.

Harmon, Frederick G., and Jacobs, Garry. Pathway to the Top. *Supervisory Management*, Nov, 1985, 30, p. 14-19.

Hill, Napoleon. *Think and Grow Rich.* New York: Fawcett Crest, 1983.

Hill, Napoleon, and Stone, W. Clement. *Success Through a Positive Mental Attitude.* Englewood Cliffs, NJ: Prentice-Hall, 1987.

Korn, Lester. Blocked! *Across the Board*, Jan, 1988, p. 54-59.

Kravetz, Dennis J. *Getting Noticed: A Manager's Success Kit.* New York: Wiley, 1985.

Manz, Charles. *The Art of Self Leadership: Strategies for Personal Effectiveness in Your Life and Work*. Englewood Cliffs, NJ: Prentice-Hall, 1983.

Morrow, Jodie Berlin, and Lebov, Myrne. *Not Just Another Secretary*. New York: Wiley, 1984.

Roger, Henry C. *Roger's Rules for Success*. New York: St. Martin's Press, 1984.

Rosen, Betty. *How to Set and Achieve Goals: The Key to Successful Management*. Englewood Cliffs, NJ: Prentice-Hall, 1981.

Skrzycki, Cindy. Risk Takers (Successful Personalities). *U.S. News & World Report*, Jan., 1987, 26, 102, p. 60-64.

Stuart-Kotze, Robin, and Roskin, Rick. *Success Guide to Managerial Achievement*. Reston, VA: Reston Publishing Company, 1983.

Ziglar, Zig. *Top Performance*. New York: Berkley Books, 1982.

18

Managing Career and Personal Life

This chapter helps improve performance in the following areas:

- Reducing conflict between career and personal life.
- Reducing stress between job and family life.
- Reducing tardiness/absenteeism due to family problems.
- Using time better for job and family matters.

Action Items for Managing Career and Personal Life

1. Make use of "quality time" with family.

Many employees lament that their time with the family is limited. The amount of family time on evenings and weekends is insufficient for many, and often mixed in with chores or other activities. One solution to this is to plan infrequent quality time with family members. This might be a three-day "getaway" weekend at a resort or wilderness area. Or weekend outing where you can spend a significant amount of time together. For many, this makes up for the lack of time during the typical work week. Think of planning these retreats with quality time if you feel family time is too limited.

2. Schedule exercise just like meetings.

Physical fitness promotes health and makes many people feel refreshed and stimulated. However, many complain that there just is not enough time to exercise regularly. One solution to this is to schedule exercise activity just as you would a meeting. What happens if a conflict occurs? Reschedule your workout just as you would with the meeting, making sure that you get in a certain number of workouts each week. This is certainly a better way to approach fitness than doing it when you have "extra time." Try scheduling if you have trouble finding time for exercise.

3. Use effective communication when career and personal conflicts arise.

There are bound to be cases in everyone's career when career and personal life are in conflict. For example, a special project requires you to work late on evenings when some family activities were supposed to occur. If these conflicts are not managed well, they could hurt personal relationships, job performance, or both. If you face such conflicts, ensure that you talk them out with the family, manager, or whoever else is appropriate. There are many more negative consequences from not discussing a conflict than bringing it out in the open. Take the initiative to have open, candid discussions with the appropriate people when these conflicts arise for you.

4. Set joint goals with family members for time at home.

Conflicts between job and home life often arise because of different expectations. A non-working spouse might expect the working spouse to be home during certain hours for family activities. When the working spouse works longer than expected, a conflict arises. If you find yourself having different expectations from your spouse or "significant other," work toward joint goals that you can both agree to. Talk out different options and see if you can find a happy medium where you are both happy. By having agreed to common expectations, the conflict between job and family life can be minimized.

5. Minimize commuting time.

We are all different in our ability to manage commuting time. Some employees can tolerate very long commutes and not find it troubling while others find even a short commute difficult. If you are having difficulty finding enough hours to do everything you want, examine how much time you spend commuting. You might save 1-3 hours each weekday by living closer to work. Obviously, there are many tradeoffs involved in deciding where to live, but if the time away from family or personal activities is too great, you might want to relocate closer to work. The extra hours you pick up might more than offset the extra cost or other negatives of living near by.

6. Explore work at home.

Work at home is a growing trend in this country. Employees, instead of coming into an office each day, perform the same job duties by working at home. Of course, only certain jobs have the potential to be done out of the home, but the number is growing every day. Think about whether you could do your job out of the home with only occasional forays into the office. If so, this might give you more time with the family and for personal activities.

Work at home is particularly attractive for those struggling with day care or disability problems. If you might benefit, present work at home to your manager. It is important to note that studies have shown employees who work at home to be more productive than those at the office, and there is a company cost savings by having people work at home. Work at home is likely to grow in the coming years.

7. Seek a balance in your life between job, family and personal activities.

We all must juggle activities that involve the job, family and personal interests. Things sometimes get out of hand when either one of the three becomes too dominant. Employees then feel they are missing something, and conflicts can arise. Evaluate the balance you have right now between job, family and personal activities. Are any of the three too dominant? If so, try to get more balance into your life. This balance is not measured in hours but is more of a psychological balance between the three. Make adjustments where you need to.

8. Explore work as a contractor.

One growing employment option for many is to work as a contractor rather than a full-time employee. The contractor may work for a defined period for a company, and may or may not come into an office. As a contractor, the individual has more freedom to set the hours of employment, the length of employment, and the place of employment. Contracting is yet another option for many who find it difficult to juggle work and family life at the same time. Evaluate hiring yourself out as a contractor if you feel this would be of assistance in your career.

9. Postpone marriage and children until a later time.

Many employees embark upon their career and are quick to get married and start a family. This may come at a time when they need to devote a great deal of energy to their career. Also, employees at this stage may not have the organization and time management skills that they will develop later. The net result is for the employee to experience a conflict from having too many responsibilities at once. If you have yet to marry or start a family, evaluate whether you can postpone these activities until your career is "up and running." When in your late twenties or thirties, you may be better able to manage the conflicting demands of family, personal and career activities. Consider this if it is a realistic option for you.

10. Minimize down time.

The lack of time for job, family, or personal activities may be hampered by having too much down time. The down time might be watching too much television, overuse of recreational activities, or idle conversation. You should take stock of the amount of down time you have in your life. Can you cut back on television, for example, and devote the extra time to career, family, or personal activities? By minimizing down time, you can pick up some extra hours each week and find time for more important activities.

11. Determine your priorities between personal and career demands.

Some employees try to do it all at once—career, family, and personal interests. As a result, they can feel themselves short-changed in not finding enough time to pursue all options. If you ever feel this way, take the time to formally list out what is of highest priority to you now in terms of career, personal, and family demands. After understanding this better, you might be able to make adjustments to accommodate your highest priorities. For example, you might postpone marriage and children if career activities are your highest priority right now. You can always readjust your activities when your priorities change.

12. Carefully explore day-care options.

Conflicts between job and family are heightened when there are day-care problems. If you are experiencing day-care problems which are affecting job performance, take the time to aggressively line up day-care sources. Think not only of formal day-care centers, but relatives, friends and others who might provide assistance. Be certain to have at least one back-up source available at all times. That way, if the primary source is unavailable, you can quickly and easily resort to the back-up. Since the day-care industry is a rapidly changing field, you need to continually stay current with available facilities. By doing so, you can ease the day-care problem, and the conflict between family and job demands.

13. Recognize that you may not be able to do it all.

Career, family, and personal demands can add up to a great deal for many people. For some, this becomes an overload situation. If you feel this way, recognize that you may not be able to do it all. Prioritize your choices as suggested in an earlier action item. Then draw a line on how many activities you can pursue at once. Some activities might have to go. For example, the Friday night card game might have to be done away with along with other less important activities. By recognizing the limited time you have, and what your priorities are, you can use intelligent planning to reduce potential conflicts.

14. Improve your organization and time management.

The conflict between work, family and personal interests is heightened when the employee needs better organization and time management. Evaluate this in yourself. Are you well organized? Do you use your time effectively? If the answer to either of the questions is no, set up some goals for improving your organization and time management. Read articles or books in the area, take seminars or college courses, use a calendar system. Also, read the chapters in this book dealing with organizing and time management. By making improvements here, you can lessen the conflict between work, family and personal demands.

15. Handle conflict by working for solutions.

If you get into a conflict with others relating to job, family and personal demands, try to keep the interaction positive. Avoid being defensive, argumentative, or rigid in your ways. Do not assume that the conflict is unsolvable. Instead, remain open and flexible in the discussion, and try to work for solutions. Seek some happy medium which keeps everyone happy even if you, like others, have to sacrifice something. Adding interpersonal conflict to the career-personal conflict will only make matters worse, so keep others on your side.

16. Explore the possibilities of part-time work.

If there do not seem to be enough hours to go around, and you have explored the other suggestions offered in this chapter, you might want to consider part-time work. By lessening the number of hours put in on the job, more time can be devoted to family and personal activities. Obviously, you have to evaluate the financial impact of changing from full-time to part-time work. With dual-career families, part-time work is a nice alternative for many. Employers have increased their use of part-time employees in recent years, with the trend likely to continue. Go to your manager or company human resources department and suggest the alternative of part-time work if it fits your needs.

17. Be candid with child care issues.

Some employees are not candid when child care (or parent care) issues affect them. For example, the employee might call in sick to care for a child when a sitter is not available. Or invent some other fictitious story for missing work or being late. This can create another problem, since many managers can see through such reasons if they are not true. Then they have to deal with not only the employee being absent or late, but the employee's lack of truthfulness as well.

Should you need time for child care or family or personal matters, explain the issue candidly to your manager. Offer to take a vacation day if need be. Managers are growing increasingly aware of family and child care issues, so it is best to discuss it candidly. The manager may also be able to offer suggestions to help you with the problem.

18. Schedule the activities in your personal life.

Though it sounds very mechanical, many people can benefit by scheduling the activities in their personal life. This can ease the problem of there not being enough time to get everything done. For example, you might set aside an hour or more certain days of the week for exercise. Or block off a limited amount of time each week for your hobbies. By using scheduled blocks, you may find it easier to get in certain activities. Free time which is left over can be used at your discretion. Try using a scheduling system for some of the more important activities in your personal life as a way to get the most out of your time.

19. Examine the possibility of flexible work hours.

Many companies have put into practice flexible work hours. Flexible hours still require the employee to put in a certain number of hours each week, but there is freedom to set the exact times to start and quit. Those wanting to have the early evening hours free can start earlier, and those wanting the early mornings free can start later. Flexible hours might help you with some of your personal and family needs. If your company does not make flexible hours available to all, explore the possibility with your manager. It might go a long way in reducing the conflict between career and other needs.

20. Be willing to compromise in managing conflict.

Some employees remain steadfast in the need to keep up certain activities in their lives. This "dig in your heels" approach can add interpersonal conflict to the situation. If you are experiencing a conflict between career and other activities, take on a more flexible attitude. Be willing to compromise in solving conflicts between career, family and personal activities. Perhaps you may give up or reduce the time spent on a certain hobby in exchange for additional family responsibilities. And your spouse may do similarly. Be willing to compromise, and resolve conflicts before they become conflicts.

21. Seek the advice of others.

When dealing with a conflict between career and other needs, it is often helpful to seek the advice of another. This other person may be able to look at your life and needs from a different perspective than you can. They might offer suggestions that you did not consider at all. If you are struggling with a conflict, seek out the advice of someone you trust. This might be a friend, current or former manager, or relative. Be candid in describing the situation, and be willing to listen to all suggestions that you receive. Adding the advice of another to your own ideas can greatly help reduce the conflict between career and other needs.

Recommended Readings

Bergsman, Steve. Part-Time Professionals Make the Choice. *The Personnel Administrator*, September, 1989, p. 49-52.

Bolles, Richard N. *The Three Boxes of Life*. Berkeley, CA: Ten Speed Press, 1981.

Cameron, Charles, and Elisorr, Suzanne. *Thank God it's Monday: Making Your Work Fulfilling and Finding Fulfilling Work*. New York: St. Martin's Press, 1986.

Connor, Tim. Your Ten-Year Plan: Pointers for Inner Success. *Management World*, July-Aug, 1986, p. 1-3.

Grieff, Barrie S., and Munter, Preston K. *Tradeoffs: Executive, Family and Organizational Life*. New York: New American Library, 1980.

Fernandez, J. P. *Child Care and Corporation Productivity: Resolving Family/Work Conflicts*. Lexington, MA: Lexington Books, 1986.

Kaye, Beverly. Career Development—Any Time, Any Place. *Training and Development*, December, 1993, 46-49.

Morrison, Ann M.; White, Randall P.; and Van Velsor, Ellen. *Breaking the Glass Ceiling: Can Women Reach the Top of America's Largest Corporations*? Reading, MA: Addison-Wesley, 1987.

Palmer, Stuart. *Role Stress*. Englewood Cliffs, NJ: Prentice-Hall, 1981.

Ribaric, Ronald F. Mission Possible: Meeting Family Demands. *The Personnel Administrator*, August, 1987, p. 70-79.

Schmidt, Veronica, and Scott, Norman. Work and Family Life: A Delicate Balance. *The Personnel Administrator*, August, 1987, p. 40-46.

Shaevitz, Margorie, and Shaefitz, Morton. *Making it Together as a Two Career Couple*. Boston: Houghton Mifflin Company, 1980.

Skrzycki, Cindy. Risk Takers (Successful Personalities). *U.S. News & World Report*, Jan., 1987, 26, p. 60-64.

Spruell, G. Business Planning for Parenthood. *Training and Development Journal*, 1986, 40 (8), p. 30-35.

Time, Goods, and Well-being. Edited by F. Thomas Juster and Frank P. Stafford. Ann Arbor, MI: ISR Publishing, 1985.

Trenille, Beverly and Stautberg, Susan Schiffer. *Managing It All: Time-Saving Ideas for Career, Family, Relationships and Self.* New York: Master Media, 1988.

19

Stress Management

This chapter helps improve performance in the following areas:

- Reducing stress on the job.
- Becoming less tense in the workplace.
- Managing tension and pressure more effectively.
- Remaining calm under difficult circumstances.

Action Items for Stress Management

1. Get involved in a regular exercise program.

There is probably no other better way to reduce stress than through exercise. By exercising, the tension can drain away instantly, leaving a person feeling relaxed and yet energetic. And then there are the additional benefits of losing weight and developing better muscle tone. Evaluate your current use of exercise. If you are not exercising regularly, start a program now. Consult a physician if you have not exercised for a long time.

For exercise to be most beneficial, there should be at least 30 minutes of non-stop activity such as walking, running, swimming, bicycling, or other aerobic sports. You may have to build up to this level if you do not exercise regularly now. Begin a program and build up to faster or longer intervals. See if you do not feel a great sense of relaxation after completing your exercise routine.

2. Reduce your intake of caffeine and nicotine.

Both caffeine and nicotine are stimulants which energize the body, and also cause stress if used in excess. While limited amounts are not harmful, care should be taken with the amounts used. Caffeine is most commonly taken in coffee, tea, and soft drinks, while nicotine is primarily ingested from smoking. Evaluate your use of caffeine and nicotine. If you have more than two cups of coffee each day, are a frequent smoker, or drink large amounts of soda or tea, you can be building up stress without knowing it. Reduce your intake or take de-caffeinated versions of these products. It can reduce the amount of stress you experience.

3. Avoid feeling that everything is a crisis.

Some employees tend to regard everything as a crisis. Whenever a problem or change needs to be made, they overreact and make it into a major event. While problems and change are inevitable in every company, they are not necessarily a crisis. If you are a person who feels your job is nothing but crisis management, try to change that attitude. Recognize that many of the issues you have to deal with are normal opportunities for someone in the workplace. Try to separate a true crisis from a simple problem that requires a solution. If you see patterns develop with problems, take the time to put in place procedures or programs to prevent a problem from becoming a problem.

4. Use deep breathing techniques.

When we become stressed and tense, our breathing rate and heart rate tend to go up. We are putting our system in high gear to deal with a perceived crisis. Some people have their system in high gear all day, and produce stress as a result. Caffeine and nicotine can keep your breathing and heart rates at quicker levels without any voluntary control on your part.

One of the most effective ways to reduce stress is to reduce your breathing rate. This in turn will bring down your heart rate, and put your body in a more relaxed state. Try using deep breathing for a couple of minutes when you feel yourself becoming stressed. Think of relaxing as you try to lower your breathing rate. If helpful, time your breathing rate or pulse rate until you notice a change. Reduced breathing levels are very effective in reducing perceived stress.

5. Become more organized and manage time more effectively.

Stress is increased when we feel we are losing control of the work day. We think only of all of the things that need to be done and the lack of time to do them. This can be improved upon by better organization and managing time effectively. You should evaluate how effective you are in these areas or ask a trusted friend for an opinion. By better organizing your work, you will feel more in control and less stressed. Similarly, by managing time effectively, you will get more done and feel less stressed. Review the other chapters in this book for specific suggestions on how to become better organized and manage time more effectively.

6. Take up a relaxing hobby.

One way to reduce stress is to take up a relaxing hobby. In particular, the hobby should be one that it is easy to enjoy and become absorbed in from a psychological standpoint. Successful hobbies from a stress reduction standpoint are those where the hours slip away quickly and you hate to break away. This relaxing hobby may be one of a number of choices, depending on what relaxes you. Examples include painting, writing, building things, crafts, model railroads or planes, automobile refurbishing, needlework, chess, astronomy, and many other possibilities. Find a hobby that is relaxing for you.

7. Use visualizing as a stress reduction technique.

You can lower your breathing and heart rates, and reduce stress, by visualizing a calm scene. What you simply do is think of a calm relaxing place for you. Perhaps that is sitting in a whirlpool, being in a boat on a lake, watching the sunset on the ocean, or sitting in your favorite easy chair. Whatever the case, when you feel yourself becoming stressed at the workplace, think of this relaxing scene for you. Envision yourself in this relaxing place and how calm and good you will feel. By doing this for a fifteen seconds or more at work, you can reduce your stress. Try visualizing as a stress reduction technique.

8. Try laughing, smiling, and joking more.

This action item sounds so easy, yet it can do wonders for reducing stress. We have all experienced relief in intense situations when someone makes a joke that causes everyone to laugh. People who can break tension with occasional bits of humor can prevent stress from building up. Ask your friends and co-workers if they see you as an intense person. If so, try to joke, laugh, and smile a bit more. We are not suggesting that you become a comedian, but that you simply lighten up on occasion to reduce your intensity and possible stress.

9. Build interpersonal relationships with those who cause stress.

Some employees find that their stress level goes up when they have to interact with a certain person. They may be stress-free at other times, but find this one individual produces stress. If you have this problem, try to build a better interpersonal relationship with this person. Try to get to know them better, and develop a working friendship. Use the suggestions we offered in the chapter on interpersonal skills to work better with the person who causes you stress. By improving the working relationship, you can reduce your stress level.

10. Develop a calm, inner resolve.

Some employees have a calm demeanor, even under very stressful events. Nothing seems to upset them or cause them to lose control. If you lack this type of style, try to develop a calm, inner resolve. This starts by convincing yourself that everything will work out fine, that everything is under control. If you can develop this skill, you will reduce your stress level and ability to handle crisis situations. After telling yourself and others that things will work out fine, objectively think through what needs to be done. Put together a plan and carry out the plan in a step-by-step way.

11. Rehearse and prepare for stressful events.

Some events cause stress in the workplace. Examples include meeting with an important client, attending a meeting with senior managers, or making a presentation to others. We can reduce the stress of these events by proper preparation and rehearsal. Put together a concrete plan for your meeting or presentation. Rehearse it several times so you know the content very well. Anticipate what sort of questions or objections those in attendance will have. And finally, visualize yourself at the meeting or presentation doing everything perfectly. That will build your confidence for the actual event itself. By advance preparation and rehearsal, you can reduce the amount of stress related to meetings or presentations.

12. Get a proper amount of sleep.

Lack of sleep can contribute to stress. While people differ in how much sleep they need, the lack of enough sleep can leave people feeling tense, irritable, and physically and psychologically fatigued. The problem is also compounded when people who did not get enough sleep drink several cups of coffee to "get them going." The caffeine itself can produce stress. The solution to all of this is to try to get the proper amount of rest for you as an individual. Proper sleep each night can do wonders in reducing the level of stress.

13. Do not take the comments of others personally.

Some employees take the suggestions and comments of others personally. They feel they are being attacked when a co-worker or manager suggests that they do things differently. This increases job stress, and for no good reason. If others make suggestions to you on how to do your job differently, do not take the comments personally. See the feedback as an opportunity to learn, grow, and improve, not as criticism or an attack on you. We all can get better at whatever we do, and you need to maintain that sort of an outlook. With this type of attitude, you can lessen your stress on the job.

14. Develop an objective versus emotional outlook.

Some employees react very emotionally to the events around them, both positively and negatively. If done all day long, this can be emotionally draining and leave a person feeling stressed and fatigued.

It is desirable to have an emotional uplift to positive things that happen around the workplace. However, if you tend to react emotionally, you will want to reduce your emotional reaction to negative events. Try to minimize anger, depression, and other negative emotions when undesirable events happen at the workplace. Instead, try to look at these events objectively and ask what can you do to make the situation better. Having an objective rather than emotional reaction can reduce the amount of stress you feel.

15. Talk out stressful events with others.

When an individual holds stressful feelings inside, the pressure can build and build. For most people, having someone to talk to can lessen the stress dramatically. Psychologists call this a "catharsis" effect, meaning that you feel a sense of relief from just having talked to someone else about your stressful situation. If you tend to hold emotions and stress within you, try letting them out more. We are not suggesting you explode at someone else, but that you calmly and objectively tell the other person what is causing you to feel stressed on the job.

The other person you have the discussion with might be a co-worker, manager, friend, or spouse. Think of someone who has knowledge of the area causing your stress, can offer good suggestions, and is a good listener. You will find a sense of relief from stress by being able to get things off your chest in a positive, constructive way.

16. Develop a support network.

You may experience stress by not knowing what to do in a certain situation. In many cases, co-workers, managers, and friends might be able to offer you helpful suggestions. At other times, it may be useful to expand your sources to include other people as well. For example, professional associations and colleagues at other companies might be able to offer you advice which adds to that you can get at your own organization. Build a support network of your own by contacting others in your field, professional associations, and community organizations. They can help your alleviate stress by providing someone else to talk to in difficult times.

17. Avoid seeing discussions as win-lose confrontations.

Some employees see meetings and discussions as a chance to get their ideas approved over those of others. This attitude leads to competitiveness and a win-lose outcome. Those who lose, and even those who win, can leave the meeting feeling stressed and exhausted. If you are a person who wants to dominate discussions and get only your ideas approved, try to change this style.

Do not view meetings as contests with winners and losers, but as open discussions with everyone sharing his/her view. The only "winning" idea is the one that works best, and this may be a composite of the ideas of several people. State your opinion clearly, but do not become stressed or frustrated if your idea is not used. That is part of the give and take of the business world. Occasionally, champion the ideas of others who may do the same with your ideas. By developing this win-win attitude, you can reduce your job-related stress.

18. Do not use alcohol or drugs as stress reducers.

It is tempting for some to use alcohol or drugs as a means of reducing stress. The idea is that by having a few drinks or a tranquilizer, you can eliminate all of the stress problems. Actually, this is a very ineffective solution. First of all, the **cause** of the stress is never dealt with when using alcohol or drugs. You only provide a short-term relief from the **symptoms,** and the problem quickly comes back to haunt you again.

Second, by escaping from stress rather than coping with it, you never learn how to deal with stress itself. Last, the use of alcohol and drugs may require larger quantities, creating health and dependency problems which increase stress. All in all, alcohol and drugs only make stress worse rather than provide an effective solution.

19. Work on reducing stress at home.

Stress at home may heighten stress on the job. Some individuals may bring the home-related stress to the workplace itself. If you feel much of your stress is due to home-related problems, apply the action items in this chapter to your home life. Also, turn to the chapters on interpersonal skills and organization and time management with an eye toward applying them at home.

Try wherever possible to spread out stress-causing events at home. Some of the most stressful events in our personal lives are moving to a new area, starting a new job, getting married or divorced, having children, or having health problems. While some events cannot be avoided (e.g., health problems), you can avoid adding to the stress by taking on other stressful activities such as moving to a new home. Keep home-related stress to a minimum wherever you can.

20. Have a well-balanced diet.

Studies have shown that people who are under stress use up certain vitamins and minerals to a much greater degree than those who are not under stress. The person who does not have a well-balanced diet may be less able to cope with stress than someone who gets their proper share of nutrients. Evaluate your diet to determine whether you are getting a well-balanced mix of fruits, vegetables, grains, fish, poultry, and meats. If you are dieting, do you have a well-balanced diet or take vitamin supplements? The key is to ensure that your body is physiologically able to handle any stress that might come its way.

21. Listen to calming music.

Still yet another way to reduce stress is to listen to calming music. For many, music can soothe and relieve day-to-day stress. You should try music as a means of temporarily relieving the symptoms of stress. Find some music that is particularly relaxing for you. Seek out a comfortable, quiet place and use headphones or speakers as ap propriate. Try to cleanse your mind of other matters and practice deep breathing as you listen to the music. You may find this an effective way to reduce stress.

22. Develop a more carefree attitude.

Some employees have a very serious, very intense approach to their work. They never seem to relax and enjoy themselves. This can increase the amount of stress which is felt. If you are this way, try to lighten up your style a bit. Develop a more carefree, friendly style. We are not suggesting that you neglect your work, but rather that you increase your interest in people and become less intense. You may well find that you start to enjoy life and work more, and are less stressful on the job.

23. Use relaxation techniques at home.

Stress can be reduced by practicing effective relaxation techniques at home. While everyone has their favorite place to relax, some of the more common are whirlpool baths, spas, swimming, sunning, lying in the sand or in a hammock, or relaxing in a comfortable chair. Whatever works best for you, having a favorite relaxation place at home can help reduce stress. Buy or build a place to help you unwind after the work hours.

Recommended Readings

Adams, John D. *Understanding and Managing Stress: A Workbook in Changing Life Styles*. San Diego, CA: University Associates, 1984.

Cavanagh, Michael E. What You Don't Know About Stress. *Personnel Journal*, July, 1988, p. 53-59.

Cohen, William A., and Cohen, Nurit. *Top Executive Performance: 11 Keys to Success and Power*. New York: Wiley, 1984.

Fink, Steven. *Crisis Management: Planning for the Inevitable*. New York: AMACOM, 1986.

Goldberg, P. *Executive Health: How to Recognize Health Danger Signals and Manage Stress Successfully*. New York: McGraw-Hill, 1979.

Goodloe, Alfred; Bensahel, Jane; and Kelly, John. *Managing Yourself: How to Control Emotion, Stress, and Time*. New York: Franklin Watts, 1984.

Greenberg, Herbert M. *Coping with Job Stress*. Englewood Cliffs, NJ: Prentice-Hall, 1980.

Jenner, Jessica Reynolds. On the Way to Stress Resistance. *Training and Development*, May, 1986, p. 112-115.

Lazarus, R. S., and Folkman, S. *Stress, Appraisal and Coping*. New York: Springer, 1984.

Miller, Annetta. Stress on the Job: It's Hurting Morale and the Bottom Line. How can Workers and Bosses Cope? *Newsweek*, April 25, 1988, p. 40-45.

Quick, J.C., and Quick, J. *Organizational Stress and Preventative Management*. New York: McGraw-Hill, 1984.

Stress: Can We Cope? *Time*, June 6, 1983, p. 48-54.

20

Confidence and Self-Image

This chapter helps improve performance in the following areas:

- Increasing personal confidence.
- Being more assertive.
- Negative feelings about yourself and your abilities.
- Developing a better self-image.

Action Items for Confidence and Self-Image

1. Attribute your successes to yourself.

Success can be attributed to different factors. For example, it can be attributed to luck or chance (e.g., being in the right place at the right time), or success can be attributed to yourself (e.g., your skills, hard work). You should evaluate how you attribute your successes to date? Are they due to things you control or due to chance?

Employees with a high amount of confidence attribute their successes to factors that reside within them. As such, they will see themselves in control of their future success, and work harder to attain more success. You should have that sort of confidence as well. Recognize that your skills, abilities, and motivation will propel you onward in your career. See yourself as skilled and in control of your career.

2. Talk like a confident person.

Employees who are confident and have a strong self-image project this in what they say. They talk like a confident person. By expressing confidence in the future, they inspire others toward higher achievements. And the fact that they believe that they will succeed motivates them toward success. We are not suggesting that you be phony in expressing confidence, but that you genuinely believe that things will work out well. And those who believe in success are much more likely to attain it than those who do not believe it.

The talk of a confident person might reflect saying things such as the following:

- "I'm confident we can get the job done."

- "I'm very pleased with the way it turned out."

- "We did a good job with that."

- "If we all work a little harder, we can get it done."
- "I know everything will turn out all right."
- "I'm happy with what I've accomplished so far."

3. Avoid negative thoughts and speech.

Some employees react negatively to any type of challenge. They are quick to focus on the "can'ts" rather than the "wills." When someone says they can't do a task they are really saying they will not even try to do the task, and that ensures failure. Furthermore, the person who thinks negatively may inspire others to think negatively as well. Avoid negative thoughts and speech when you hear of a new challenge. Focus on the positive at first. If your reaction is negative overall, let that be a balanced reaction that is thought out.

Negative language to avoid includes the following examples:
- "I don't think we will be able to do it."
- "The reasons I couldn't get it done are. . ."
- "We've never done it that way before."
- "I tried hard, but. . ."
- "We'll never get this done on time."
- "Gee, I never seem to do anything right."

4. Present your good ideas to others.

Some employees quietly work away on their own. They may have excellent ideas for improving the area, but lack the confidence to present those ideas to others. Or they merely tell their co-workers instead of their manager. If you tend to be inhibited or shy in presenting your ideas, recognize that managers are always interested in hearing of new ideas that will improve the department. Even if they do not use every idea, this does not mean that they do not want to hear more.

Go forward in presenting your ideas to management. If easier for you, write up the idea and send it to others rather than present it verbally. But have the confidence that what you have to say is important and valued by others. Do not let your own lack of assertiveness hurt your career. Only positive things can happen from sharing out good, constructive ideas. Muster the courage to go forward and say what you think is right.

5. Recognize your personal strengths.

An excellent way to build self-confidence is to recognize your personal strengths. List out your special skills, abilities, knowledge, personality traits, and other strengths that separate you from other people. Review the list and recognize that you have some valuable and important skills that many others might lack. Use this list as your foundation to build self-confidence. Review the list periodically and add to it as you acquire additional strengths.

6. Visualize yourself being successful.

The technique of visualizing can help in building confidence and attaining success. Visualizing involves seeing yourself in the future attaining great success—success being defined any way you choose. By spending ten minutes every evening seeing yourself doing successful activities, you will convince your inner self to attain this level of success. Your aspirations for success will become reality if you repeatedly envision this success and the good feelings associated with it. Use visualizing as a technique to boost your inner confidence and self-image.

7. Build more knowledge in your area of expertise.

Some individuals lack self-confidence in their area of employment. They are uncertain of knowing what to do and when to do it. If you are ever troubled by this problem, aggressively set out to change. Build a high level of knowledge in your area of expertise. Resolve to know more about the field than anyone else. Read books and articles in the field, join professional associations, attend seminars, network with other professionals, and in other ways build up you knowledge level. This added knowledge will do wonders in boosting your confidence and self-image.

8. Dress the part.

Self-image can be helped or hindered by the clothing and grooming shown by an employee. It helps if someone aspiring to be a senior manager **looks** like a senior manager. Others at the company will start to think of the person like they would think of a senior manager. We are not suggesting that clothing and grooming is all there is to getting ahead, but that looking the part can help your career, and not looking the part can hamper your progression.

Each job and company will have its own standards for clothing and grooming. You should carefully study the dress and grooming of people who are in jobs that you aspire to. Particularly pay attention to the people you admire and are very successful. If uncertain as to where they buy their clothes, compliment them on their outfit and ask where they bought it. By improving your dress and grooming you will project a better self-image and enhance your career progression.

9. Seek out feedback from others on your confidence level.

It helps to know how other people see your confidence level and self-image. By getting this feedback, you will know where to make adjustments. Ask co-workers or friends for their candid opinions. Remain very open to what they say. Do others see you as confident of yourself or uncertain? Are you perhaps lacking in confidence in just certain situations? By knowing the answers to these questions, you can learn how to change your behavior and project better confidence.

10. Recognize that we all have strengths and weaknesses.

Employees who lack confidence might do so because of an unrealistic viewpoint. They may focus on their weaknesses, and regard those weaknesses as making them inferior to others. In reality, **everyone** has both strengths and weaknesses, though the exact combination is different for each person. By simply recognizing that you are no different from others in this regard can do wonders for instilling better confidence. If you need to dwell on any aspect of your behavior, focus on the positive elements, those things you do well. Avoid focusing on the weaknesses, and regard yourself as having a unique mix of strengths and weaknesses just like everyone else.

11. Accept the suggestions others might give you.

It is ironic that people who need help the most are sometimes the most reluctant to take advice. When someone lacks confidence, they may see the helpful suggestions of others as personal attacks. They defend themselves because they do not want their fragile ego to lose any more confidence. And those who have loads of confidence will easily accept feedback since their ego will not suffer regardless of what they hear.

Evaluate your reactions to the suggestions of others. Are you receptive to the feedback you get during performance appraisals or at other times? If not, try to build up your confidence enough to listen to the feedback. Others are trying to be helpful, not destructive. Recognize that by learning from the suggestions and making changes you become a better employee and more confident.

12. Learn new job skills.

Employees with limited or dated job skills may lose confidence in themselves. The world may be passing them by while they are standing still. Evaluate how confident you are of your job skills. Are you current and up-to-date in your field? Can you use the latest technology, be it computers or other equipment? If the answer is no, set a goal to increase or build additional job skills. List out the skills most important for your area and start a developmental plan. That developmental plan might include training, seminars, workshops, teaming up with an expert, or reading on your own. Use the learning of new skills as a means to boost your confidence.

13. Take up new sports or hobbies.

Confidence and self-image can be built up by away-from-work activities. By learning new skills and knowledge away from work, you can carry over your enhanced confidence to the job itself. Think of ways you might enhance your confidence away from the job. Are there new sports you can learn to play? New hobbies you can learn? New skills you can acquire? Recognize that you will not be highly proficient at these new activities right away. However, acquiring basic proficiency when having very limited skills to start should make you feel more confident in your ability to learn and grow. Try new sports or hobbies as a way to expand your self-confidence.

14. Seek out more job responsibilities.

Another excellent confidence builder is to seek out and expand your job responsibilities. By expanding into new areas, and succeeding at them, you can enhance the way you feel about yourself. Try doing this by first listing out those job responsibilities you could add without creating problems at your company. Perhaps there are special projects that need to be done or overflow work in an adjacent area. Seek out your manager with the idea, saying that you see the added responsibilities as a means to grow and learn. If given the increased responsibilities, reward yourself for successfully learning and performing new activities. Recognize that you are capable and confident of learning and doing more.

15. Recognize it is your opinion of yourself that counts.

Confidence is ultimately a very personal and individualized feeling. It is, however, shaped by the opinion others have of you. For some employees, a critical opinion of them expressed by someone else becomes overwhelming. They do not have the personal self-confidence to overcome the blow. Recognize that your opinion of yourself is more important than the opinion others have of you. If you think highly of yourself, and everyone should, the opinion of someone else should not matter that much. Even if one person is damaging, you should be able to move away from that and still be confident in yourself. Make sure your opinion of yourself is positive and you do not let that change.

16. Learn from your failures.

Everyone experiences failure in life, however people react very differently to it. Some blame and criticize themselves for failure, lowering their confidence and self-esteem. You should avoid reacting this way to failures that you experience i 1 your career. Instead of blaming and criticizing yourself, analyze what went wrong. Learn and grow from the failure by adding new knowledge, skills and experience. If you treat failure this way, your confidence will not be shattered. In fact, it may even grow since you will come to feel that you know the ropes much better than you did before. Recognize that failure is inevitable, but do not let it diminish your confidence.

17. Listen to motivational and inspirational tapes.

A good self-confidence builder is to listen to motivational and inspirational tapes. Hearing the speaker's personal message is like having your own coach or mentor. There are many excellent ideas to be obtained from such products that you can put into practice. These tapes are relatively inexpensive and can help you increase your self-esteem. Seek out audio or video tapes th;·t build self-confidence. Use the ideas to improve your skills and how you feel about yourself.

18. Start an exercise program.

You self-image can be enhanced a great deal by starting and maintaining an exercise program. An exercise program can help lose weight, develop muscle tone, increase stamina and energy, and reduce stress. Add to that the benefit of gaining confidence from being able to do certain exercises or participate in certain sports. All of these benefits work to build a better self-image. Start an exercise program that is right for you, consulting a physician first if you are not used to exercise. Aerobic sports, with thirty or more minutes of constant motion, have been found to be the most beneficial from a cardio-vascular standpoint. Mixing aerobics with certain muscle-shaping exercises (e.g., weight work) can be an excellent way to improve your self-image.

19. Think positively.

This action item sounds basic, but this general mental attitude can do wonders. At least fifty percent of succeeding stems from believing that you can succeed, so this is your essential starting point. Think positively about yourself and succeeding. Confident employees focus on positive success rather than on problems or failures. They commonly think and say things like "I can," or "I will." For many the word "can't" does not exist. Try to think positively in your career.

20. List out your accomplishments.

Some people are quick to forget how much they have accomplished in life. It can boost their self-confidence to reflect back occasionally. List out the accomplishments you are most proud of in your life. These might be on-the-job accomplishments or those done away from the job. For example, you might list getting a certain promotion or performance appraisal rating, completing school, serving in a volunteer leadership role, or perfecting your skills at a particular hobby. After your list is complete, go back over it and reflect on how many accomplishments you have made already. Let that list stimulate you to even greater accomplishments as you go forward.

21. Maintain a diary of achievements.

Your confidence can also be helped by compiling a diary of achievements. Once a week or once a month, list out the important achievements you have made. Occasionally, go back and re-read your progress in earlier years to see the big picture. The use of such a diary can help you feel good about what you have already done, and help you set goals for the future. Try maintaining a diary of achievements to enhance your self-confidence.

22. Maintain a good body posture.

The self-image you project to others is dependent, in part, on how you sit or stand. If you tend to slouch or lean, others may conclude that you are not a confident, fit person. This conclusion may be wrong, but we all interpret others by what we see. Evaluate your body posture when sitting or standing. Try to sit and stand more straight and erect, with the trunk of your body in an upright position. Develop an awareness of how body posture affects your self-image and do what you can to have an effective body posture.

23. Greet people warmly.

The manner is which we greet new people can affect how others see our self-image. Warm and friendly greetings are associated with strong self-confidence while a reluctant or weak greeting is associated with limited self-confidence. Evaluate how you greet new people upon first meeting them. If you need to make improvements, start by using a warm smile and firm handshake. Try to be friendly and engage the other person in conversation, if even about trivial matters. Be willing to introduce yourself to new people if no one else is there to introduce you. These effective greeting techniques will project an image of being confident.

24. Use a body language which shows confidence.

We have all seen a speaker whose body language showed little confidence. The person might have had their hands in their pockets, nervously adjusted their tie or coat, rocked back and forth, or hid behind the podium from the audience. We thought to ourselves that this person lacked confidence in what they were doing. Think of your body language as you interact with others. Does it show confidence or a lack of confidence? Generally speaking, confident people use gestures, look someone in the eye, have a firm voice, can face people and stand close to them without feeling uncomfortable, and have good posture. Try to improve your body language where you can to show more confidence.

Recommended Readings

Alberti, Robert E., and Emmons, Michael. *Your Perfect Right*. New York: Impact Publishers, 1988.

Back, Ken, and Back, Kate. *Assertiveness at Work*. London: McGraw-Hill, 1982.

Calano, Jimmy, and Salzman, Jeff. *Career Tracking: 26 Success Short-Cuts to the Top*. New York: Simon and Schuster, 1988.

Cuming, Pamela. *The Power Handbook: A Strategic Guide to Organizational and Personal Effectiveness*. New York: Van Nostrand Reinhold, 1981.

Fritz, Roger. *You're in Charge*. Glenview, IL: Scott, Foresman and Company, 1986.

Hill, Napoleon. *Think and Grow Rich*. New York: Fawcett Crest, 1983.

Hill, Napoleon, and Stone, W. Clement. *Success Through a Positive Mental Attitude*. Englewood Cliffs, NJ: Prentice-Hall, 1987.

Kravetz, Dennis J. *Getting Noticed: A Manager's Success Kit*. New York: Wiley, 1985.

McKain, Robert J. *How to Get to the Top . . . and Stay There*. New York: AMACOM, 1981.

McKay, Matthew, and Faning, Patrick. *Self Esteem*. New York: St. Martin's Press, 1987.

Morgan, Phillip I., and Baker, H. Kent. Building a Professional Image: Learning Assertiveness. *Supervisory Management*, Aug, 1985, 30, p. 14-20.

Rubin, Theodore. *Overcoming Indecisiveness*. New York: Harper, 1985.

21

Balancing Independence and Dependence

This chapter helps improve performance in the following areas:

- Working on one's own.
- Having the confidence to work independently.
- Working as part of a team.
- Focusing on the group versus one individual.

Action Items for Balancing Independence and Dependence

The first part of this chapter contains action items on working independently. For action items on dependence and teamwork, see the second half of the chapter.

Increasing Independence

1. Be confident of yourself.

A starting point for increasing independence is to be confident of yourself. Recognize that you are a professional at what you do, know your job well, and an important part of the company. Your ideas are just as important as anyone else's ideas and deserve to be heard. By having this basic confidence in yourself, you can begin to take actions which are more independent. Work on building your confidence and self-image. Carry out the action items suggested in the chapter on confidence and self-image.

2. Present your ideas more aggressively.

Some employees are reluctant to present their ideas at meetings. They may fear saying something wrong, or losing the friendship of someone else. You can rarely advance in most occupations without being able to present your ideas to others, and be willing to do so in an open forum. If you cannot act independently in this regard, then build the confidence to present your ideas more aggressively. Do so in a non-argumentative way, but try to say a bit more than you have in the past.

If others challenge your ideas, do not back off at first unless you feel this is the thing to do. Instead, acknowledge the other person's ideas by saying something like, "I can understand why you feel the way you do." Then expand upon your position a bit more, and why you feel it is the best way to go. By gradually increasing your assertiveness in expressing your ideas, you will see that there is nothing to fear. While there is always a good point to drop an idea, do not do so quickly if this has been a problem in the past. Your ideas are important for all to hear.

3. Make more decisions on your own.

When faced with a decision, some employees are quick to run to their managers. Rather than make the decision on their own, they delegate upward and let the manager make the decision. When this occurs for very trivial decisions, the manager's valuable time may be used up and the employee is not carrying out the job responsibilities. Review your tendency to go to your manager for decisions. Do you do this for virtually everything that goes on in your area? If so, try to make more decisions independently. Have the confidence and independence to carry out most minor decision-making on your own. Escalate only important or complex decisions to your manager.

4. Draw up plans and goals for yourself.

Some employees are good at carrying out the plans and goals of others, but do not take the initiative to draw up their own goals. They are overly-dependent on others for direction and goals. Take stock of whether you have set any goals and plans for yourself and your job. If the answer is no, draw up some goals and plans right now. Think of what is important to achieve in your job and your personal development that has not been done to date. Once you have written up your goals and plans, present them to your manager or others as appropriate. Get their approval and work towards attaining the goals. Continue to do this on an ongoing basis. It is an excellent way to show that you are more independent and capable of working on your own.

5. Recognize that you know your area well.

It is helpful in asserting independence that you know your job well. If you are comfortable in carrying out your job, you are more capable of acting independently. Assess how well you know your current job. If not well, aggressively go out and learn more through reading, professional associations, or contacts with experts or former job incumbents. This will build your confidence in how you do your job and your ability to work independently.

If you currently know your job well, recognize this. Tell yourself that you know the job better than anyone else from your experience and job knowledge. By accepting this, there is no reason why you cannot operate more independently in carrying out the job. You are fully capable of making decisions, making plans, and working independently in carrying out your job responsibilities.

6. Use your boss as a sounding board rather than problem solver.

Some employees use the "dump and run" technique. They dump a problem in their manager's lap and then run and wait for a solution. Making others aware of a problem is only half of the battle—solutions are needed as well. You can take on a more independent role by identifying both problems and solutions that arise in your area. If your manager needs to be involved in the decision, go to your manager with your suggested solutions. Discuss the advantages and disadvantages of each solution if helpful. In this way, your manager is used more as a sounding board rather than problem solver. The manager can critique your ideas and let you carry out the action you presented. By doing this, you will be helping your manager and showing that you are capable of independently carrying out the job.

7. Do not back off or compromise too quickly.

When employees present ideas at a meeting, it is interesting to see how they react if someone challenges the idea. Some back off very quickly, regardless of what the other person suggests. By doing so, they are indirectly telling others that they are not confident of their idea, and that the idea was a poor one. Others may persist with their idea for a long time, and not buy off or compromise. There is a happy medium between abandoning an idea too quickly and sticking with it too long.

Evaluate your reaction when someone challenges your ideas. Do you quickly back off, saying something like, "well, that was just my suggestion, but I know there are others." If so, stick with your ideas longer until you are really convinced that it is time to change or compromise. Recognize that part of the give and take of the business world is that people will have different ideas, and discuss the ideas openly with others. Assert your independence by willing to present and discuss your ideas as long as appropriate.

8. Be willing to take an unpopular position.

There is always some risk involved in being the first to offer an opinion or expressing an unpopular opinion. To do so requires more confidence and independence than in many other situations. Some employees can never do this regardless of the circumstances. You should review whether you have a tendency to be this way. If so, recognize that your ideas should be heard as well those of others, even if your ideas are unpopular.

As long as you are tactful and professional in what you have to say, people will respect your right to say it. Gather facts and information to support your viewpoint. Have the confidence and independence to say what you feel, and recognize that your self-esteem will not be lowered by speaking out. You may even feel a great sense of relief in saying what you feel.

9. Take on some projects by yourself.

Many projects in organizations have multiple employees working on them. This may enable a variety of ideas and skills to be brought into play. There are, however, many smaller projects that could be

done by just one person. If you have a reluctance to work independently, your manager may be hesitant to delegate to you these
sorts of projects.

You need to prove to your manager that you are independent
enough, and skilled enough, to handle projects on your own. You
might have to first establish this by your work on a team. Convince
yourself that you can carry out a project that you or your manager
feel needs to be done. Then go to your manager with a proposal
that you be given the project on your own. You may have some
anxiety in the early stages, but be confident of your skills and
abilities to handle the project. What you learn from the first project will help build further confidence at working on your own.

10. Take the extra step on your own.

You can show your independence by taking additional steps on your
own. For example, a customer might have a problem that needs solving. Instead of going to your manager for a solution, you might take
some extra actions on your own to solve the customer's problem.
In this case, you have worked independently and gone beyond what
you would normally do to help the customer.

Evaluate whether you take such extra steps in carrying out your job.
If not, try to go further in performing your responsibilities. This
will enable you to grow, become more confident, and help your
manager out. All managers appreciate employees who will go the
extra step. What you need to ensure is that you keep your manager
posted on what you did, and that you do not ultimately overstep
your authority.

Increasing Dependence and Teamwork

11. Seek out the ideas and input of others.

You can work better as part of a team by seeking out the ideas of others. Some employees are reluctant to seek out the ideas of others, thinking it will be seen as a weakness on their part. Actually, the ideas of others can always improve upon the ideas you have of your own. And your co-workers will appreciate being asked their opinion. They will not see this as a sign of weakness. Try to increase your use of the ideas of others. Recognize that everyone can potentially contribute ideas; seek others out for their opinion.

12. Do not withdraw from a group if your ideas are rejected.

Some employees react negatively when their ideas are rejected. They may withdraw psychologically by not interacting with others in the group. Employees might also physically withdraw by isolating themselves and avoiding others. These types of reactions will hurt team dependence. Reflect back on how you react if your co-workers reject one of your ideas. Can you accept that or do you withdraw in some way? If you withdraw, try to change this by first recognizing that it was you idea someone did not like, not you. There may be many other ideas that you have that the group will like. Your withdrawal will only put a strain on the group, so remain an active part of the team and accept what happened as an event that happens to all of us from time to time.

13. Work for a consensus versus pushing your own ideas.

Teams which form a bond together tend to use consensus decision making. Rather than push their individual ideas, the group listens to all and forms a consensus of which way to go. To be more of a team player, you should adopt this strategy as well. Rather than

try to get your ideas approved, look openly at every idea on the
table. See if a group consensus exists, and if not, work for a consensus. Be willing to accept and buy off on whatever idea is supported by the group consensus, even if it does not match your initial
idea. By using consensus decision making, you will form a stronger
team and be more dependent upon one another.

14. Cross-train with your co-workers.

Teams work more effectively together when they understand each
other's jobs. This enables better appreciation of the work of others,
and permits better coverage when someone is away. If there is no
formal cross-training at your company, take the opportunity to do
some informal cross-training on your own. Learn the basics of
another co-worker's job and provide the same training for your job.
This builds a stronger dependency between you and another co-
worker, and enables you to help each other out as part of a team.

15. Use effective interpersonal skills.

Team building and mutual dependency are helped by effective interpersonal skills. You must be able to get to know and work effectively with others if you are to become a team. Evaluate your
interpersonal skills. If you are difficult to get along with, or not very
friendly, work on improving your interpersonal skills. Turn to the
chapter in this book on interpersonal skills and implement the action items contained there. That will help you get along better with
others and work more as a team.

16. Seek out the ideas and suggestions of others.

Some employees are too independent and try to solve all problems
on their own. They feel if they cannot figure it out, then no one
else can either. That extremely independent attitude can make it
difficult to work with others and build a team. Are you the independent type who would rather work on your own? If so, try to seek

out others from time to time to get their ideas and suggestions. There should be a balance where you avoid going to others all of the time or none of the time. If you are reluctant to seek the help of others, recognize that they will appreciate it if you ask their opinions, and you may get some additional ideas that you never thought of before. The net result is a better solution and a stronger team.

17. Use more teambuilding activities.

There are many informal teambuilding activities that employees can engage in. They will help build a team and enable employees to get to know each other better. These teambuilding activities include taking lunches and breaks together, participating in away-from-work social events, complimenting others for a job well done, and being more friendly and open. You might want to evaluate how often you use these teambuilding activities. Make an effort to do more of them to develop a team.

18. Encourage others to run ideas by you.

You can develop more of a mutual dependency with co-workers by asking others to run their ideas by you. When team members feel free to share ideas with each other, more dependency and common approaches will develop. Tell others to feel free to stop by whenever they want to run ideas by you. Practice the open-door policy when people stop by. Put aside whatever you are working on and practice good listening skills. By encouraging others to run their ideas by you, you will establish more camaraderie and teamwork.

19. Offer to train others.

Teamwork and joint dependency can be increased by offering to train people on how to do their jobs. The prime opportunity for this is when a new employee starts a job similar to your own. Do you take the time to show the new employee "the ropes?" If you do, the two of you will become more of a team and work effectively together. Think back to whether you have gone out of your way to help new people get up to speed. If not, make this a goal for the future.

20. Be willing to compromise.

Some employees are reluctant to compromise in decision making. They see decisions as all-or-none situations, with their ideas being used or someone else's. That type of attitude makes it difficult for teamwork and mutual cooperation. You should avoid such an attitude if you currently have one. Instead, be willing to compromise in decision making and problem solving. See the group being more important than any individual, be that yourself or anyone else. Be willing to change and modify any of your ideas if the group comes up with suggestions to improve the idea. Compromise is important ingredient for team success.

21. Use joint goals.

Very independent employees are used to having personal goals rather than joint goals with others. While that makes for high personal accountability, it does not do much for building teamwork and mutual cooperation. Review the types of goals that you have for the coming year. Are they all personal goals or are some joint goals with others at your organization? We recommend that there be a mix of goals, some being personal goals and some being joint goals with others. If your goals are too extreme in the personal direction, turn some of them into joint goals with others.

22. Give feedback and coaching to peers.

In organizations that are poor on teamwork, feedback and coaching are solely the responsibility of an employee's manager. In organizations with strong teamwork, employees help out their peers by providing feedback and coaching. Obviously, this is a two-way street, with employees both providing and receiving feedback. Review the status of feedback and coaching in your area. Do you do this for any of your peers?

The feedback and coaching can take many different forms. You can share out feedback on what the company is doing or how your co-worker is performing. Coaching can include how to improve job performance or the learning of new skills or abilities. Go carefully and slowly if you are providing feedback and coaching to a co-worker for the first time. Make it clear that you are only trying to help the person. Most employees are receptive to this type of assistance though it may be new for them. Use feedback and coaching as another means of building teamwork.

Recommended Readings

Adair, John. *Effective Teambuilding*. Brookfield, VT: Gower Publishing, 1986.

Back, Ken, and Back, Kate. *Assertiveness at Work*. London: McGraw-Hill, 1982.

Bolton, Robert and Bolton. Dorothy Grover. *Social Style/Management Style: Developing Productive Work Relationships*. New York: AMACOM, 1984.

Costley, Dan I., and Todd, Ralph. *Human Relations in Organizations* (3rd ed.). St. Paul, MN: West Publishing, 1987.

Cuming, Pamela. *The Power Handbook: A Strategic Guide to Organizational and Personal Effectiveness*. New York: Van Nostrand Reinhold, 1981.

Fritz, Roger. *You're in Charge*. Glenview, IL: Scott, Foresman and Company, 1986.

Galagan, Patricia. Work Teams that Work. *Training and Development*, Nov., 1986, p. 33-35.

Galagan, Patricia. Between Two Trapezes. *Training and Development*, March, 1987, p. 40-50.

Guest, Robert H. *Work Teams and Team Building*. New York: Pergamon Press, 1986.

Hobbs, Charles R. *Time Power*. New York: Harper & Row, 1987.

Moskowit, Robert. *How to Organize Your Work and Your Life*. Garden City, NY: Doubleday & Company, 1981.

Pollock, Ted. Organize Yourself. *Production*, Jan, 1988, 100, p. 33-35.

22

Selling and Negotiating

This chapter helps improve performance in the following areas:

- Improving sales skills with clients and customers.
- Selling ideas to internal company employees.
- Being more persuasive.
- Being more effective at negotiating.
- Improving presentations to others.

Action Items for Selling and Persuading

1. Analyze the needs of your clients (or internal audience).

Selling is greatly enhanced by first understanding the needs of your clients. By knowing what they want and need, you can adapt your sales presentation to meet their needs. This is just as true for in-house "selling" to your manager as it is for external selling to clients. Evaluate whether you take the time to assess and analyze the needs of your individual clients versus giving them a canned presentation that you have used many times before.

What sorts of factors should you consider in analyzing the client's needs? The following are samples:

- What does the person know about my products/services?.

- What does the person **want** to know about my products/services?

- What goals does the client have in the coming year?

- What are their main "drivers" (cost, quality, timeliness, service)?

- How do my products/services benefit this client?

By knowing the answers to questions like these, you can tailor your presentation to the particular client's needs.

2. Organize your ideas into a persuasive flow.

Some employees fail to persuade others because their is no flow to their ideas. The ideas just seem to be a collection of facts, figures, and anecdotes that do not lead to anything. You should ensure that all of your presentations build to a logical conclusion and persuade the individual to buy what you are selling. It makes no difference if you are making a one-on-one sales pitch to your boss or a formal presentation to a roomful of people.

There are many ways to organize your ideas into a persuasive flow. The following are examples:

- Compare and contrast your product with others, leading to the conclusion that your product is best to buy.

- Present an ordered series of facts which support your product. These facts build toward a general conclusion of buying what you are selling.

- Start by describing a problem that the client has, then how your product or service is the solution to that problem.

3. Read the body language of your audience.

Good sales people take the time to read the body language of their audience. Rather than plod along without reacting to body language, effective presenters will adapt to what they are seeing. As a simple example, if the audience looks confused, the presenter will stop to ask if there are any questions. Similarly, other body language signs are read and reacted to.

You should learn how to read the body language of others. In particular, learn to recognize signs of objections and agreement. In general, people who object may be leaning away from you, avoiding eye contact, folding their arms, shaking their heads, or frowning. If you see this, you should stop and try to resolve the objections or concerns. Those who are positive and in agreement are likely to be leaning forward, smiling, nodding, looking you in the eye, and have an open posture. You can continue with your ideas when you see this. Learn to recognize and deal with the body language of an audience.

4. Show empathy in response to objections or emotion.

Some employees fail to show empathy with a client's objections or emotions. If an objection is raised, they merely come back with their opinion or provide facts and figures. This can make the client feel they were not listened to, and emotionally uncomfortable. A better response is to show empathy whenever a client objects or says something emotional.

You show empathy by saying words which indicate you know how the person feels, and can understand their reasons for feeling this way. Empathy does not indicate agreement, but an **understanding.** Sample empathy statements include:

- "I can understand your reasons for feeling that way."

- "I know it can be upsetting if you felt it took too long."

5. Sell to make the client happy, not to make you happy.

Employees often sell to make themselves happy. They think of the money, commission, prestige, or salary increase they will get by selling something, and many forget about the client. An alternative is to think constantly of the client and how you can make that person happy. If they are a happy buyer, you will be happy as well from getting the sale, but the initial focus is on the client. Try to use this approach when selling ideas or products to others—focus on how you can make them happy with what you have to offer.

6. Practice your presentation.

This action item sounds awfully easy, but many employees do not rehearse what they are going to present to someone else. As a result, they may not give a crisp presentation, or be unprepared for certain questions or comments. You should review whether you rehearse your sales presentations. If not, change this immediately. Find a room where you can privately rehearse in your mind if not by actually saying the words. Visualize the presentation itself, and think of what kinds of questions and concerns might be raised and how you will handle them. By rehearsing and preparing, you will be much more effective in selling to others.

7. Adapt your presentation to the personality of the client.

People have different personality traits, and a single selling approach will not appeal to everyone. For example, some people are very numbers oriented and always thinking about costs and budgets and the like. If your presentation does not address this, you have less chance of making the sale. Do you adapt your presentation to the personality of the client? If not, think of a specific person in advance and what drives them. Then tailor your presentation to this person. The more common personality types are:

- Those who are concerned with figures, numbers, and costs.

- Those who are very people oriented and need to be comfortable with the people they are dealing with.

- Those who are power and control oriented and want to be seen as decisive and leading others.

- Those who are cautious and analytical and want to avoid mistakes by getting many details.

8. Practice active listening.

Those who are effective at selling practice active listening. They show the other person that they are paying attention to what is being said. Evaluate your listening skills. If you are not practicing active listening with others, try to improve in this area (see the chapter on listening for details). Ways to show active listening are as follows:

- Maintain good eye contact.
- Lean forward to show interest.
- Face the person directly.
- Nod to indicate understanding.
- Make notes on what someone has said.
- Summarize what the person has said at various points.
- Avoid distractions when listening.

9. Tape yourself making a presentation.

Many people are surprised at how they look when they present to others. They may be totally unaware of certain habits they have or nuances in their speech. You can better prepare for your presentations by taping yourself. Cameras can be rented which easily hook up to a home video recorder. You can tape yourself many times, perhaps some in a more formal stand-up presentation and others while sitting down as in a meeting. Critique your own presentation and work on improving where needed. Taping yourself can be a very valuable aid in giving better sales presentations.

10. Listen more than you talk in sales meetings.

Many people envision those who are good at sales as being people who talk nonstop. Actually, very good sales people are effective listeners who find out what a client needs and sell this to the person. Evaluate how you spend your time in a sales presentation. Do you have a balance between speaking and listening or do you do most of the talking? Try to find that happy balance. Force yourself to ask more open-ended questions of your clients, and listen to what they have to say. You will find that you can learn a great deal by doing this, and use this to sell more effectively.

11. Do your homework on the company and its employees.

Some employees fail to do any homework in advance on a company that they are selling to (the same is true of in-house presentations to managers). As a result, they may be surprised when bits of information come up that they are unprepared to handle. Before selling to others, you should always do your homework in advance. Find out about the company from written sources or other people. Determine the type of business they are in, where they are going, who their competition is, and what there needs might be. Also do some homework on the employees in the company, particularly the people you will be presenting to. Find out about their backgrounds and interests, and what they are looking for. Doing your advance homework helps you tailor your presentation and do a more effective job at selling.

12. Follow up and be persistent.

Selling ideas or products is rarely a one-shot effort. Oftentimes you will have to go back and present a number of times. Someone who is not buying on one day might be in the market the next day. Effective sales people will make follow ups on a periodic basis to check on someone's needs. They usually place a follow-up note in their tickler files or on their calendars. You should use this system as well and make routine follow ups. Persistence often pays off in the form of a sale at a later date.

13. Strive for a long-term client relationship.

Some sales people look for the one-time-only sale for maximum profit. They keep going from lead to lead with this in mind and eventually find themselves out of leads. Their former clients do not care to do business with them because they see the relationship as one-sided, and new clients are limited. An alternative is to try to develop a long-term relationship with each client and generate repeat sales. Individual sales might be for less than maximum or typical profit. However, the focus is on repeat business for years to come. You should try and develop this long-term perspective as well. Be willing to sacrifice a larger sale or more profitable sale today for a large number of smaller or less profitable sales down the road. Effective sales people develop this type of relationship with their clients.

14. Make selling and negotiating a win-win situation.

Many people look at selling and negotiating as a win-lose situation. They want to win as much as they can at someone else's expense.

The more you win the better, even if your client loses more and more. That type of attitude and style is very short-sighted, for the losers do not like to lose. They may refuse to do business with you again if they feel they were taken advantage of, and may speak negatively of you to others. The net result is that the "winner" in the negotiations is a loser as well.

An alternative approach which has gained great acceptance is to make selling and negotiating win-win if at all possible. You should adopt this strategy as well. Look at what you are selling from the standpoint of the buyer. Is this person going to win from the association? Are they getting a good deal and the things they really want? List out on paper how the buyer is winning. If they are winning, you are winning as well, and are more likely to get repeat business from this client and referrals to other clients.

15. Develop sales plans.

In many cases, selling is enhanced by developing sales plans. Planning forces the sales person to think through the company and people to be dealt with, and a particular strategy for effectiveness. With this advance planning, people are likely to be more effective in fine-tuning their sales presentation, and making follow-ups. Suggested items to include in a sales plan are the following:

- The type of industry the client is in, and industry characteristics (size, growth, etc.).

- Company background information—size, growth, standing in industry, uniqueness.

- Characteristics of the key people at the company you are dealing with and the CEO.

- Company needs in regards to your products and services.

- How you can help the company (improve productivity, reduce costs, save time, etc.).

- Your strategy for presenting to the client.

16. Increase the number of leads that you have.

Less effective sales people wait for leads to come to them from referrals or people who look them up in the directory. While this produces some activity, a better strategy is to aggressively go out after leads. There are many ways to do this. There are listings of companies such as produced by Dun and Bradstreet, phone directories, professional association directories, mailing lists, cold calling, and other sources. Evaluate how aggressive you are in generating leads. To attain more leads, think of where to find the people who are your typical clients. Then obtain the sources to generate more names and companies and work through them.

17. Handle complaints by dealing with emotions first, then facts.

Upon hearing a complaint, many employees reply with a factual answer. For example, an agitated client might say, "Do you know how long I've been waiting for your product?" And the employee might say, "Yes, you've been waiting sixty-three days." Assess how you deal with a complaint—what are the first words out of your mouth? If you reply with a factual answer, you will leave the client upset and feeling that you are not dealing with their emotions.

Whenever you hear a complaint, deal with the client's emotions first, then give them whatever facts are needed to resolve the matter. You deal with the emotions by showing empathy, saying things like, "I know it must be very frustrating for you to have to wait so long." After getting the client calmed down, you can move from dealing with their emotions to dealing with solving the problem at hand.

18. Always maintain a positive, upbeat attitude when selling.

It is easy for sales people to get discouraged with the selling process since they get rejected so often. Yet effective sales people never let this show. They are positive and upbeat with each sales call.

Though they may statistically succeed with only a small percentage of their leads, they are optimistic that each call will be successful. Their attitude itself leads to increased success. How positive and upbeat are you with prospective clients? Are you positive only once in a while, or are you this way every day? If necessary, change your attitude by making it more positive. Recognize that your attitude itself can enhance or decrease your sales success rate regardless of who the client is or what their needs are. Be positive and optimistic all of the time.

19. Recognize that rejection is a part of the job of selling.

Ineffective sales people cannot handle being rejected so often. They take the rejection personally, as if **they** were ineffective and worthless. Effective sales people regard rejection as a part of the game. They simply understand that only a small percentage of all leads will lead to a successful sale. When rejection occurs, they do not take it personally or get depressed over it. They respond by generating more leads. You should use a similar approach in regarding rejection as a normal part of the job and not to be taken personally. Remain optimistic and confident throughout.

20. Use effective visual aids when presenting.

We have all heard the saying that "a picture is worth a thousand words." And this is very true when selling your ideas or products. You will find it useful to develop visual aids to go along with your verbal presentation. Think of how you can present your ideas to make them visually interesting. Perhaps you can use a few charts or graphs which are colorful, brief tables, photos, wall charts, or product samples. Keep the visual aids simple, and do not overuse them as might occur with a one-hour slide show.

21. Be aware of your competition.

You can sell more effectively by knowing your competition well. This enables you to understand your niche versus those of your competitors. If you currently lack information about your competitors, aggressively go out and get more information. Obtain brochures and ask your clients what they think of the competition. Then create a chart listing each competitor and the strengths and weaknesses of each. Be candid in charting your own company as well.

In situations where you know your client is looking at a competitor as well, sell those **positive** areas where you are better than the competition and get the client to focus on this. This can help you get the sale by being able to show the competitive advantages of your firm. Take the time to know and stay current on your competition.

22. Look for compromises in negotiation.

Ineffective negotiators try to dig in their heals and engage in a waiting contest. Eventually, the other party or they will give in. This type of approach produces winners and losers, and alienates one if not both parties. Is this the approach that you have to negotiation? It is more effective to approach negotiation up-front as a process requiring compromise. Having this attitude, you will suggest compromises throughout the negotiating sessions, and see the relationship with the client as one of give and take. Search for some happy medium that is satisfying to both parties. Make compromise an integral part of your negotiations.

23. Use effective phone skills.

Many employees come across differently over the phone than they do in person. They may sound less friendly, less helpful, more boring, or less clear. In part, this may be due to their treating the phone as an annoyance rather than a aid, and in speaking while doing other things. You should periodically evaluate your "phone voice" by listening to yourself on a recording. As for effective techniques, try to imagine that the person you are talking to on the phone is stand-ing right next to you. This will generally put more energy and en-thusiasm into your voice.

Some people stand when taking phone calls since the act of stan-ding may enable them to project their voice better. Try also to see the phone as a desirable "interruption," answer by the third ring, and be quick to sound friendly and offer assistance. By using effec-tive phone techniques such as these, you can increase your sales effectiveness.

24. Use good presentation delivery skills.

Some people have a good sales plan and knowledge, but are short on delivery. They have difficulty with the mechanics of presenting well. Good presentation skills include using natural gestures to match your speech, using a straight and effective posture, and projecting your voice effectively. Good presentation skills also include effec-tive eye contact—holding contact for five seconds or more with each person in the audience, then moving to the next person. And last is verbal delivery, having animation in your voice and speaking at a proper rate. You should evaluate yourself in these areas by videotap-ing a presentation. If needed, enroll in a course to help you sharpen your skills in this area.

25. Have a high degree of confidence.

Effective sales people are effective, in part, because they have a high degree of confidence. They expect to succeed, and because of this, they do succeed. If you stop to think about it, it is impossible to succeed where you feel you cannot succeed, because you will not even **try** to succeed. On the other hand, expecting success is half of the way to succeeding itself. Have you ever been guilty of ap-proaching a client with low expectations, feeling "I doubt that anything will ever come of this." If so, change by having a higher confidence level. It will lead to a higher success rate.

26. Know your company's products and services well.

It is difficult, if not impossible, to sell your company's products and services if you do not know them well. For how can you explain features to a client, or explain how you differ from your competitors, if you do not know the product yourself? Make certain that you know your company's products and services inside and out. Know the benefits and disadvantages of your products versus someone else's. This is a never-ending process—you must continually update your information. If you are not getting the information yourself, go to others in the company and get it directly.

27. Use relationship selling.

An increasingly popular sales technique is relationship selling. Rather than focus on your product or service, you focus on the people and the company you are selling to. By knowing them very well, and their needs, you can be more helpful and increase your sales effectiveness. Relationship selling focuses on the long term, and starts by doing your homework on the company and the people in it. After getting the basic information, continually add to it each time you interact with the client. Build a lasting relationship of trust and mutual respect that will make the selling easier. Use relationship selling if you are not currently doing so.

28. Serve as an information source for your clients.

Oftentimes, clients need information to help them do their jobs. They may need to turn to someone as a resource for this assistance. Effective sales people try to serve as this resource for their clients. Even if they are not receiving a fee for providing the advice, they will give out information to the client. This enables the sales person to relate better to the client, builds trust and respect, and eventually leads to more sales. Evaluate whether you take on this role with your clients. If not, try to expand your role to that of a resource person and encourage the client to contact you for help in certain areas. It greatly aids relationship building and sales effectiveness.

29. Expand an existing relationship into other areas.

Many times sales people think of a client only in relation to the products and services that **they** are selling to the individual. Yet within their company there are other products and services which might also be of value to the client. The secret is to merely use the existing relationship to broaden into other areas. Think of doing this with your current clients. Make them aware of other products and services that your firm provides. Ask them to introduce you or others at your company to the people who might use these products and services. The key is to expand an existing relationship into other areas so your company is more of a total resource to the client.

30. Know the decision makers and decision process.

Some employees may lose a sale by selling to the wrong person. They may sell to someone who does not have the decision making authority and be wasting their time. Early on, try to identify who the decision makers are at the client company. Also try to understand how the decision will be made. By knowing the decision maker and the process, you can do a more effective job at selling itself. You can ensure that you are targeting the right person and fitting your proposal to match the decision making process.

31. Show how your product meets the client's needs.

One of the most effective ways to make sales is to link your product to the client's needs. By knowing what the client needs and wants, you should be able to easily determine how your products and services meets those needs. Then, in your presentation or proposal, emphasize this linkage between the client's needs and your product. Continue to mention this in subsequent conversations until the final decision is made. Use this approach in your sales efforts if you are not currently doing so. Make a linkage with what you have to offer with client needs to solidify your responsiveness to the client's needs.

Recommended Readings

Alessandra, Anthony. *Non-Manipulative Selling*. Reston, VA: Reston Press, 1981.

Alessandra, Anthony, and Wexler, Phil. Breaking Tradition: The Sales Pitch as Customer Service. *Training and Development*, November, 1985, p. 41-43.

Berlew, David E. How to Increase Your Influence. *Training and Development*, Sept, 1987, p. 60-63.

Byrnes, Joseph F. Ten Guidelines for Effective Negotiating. *Business Horizons*, May-June, 1987, 30, p. 7-12.

Evered, James F. *A Motivational Approach to Selling*. New York: AMACOM, 1982.

Fisher, Roger, and Ury, William. Getting to Yes. *Management Review*, Feb, 1982, p. 16-21.

Girard, Joe, and Brown, Stanley H. *How to Sell Anything to Anybody*. New York: Warner Books, 1979.

Guder, Robert F. *Negotiating Techniques*. Fairfield, NJ: The Economics Press, 1985.

Hawver, Dennis A. Plan Before Negotiating . . . and Increase Your Power of Persuasion. *Management Review*, Feb, 1984, p. 46-48.

Hopkins, Tom. *How to Master the Art of Selling*. New York: Warner Books, 1982.

Karrass, Gary. *Negotiate to Close*. New York: Simon and Schuster, 1986.

Kennedy, Gavin. *Everything So Negotiable: How to Get a Better Deal*. Englewood Cliffs, NJ: Prentice-Hall, 1983.

LeRoux, Paul. *Selling to a Group*. New York: Harper & Row, 1984.

Ley, D. Forbes. *The Best Seller*. Newport Beach, CA: Sales Success Press, 1986.

Morgan, Rebecca L. *Professional Selling: Practical Secrets for Successful Sales*. Los Angeles: Crisp Publications, 1988.

Nirenberg, Gerard. *How to Sell Your Ideas*. New York: McGraw-Hill, 1984.

Nirenberg, Gerard. *Fundamentals of Negotiating*. New York: Hawthorn Books, 1973.

Qubein, Nido. *Nido Qubein's Professional Selling Techniques*. Rockville Center, NY: Farnsworth, 1983.

Riley, Tom. *Value-Added Sales Management*. Chicago: Contemporary Books, 1993.

Shea, Gordon F. *Creative Negotiating: Product Tools and Techniques for Solving Problems, Resolving Conflicts, and Settling Differences*. New York: CBI/Van Nostrand Reinhold, 1983.

Smith, Terry C. *Making Successful Presentations: A Self-Teaching Guide*. New York: Wiley, 1984.

Swets, Paul W. *The Art of Talking So That People Will Listen*. Englewood Cliffs, NJ: Prentice-Hall, 1983.

Willingham, Ron. *The Best Seller: The New Psychology of Selling*. Englewood Cliffs, NJ: Prentice-Hall, 1984.

23

Customer Service Skills

This chapter helps improve performance in the following areas:

- Providing better customer service.
- Improving relationships with customers and clients.
- Working better with peers and others in the company.
- Doing a better job with phone and face-to-face communications.

Action Items for Customer Service

1. Show empathy when handling complaints.

When receiving complaints from customers, the best approach is to show empathy. The first words out of your mouth should indicate an understanding and identification with what the customer is going through. Empathy does not indicate agreement with what the customer is saying, but an understanding of what they are feeling. Showing empathy is the single best way to calm down an irate person. Examples of empathy statements are as follows:

- "I can understand why you feel the way you do."

- "I know it must be frustrating if the product isn't working properly."

- "I realize the cost may seem like a great deal to you. . ."

Evaluate your first reaction to a complaint. If you provide excuses or focus only on a solution, your customer may feel that you did not deal with their feelings, that you did not understand them. A better approach is to show empathy when you first hear the complaint. Make it a part of your customer service.

2. Conduct follow-ups with customers.

Some employees do not follow up with customers. They sell or repair a product, or provide a service, then do not get the customer's feelings later. The net result is that the employee does not learn how to improve products and services, and minor problems may grow into larger ones before the customer complains. Try to evaluate how often you follow up with customers. Would you, for example, call a customer back to see if their complaint has been properly handled? If you do not do this very often, make it a part of your regular activities. Make follow-up phone calls or use written surveys to find out how your customers feel. Act on the suggestions they make to improve your products or services.

3. Use effective phone skills.

Customer service is handled over the phone in many cases. This creates a problem in that many people treat the phone as an annoyance or interruption rather than as an opportunity. The tone in their voice, and the help they provide may then be less effective than if the service were done face-to-face. Try to use effective phone skills whenever you interact with customers. The basic ways to do this are as follows:

• Answer calls by the third ring.

• Treat calls as important and a pleasure, not an annoyance.

• Put a "smile in your voice"—be pleasant, friendly, engaging.

• Identify yourself and be quick to offer assistance.

• Imagine that the caller is standing in front of you.

• Try standing when taking calls to improve the sound of your voice.

4. Create accurate expectations.

Customers can find it very frustrating when they do not know what to expect after presenting a problem. If they are unclear as to what will happen and when, their feelings about the service they get will be negative. Review how you leave off with customers. Are you clear and concise in stating what will happen, or vague and non-committal? Try to leave the customer feeling comfortable by ending each conversation with a summary of what will happen. The summary can include, but is not limited to:

• What will happen next—specific steps to be taken.

• Specific times when the steps will occur.

• Who will do what—action items for both your company and the customer.

• Contingency plans should something else happen in the interim.

5. Deliver on the expectations you set.

Customers can become very irate if their expectations are not met. If they were told, for example, that a product would be delivered on Tuesday and it does not arrive until Friday, this results in very negative feelings. Perhaps the customer would have not minded waiting until Friday if this is what they were told in the first place. Failing to deliver as expected is what caused them to be upset.

If you have ever been guilty of failing to deliver as promised, try to correct this problem. Do not quote the customer "best case" delivery dates if you can only deliver these if everything goes right. Instead quote them dates or other terms that you are very confident can be met. If the product is delivered sooner, the customer will find this a pleasant surprise. That is much better than quoting an early date, and being late. Make sure you can deliver on all of your promises. If you cannot, simply do not promise it.

6. Error in the direction of the customer.

Occasionally in customer service, a borderline decision has to be made. There is no clear precedent on what to do, and the decision can be made to benefit the customer or the company. If you are ever faced with this dilemma, always error on the side of the customer. That will likely lead to a long-term customer and additional customers. If you try to make the decision in your behalf, you may gain a few extra dollars short-term, but might lose a customer or business referrals. Have the customer get the benefit of the doubt in all toss-up situations.

7. Make negatives into positives.

Some employees have a habit of saying the negatives too often. Examples of this are "I can't help you with that," or "It's not my job." These negatives make the customer feel that they are not important and not getting good service. The statements direct attention to what is upsetting rather than to what is helpful. Many of the negatives can be turned into positives by focusing on the activities that can be done to help the customer. The following are examples:

Negative	Positive
"I can't help you with that."	"Joe Smith can help you with that."
"It's not my job."	"Betty Turner has the information you need."
"Our policy says we can't do that."	"What we can do for you is the following..."

Evaluate how often you use negative statements in dealing with customers. Convert those statements into positive ones wherever you can.

8. Deal with emotions first, then facts.

One of the most important things to avoid with customers is getting into an argument. This can easily happen if the customer is emotionally upset. It can also happen if the employee tries to deal with facts before the customer has settled down. That will be ineffective when the customer is emotional. Try to think of how you react when in this type of situation. Do you quote the company policy when the customer is upset, debate the issue with them, or try to find a quick solution? If so, you might leave the person upset.

Effective customer service people deal with the customers emotions first, then facts and a solution later. They deal with emotions by showing empathy as described in an earlier action item. When the customer's emotions have gone away, they then deal with facts and finding a solution. Try to make this your approach as well. Deal with emotions first, then facts.

9. Stay on the phone until calls are transferred.

We have all had the experience of being cut off when our call was transferred to someone else. That can be very frustrating and represents poor customer service. Those who transferred the call should not have merely dialed someone else's number and hung up. A better procedure would be the following:

• Ask the caller if it is all right to transfer them.

• Give them the name and number or the person they are being transferred to.

• Stay on the line until the two parties are talking to each other.

Make this your procedure for handling transferred calls. It is still yet another way to provide better customer service.

10. Put the emphasis on quality in customer service.

Quality has perhaps been one of the most talked about areas in recent years. Quality has become the basic foundation of many customer service programs. You should place your emphasis on quality service as well. Continually ask yourself if you could do anything different or better in providing the service that you do. Walk a mile in the customer's shoes, and ask if you would have been content with the service or wanted anything more. Quality is not fancy company programs or slogans, but day-in and day-out work by individual employees to make the quality as high as possible. Make the changes you feel are necessary in your area. Set high quality standards and work toward them every day.

11. Assist your co-workers.

This suggestion relates to helping your co-workers, but has a major impact on service provided to a customer. There are many occasions in the workplace when co-workers are away from their desks or tied up with a customer when another call comes in. Co-workers with a "it's not my job" mentality will not help out, resulting in poor customer service. You should evaluate how often you will grab that ringing phone or help a visitor or customer when one of your co-workers is tied up. This is definitely a two-way street—your helping others will encourage them to help you. Make it a point to assist others whenever the need arises.

12. Admit it when you are wrong.

Some employees have a tendency to become defensive when they, or their companies, have made a mistake. They may deny that anything was done wrong or provide a list of excuses that do not make the customer feel any better. The more effective approach is to admit, in clear, uncertain words, when you or the company were wrong. Then go on with finding a solution if needed. Think of the last time a customer or co-worker confronted you with something that was done incorrectly. Did you get defensive or acknowledge the mistake and go on from there? Be willing to admit it when you are wrong as a way to improve customer service.

13. Make "value-added" your standard.

Customers feel that the service is excellent if a company goes an extra step. For example, a printer might toss in some free note pads with a large order, or a company may make several follow-up calls to check on the services they provided. These "value-added" activities make the customer feel they are being treated special, and getting more than they actually paid for.

Think of how you can provide value-added services in your job. What other services or products can you provide that others would not do? Then add these value-added services to your basic job responsibilities. Make value-added your standard way of doing business and see if customer service does not improve.

14. Train your peers.

New or less experienced employees may have more difficulty helping a customer. Some of their co-workers may look the other way, feeling it is up to the manager to train the person or up to the employee to learn quickly. Others will chip in and do a little informal training with a new or less experienced employee. Evaluate whether or not you do this on an ongoing basis. If not, take some time to train your co-workers on their jobs, even if you are not asked to do this. This will help build teamwork and result in better service to the customer.

15. Practice active listening.

When customers are ventilating, they want to feel they are being listened to. The employee who shows active listening will be seen as providing good customer service. How do you provide good active listening? The following are examples:

- Maintain good eye contact.

- Lean forward to show interest.

- Face the customer directly.

- Vary your facial expressions during the conversation.

- Nod your head to indicate understanding.

- Make notes on what someone has said.

- Summarize the customer's key points during the conversation.

Take a hard look at how well you practice active listening. If uncertain, have a co-worker give you some feedback on how they see your listening skills. Change your practices to improve active listening and improve your customer service.

16. Read the customer's feelings as well as the content.

Some people listen only for the content of a customer's message. They fail to read the feelings and emotions that go with the words. As a result, they are less able to address the concerns of the customer and provide excellent service. A more effective procedure is to try and read the feelings as well as the words. Pay attention to the body language, facial expressions, gestures, and voice inflection when the customer speaks. Try to read these as well as the words, and ask clarifying questions when the voice may not agree with the words. Adding the ability to read the customer's feelings can greatly enhance the quality of customer service.

17. Engage the customer in friendly conversation.

Employees who are good at customer service will take the time to engage the customer in friendly conversation. It makes no difference if the interaction is brief or routine, they will say a few words to find out how the person is, how their day is going, the weather, etc. This bit of conversation makes the service seem more personal, more friendly, and more people oriented. Customers like being asked a few things about themselves as long as the questions seem genuine. Try to engage your customers in friendly conversation when you interact with them. It is a great way to improve your customer service skills.

18. Get close to the customer.

Effective customer service can be provided by getting close to the customer. Employees who do this well are always interested in finding out more about what the customer is thinking and feeling. They can then address the matters that they identify. Try to spend more of your time getting close to the customer. Practice "management by walking around," for example, by wandering the aisles of the store and seeing what customers think of the products and service. Or seek out feedback from customers by dropping in on them or giving an unexpected call. Those who have a smaller number of customers might try lunches or other social activities that have a sole purpose of better understanding the customer's needs and feelings. Use these and other techniques to get close to your customers and know how they feel about service at your company.

19. Use care when putting people on hold on the phone.

It can be very frustrating when customers are put on hold on the phone and feel like they are forgotten. This builds frustration and can make the person upset with the service they are getting. There are several basic steps which should be followed to put callers on hold. These steps are as follows:

- Give the caller options rather than just put them on hold.

- If you think the person will be on hold for a long time, tell them this and suggest that you call them back later.

- Check back with people on hold every thirty to sixty seconds.

Evaluate your practices for putting people on hold versus those listed above. Improve where you can to use the phone more effectively in providing good customer service.

20. Make "no surprises" your motto.

Customers can become very upset with a company when they are given unpleasant surprises. For example, they might be told that an item costs so much and then find a bill for larger than that, or find they are charged for shipping when they were told it was free. The more effective approach is to never surprise the client. Tell that what to expect, and if you are uncertain, do not make a commitment. Instead, check the information out and then get back to the customer. Review your dealings with customers to see if you have ever heard people say they were surprised by something which was done. Make "no surprises" your motto in providing good customer service.

21. Adjust "policy" where it makes sense to do so.

We all feel upset as customers if a company will not change because of "policy." This is particularly frustrating when it makes sense to change the policy or make an exception. Ineffective employees cling to policy even when it is unwise to do so. They give customers a "no can do" answer and defend this on the basis of policy. When you deal with customers, look at policies and procedures with an open mind. Certainly, you should not change policy for each customer, but be willing to modify or make exceptions where it makes sense to do so. Discuss it with your manager or others if you are uncertain. By adjusting policy where needed, the customer will feel their personal needs are being addressed and feel more satisfied as a result.

22. Keep the customer updated on long-term assistance.

Some employees might fail to update a customer on long-term assistance. For example, the company might be manufacturing a custom product for the customer which might take six months to produce. Rather than update the customer, the employee lets there be a long period of silence until the product is complete. Try to avoid this in dealing with your customers. Give them periodic updates on the status of the product. This will keep the customer feeling comfortable that progress is being made and they can expect the product on time. They will see these updates as an important service from the company. Try using such updates whenever you can.

23. Make your customer service more personal.

Some employees fail to get to know their customers well. Without trust and rapport being present, it may be hard to find out how service can be improved or get additional sales from the customer. Try to get to know your customers as well as possible. The more you know about them and their company, the more personal you can make your service. For example, try to at least recognize your customers and call on them by name when you see them. Try to know and recall some personal item—where they live, how large a family they have, etc. You may discover a number of items about someone who you interact with often, and use them to build a good rapport and comfort level. It will make your customer service better and help your company with additional sales.

24. Say something nice in each customer interaction.

Effective customer service employees look for something nice to say to clients each time they interact with them. They make some compliment or at least say something nice about the weather or other neutral area. This leaves the customer feeling good about the interaction and the company. We are not suggesting that employees be phony in giving out praise, but that they be genuine. It is all to easy to find at least one nice thing to say about a person or some event in the news. Try to say something nice to each of your customers. See if it does not make them want to interact with you more often and regard you as a friendly, effective employee.

25. Look for more interactions with customers.

Some employees make the mistake of being too busy to interact with customers. They regard paperwork or other activities as more important than interacting with a customer by phone or in person. Take the time to evaluate your priorities. Are paperwork or administrative details more important to you than customer interactions? If so, try to change this by looking for more interactions. Seek out your customers more. If they come into your work area, do not bury yourself in papers or other desk work. Look more friendly and approachable and be more assertive in getting to the customer.

Recommended Readings

Bacas, H. Making it Right for the Customer. *Nations Business*, Nov, 1987, 75, p. 49-51.

Blume, Eric R. Customer Service: Giving Companies the Competitive Edge. *Training and Development Journal*, September, 1988, p. 24-32.

Butterfield, Ronald W. Deming's 14 Points Applied to Service. *Training*, March, 1991, 50-59.

Desatnick, Robert L. *Managing to Keep the Customer*. San Francisco: Jossey-Bass, 1987.

Lee, Chris. The Customer Within. *Training*, July, 1991, 21-26.

McDermott, Lynda and Emerson, Michael. Quality and Service for Internal Customers. *Training and Development*, January, 1991, 61-64.

Moosbrucker, Jane, and Berger, Emanuel. Know Your Customers. *Training and Development*, March, 1988, p. 30-34.

Wilcock, Keith. Customer Service Behavior Spelled Out. *Training and Development*, November, 1989, 79-82.

Witwer, B. Thank You for Calling (Techniques for Handling Customer Phone Calls). *Management World*, Jan-Feb, 1988, 17, p. 8-9.

Zeithaml, Valerie; Parasuraman, A. and Berry, Leonard. *Delivering Quality Service*. New York: Free Press, 1990.

Zemke, Ron and Anderson, Kristen. Customers from Hell. *Training*, February, 1990, p. 25-33.

Zemke, Ron and Schaaf, Dick. *The Service Edge: 101 Companies that Profit from Customer Care*. New York: New American Library, 1989.

24

Developing
a Business Focus

This chapter helps improve performance in the following areas:

- Having more of a business orientation.
- Being more pragmatic and results oriented.
- Being in tune with the company's goals.
- Becoming less technical.

Action Items for Developing
a Business Focus

1. Know your company's products and services.

Many employees fail to understand what their organization does. They have only a limited knowledge of the products and services the company provides. This greatly restricts the employee's ability to do a good job. As an example, how well could a programmer write software for a business unit of the company if there is a limited understanding of what the unit does? How well could a secretary in a sales department assist customers if there is a limited knowledge of the company products?

How well do you know your organization and what it does? Could you describe the products and services as well as a salesperson might? If not, go out and learn more about your company and what it does. Aggressively read and talk to others so that you have an excellent understanding of the products and services the company offers. Keep up on this knowledge and use it to do your job better.

2. Spend time with employees in other departments.

Some employees fail to understand much about their company beyond their own department. As such, they have a limited perspective which others might see as very narrow. One solution to this is to spend time with people in other departments to find out what they do. Most employees are more than willing to take a few minutes to tell you what they and their departments do. You only need to ask them to give you some information. If you are in a staff department, seek out people in the line operating areas to find out what they do and how they do it. Line people might do the same with staff departments such as sales and human resources. By learning more about other departments, you will develop a broader business perspective.

3. Read the company annual report.

Nearly all companies prepare an annual report which summarizes their financial and other results for the year. If they do not give a copy to each employee, a copy can easily be obtained by request. You should take the time to read the annual review, and quarterly updates, if you do not already do so. Try to understand as much of it as you can, without worrying about understanding all of the financial results. The main area to look for is where the company is going and what it does. You might want to look up or ask about terms you are unfamiliar with so you can learn from the experience. By knowing the challenges and opportunities your company faces, you will have a stronger business sense and orientation.

4. Take business courses at colleges or universities.

Another way to broaden your business knowledge is to take courses at local colleges or universities. You need not have to get a degree— most schools allow you to take individual courses if that is all that you want to do. If you are concerned about grades, you can merely audit the course, which eliminates any pressure to get a certain grade. Courses to focus on include business, management, accounting, finance, and economics. Look in particular for non-technical courses that have a broader perspective. Try to relate what you learn to your own organization.

5. Think of the bottom-line impact of what you do.

Some employees focus on their jobs strictly from a technical stand-point. For example, a programmer may focus only on what is the technically preferred way to write a program. Similarly, this might be the focus of accountants, attorneys, auditors, and any other job at the company. This technical focus might seem insensitive to business reality for those outside the field. For example, requiring every employee in the company to fill out a lengthy form with documentation can be costly and time consuming. It might make an attorney happy, but makes the employees unhappy. It should not be requested unless absolutely necessary.

Rather than have a strictly technical viewpoint, some employees look at the bottom-line impact of what they are advocating. They think of the time, costs, and other factors before suggesting what is proper to do. They balance the technical side with the bottom-line business side. Try to make this your perspective as well. Look at time, costs, benefits, resources, and other issues before recommending a course of action. Use both a bottom-line focus with your technical knowledge for greater success.

6. Relate your work to company goals.

A business focus can be improved by relating company goals to individual employee jobs. Everyone should be able to see some link between their work and company goals, but many employees never take the time to think about it. You should relate what you do to your organization's goals. First, take the time to find out what the company's goals are for the coming year. Next, relate your work to some or all of these goals. Emphasize this relationship to your peers, manager, or subordinates when you meet with them. By studying the goals, you might also get additional ideas on what you can do to help attain those goals. Present these ideas to your manager or others at the company. You can greatly improve your business focus by relating your work to company goals.

7. Read business publications.

Your business focus and perspective can be greatly enhanced by reading business publications. Some of the more popular business publications include Forbes, Fortune, Business Week, and The Wall Street Journal. Try to read these regularly as well as the business section of your local newspaper. Look up terms you do not understand or ask others to explain them to you. Relate what you read to your own organization wherever possible. By reading business publications regularly, you will build up your business knowledge and orientation.

8. Use goals and objectives in your work.

Business people in general use goals and objectives in their work. These goals might pertain to production volume, quality, timeliness, cost, sales, or other factors. Using goals on an ongoing basis leads to having a stronger business focus. If you currently do not use goals and objectives, try setting goals and objectives for your job. Think of setting targets for the key activities that you have in the coming year. Manage yourself against the goals and objectives that you set. By doing so, you will be developing a stronger business perspective.

9. Learn more about management jobs.

You can enhance your business focus by learning more about management jobs. Since managers typically have a broader business perspective, learning more about what they do and how they do it can give you a broader business perspective. Find out what managers do at your company. Spend time with managers and have them explain what their responsibilities are. Enroll in seminars or workshops which are intended to build management skills. Read more about management in your free time. By increasing your knowledge and appreciation of management, you will be able to have a stronger business perspective.

10. Follow stocks and bonds.

Another way to learn about business is by investing in the stock market. You need not invest actual money—you can make a ''pretend'' purchase of some company stock you chose. Then follow that stock very closely over the next couple of months. See what happens to the price of your stock and the market in general. Read in the daily newspaper why the stock market is rising or falling. Also, try to figure out why your stock is going the way that it is. You can do the same with corporate bonds. By understanding trends in stocks and bonds, you will develop more business knowledge.

11. Watch business television shows.

There are a number of television shows pertaining to business and industry. They range from news item stories on the evening news to series or lengthy specials on certain industries. Try increasing your watching of business television shows if you currently do not do so. Many of the shows appear on public broadcasting stations, so look at the listings of these stations. Try to apply what you learn to your company or your industry. Adding an hour or two of business shows per week can greatly increase your knowledge of the business world in general.

12. Use budgets and goals at home.

Just as you can develop a business perspective by setting goals at work, you can do the same at home. First, think of setting goals for activities at home. A goal might be a fix-up project, increasing your income through a hobby, increasing your reading, or any of many other activities. Monitor your progress on the goal and reward yourself for achieving what you set out to do.

You might also monitor your home budget and expenses more carefully, just as managers in an office do. First, figure out what you spend each month on home costs, food, clothing, insurance, cars, and other items. Then draw up a budget based upon your income. Then track and monitor expenses against the budget you have set up. See where you overspent and take action to control expenses. By using budgets and goals at home, you can apply this back on the job.

13. Follow economic trends.

Another effective way to become more business oriented is to follow economic trends in the country. Read and find out more about the major trends in our economy such as inflation, the trade deficit, the price of the dollar relative to other currencies, interest rates, and unemployment rates. In particular, develop an understanding of how changes in these economic trends affect businesses including your company. Knowledge of what these trends are can increase your company business perspective.

14. Join professional and civic business organizations.

Business knowledge can be improved by joining organizations with a business orientation. There are local and national professional associations of this type, as well as local and national civic organizations composed of business people. By joining one or more of these organizations you can receive their publications and get to interact with business people on a social and professional basis. This is one of the easiest ways to build up business knowledge. Try and join such organizations if at all possible. Use this as a means to increase your business focus.

15. Balance technical and business approaches.

Some employees are too technical in their jobs. They might be very professional in their field, but are not very practical and business oriented. Others may see them as "too academic" or "too technical." As a result, their careers might suffer, particularly when under consideration for management positions. Evaluate whether others see you this way. If uncertain, ask your friends for a candid opinion.

If you are too technical, work for some balance in your orientation. Try to look at issues from not only a technical standpoint, but a practical business standpoint as well. Think more like a business person in looking at costs, benefits, and resources required in addition to the technical correctness of a solution. By having this balance, you will cut down on the tendency to be seen as too technical.

16. Look more like a business person.

While this action item may seem very simple, grooming and dress do have an effect on someone's business success. If people do not look like business people, others may assume they are not business people, and therefore avoid discussing or doing business with them. Evaluate your grooming and dress in comparison to others at your company. While there are different standards for different jobs, you should try to look like a manager as much as possible if this is appropriate in your job. Looking like a business person will cause others to see you this way, and you may come to think of yourself this way as well. This will help you in taking on a stronger business perspective.

17. Find out more about (or run) a small business.

One more way to develop a stronger business focus is to get involved in a small business. Perhaps you have a friend that you can spend time with who runs a small business. Ask your friend to tell you about how they run their business; how they handle sales, marketing, cost of products and services, customer service, and other areas. Try to look at the big picture and understand more about what is involved in running a business.

You might also take the plunge yourself. We recommend that you do this the easy way by turning a hobby into a moonlighting job. You might approach one of your hobbies as a small business, and try to make a profit with it. Even a part-time small business will give you a much stronger business perspective and knowledge of how sales and profits are made. You can then apply this knowledge back on the job.

18. Take on special projects that broaden you out.

Some employees fail to develop a broad business perspective because of a limited opportunity to know and work with those in other parts of the company. If this has been the case for you, try to take on special projects that broaden you out. In particular, identify projects that cross the line-staff boundary, regardless of what side you are on now. By working with others with a different perspective and different orientation, you can develop a much stronger sense of your company's overall business. Volunteer for such projects as they come up in your department or identify projects that you think need to be done and present them to your manager.

19. Avoid jargon and technical language.

A number of employees simply do not talk like business people. They use a great deal of jargon and technical language that quickly tells you they are not business people. Evaluate whether you have a tendency to use technical jargon in your conversations with others. Ask others to give you candid feedback if you are uncertain. If you do use more jargon than you should, become conscious of when you do this and cut back. This is particularly important when interacting with others outside your department, but needed within the department as well. In place of jargon, add more "business language" by talking more about costs, return on investment, and similar areas.

20. Use cost/benefit analyses.

Business people usually approach projects with a cost/benefit perspective. They ask what will it cost to do this project in terms of equipment, people, supplies, and overhead. Then they ask what will we get in return in terms of more sales, improved productivity, improved quality, or other benefits. The decision is made to go forward or reject the project on the basis of the cost/benefit analysis.

Use a cost/benefit approach in your work if you do not currently do so. This should be thought of for evaluating projects, changes in the work area, job re-design, and the purchase of new equipment, among other activities. By doing a cost/benefit analysis and presenting this to others, you will present a much stronger business orientation.

21. Develop an understanding of basic business financial information.

It is important for employees to understand at least very basic financial information. Such information includes profits, profit margins, return on equity, earnings per share, and related business statistics. There is no need to become an expert, but merely be able to understand what the more basic numbers mean that you would find on a company financial report. If you are uncertain of these terms, buy a basic book in the area or get a glossary of business financial terms. As an alternative, seek out someone who is an accountant or finance professional and have them explain the basic information to you. By developing this basic financial understanding, you will have a much stronger business perspective.

Recommended Readings

Campsey, B. J., and Brigham, Eugene F. *Introduction to Financial Management*. New York: Dryden, 1985.

Donnelly, James H., Jr.; Gibson, James L.; and Ivancevich, John M. *Fundamentals of Management: Functions, Behaviors, Models* (5th ed.). Plano, TX: Business Publications, 1984.

Elgood, Chris. Games Managers Play. *Supervisory Management*, April, 1986, p. 2-7.

Evans, Frank C. How to Read Your Company's Financial Report. *Managing Solutions*, Dec, 1986, 31, p. 23-33.

Halloran, J., and Frunzi, G, *Supervision: The Art of Management* (2nd ed.). Englewood Cliffs, NJ: Prentice-Hall, 1986.

Hax, A., and Candia, D., Jr. *Production and Inventory Management*. Englewood Cliffs, NJ: Prentice-Hall, 1984.

Henderson, Bruce D. *The Logic of Business Strategy*. Cambridge, Mass: Ballinger Publishing Company, 1987.

Hoffman, W. Michael and Mills, Jennifer. *Business Ethics: Readings and Cases in Corporate Morality*. New York: McGraw-Hill, 1990.

Horngren, Charles T. *Introduction to Management Accounting* (6th ed.). Englewood Cliffs, NJ: Prentice-Hall, 1984.

Jackson, John H., and Musselman, Vernon A. *Business: Contemporary Concepts and Practices*. Englewood Cliffs, NJ: Prentice-Hall, 1987.

Johnston, Kenneth. *Busting Bureaucracy: How to Conquer Your Organization's Worst Enemy*. Homewood, IL: Business One Irwin, 1993.

Kaufman, Henry. *Interest Rates, the Markets, and the New Financial World*. New York: Times Books, 1986.

Mayer, Raymond E. *Production and Operations Management* (4th ed.). New York: McGraw-Hill, 1982.

Neveu, Raymond. *Fundamentals of Managerial Finance* (2nd ed.). Cincinnati: South-Western, 1985.

Stoner, James A. *Management* (3rd ed.). Englewood Cliffs, NJ: Prentice-Hall, 1986.

25

Technical Job Knowledge and Skills

This chapter helps improve performance in the following areas:

- Staying current in one's field.
- Doing the technical aspects of the job better.
- Becoming more professional and expert in one's field.

Action Items for
Technical Job Knowledge and Skills

1. Join professional associations.

One of the very best ways to build technical job knowledge and skills is to join a professional association in your field. Professional associations work toward keeping employees current in their area of expertise. Many associations publish journals, magazines, and newsletters in addition to offering seminars and workshops. Professional associations also provide an opportunity to get to know other professionals in your field. Many companies will pick up the cost of professional association memberships up to a certain level.

You should look into joining professional associations in your area if you do not currently belong. There are both national and local associations in many cases. The national associations will generally be more helpful in providing publications and seminars, while the local associations will provide more local contacts for you to get to know. Join the associations that best meet your personal needs.

2. Network with others in your field.

There is a rich source of technical knowledge that can be tapped from others in your field. They may have excellent skills and knowledge in exactly the areas you are trying to build. If you try to build this knowledge on your own, you may find it more difficult than with the help of others. Try to build up a network of other professionals that you can interact with informally. The easiest people to network with are those at your own company who do similar work, but you do not see very often. Try to build more contacts with them and trade notes.

You might also consider networking with employees at other companies who do similar work. Try to contact them through associations or mutual friends and meet or talk periodically. Networking with others can provide a rich source of information to help build technical knowledge.

3. Broaden your current job.

Some employees merely do the same tasks over and over and become somewhat stagnant in their field. They see broadening out as somewhat risky or requiring extra effort that they do not care to put forth. Others try to broaden themselves out by taking on new projects or taking on larger responsibilities. Admittedly, any time you broaden out there is some risk involved since you are moving into new territory. However, that is essential any time you learn something new. You should not limit yourself through fear of learning something new, or simply avoiding extra work.

Develop a list of ways to broaden your current job. Discuss your ideas with your manager, who will likely have additional suggestions. Perhaps your manager can delegate a project to you or give you a short-term assignment that can enable you to learn and grow. Come up with some agreed-upon actions and implement your plan.

4. Build new skills.

Set a goal for yourself to acquire new technical skills during the coming year. List out those skills you feel you most need to build, getting the input of others if that is helpful. Then draw up plans for building these skills. Think of readings, professional contacts, seminars, courses, and any other means that might be helpful. Then try to put the new skills into practice and reward yourself for the progress you have made. You should look at adding new skills as a never-ending assignment. The results of this will make you a more technically competent individual in your field.

5. Enroll in college courses.

Another great way to stay current in your field is to enroll in college courses. You can take courses in your current field to increase your depth of knowledge or take courses outside your area to broaden out. If you are hesitant to return to school, remember that you do not have to work toward a degree or do not have to take a course for a grade (you can merely audit the course if you choose).

Being exposed to fresh ideas in the field should stimulate your performance back on the job. Think of enrolling in college courses to increase your technical knowledge and skills.

6. Read journals and magazines in your field.

There is a great deal being written all of the time in any field of endeavor. Some employees read a great deal and others never read at all. You should evaluate how often you read magazines and journals in your field. If your read very little, start by subscribing to at least a couple of publications that you think would be useful. If you cannot find time to read on the job, try to do so at lunch or during the evenings or weekends at home. You should be able to find the time to at least scan the articles in each issue, and read in detail the couple that are of most interest. Use journals and magazines in your field as a way to stay current and keep your technical edge.

7. Find a mentor.

Nearly everyone's career can be enhanced by having a mentor. The mentor is a more experienced employee at your company who is highly respected and knowledgeable in his/her field. This person serves as sort of a coach and counselor for employees, giving not only technical assistance, but emotional support as well. Many large companies have formal mentor programs while many others have an informal process.

Think of people in your company who might serve as your mentor. Individuals to consider are those who have solid technical skills and are successful in their careers at the company. Seek out a person of your choice and ask if the two of you could meet periodically. Most people are flattered to be asked to do this, but be sensitive to time limits that the person might have. Arrange to have candid discussions with your mentor periodically either through meetings or social occasions such as lunch or breakfast. Using a mentor can be of great assistance in building your technical competence.

8. Consider rotating to another job.

Technical knowledge and skills can be enhanced by moving into another job. If promotional opportunities are not immediately available, you might think of rotating into another job at the same level as your own. This would broaden your technical skills and provide a new sense of excitement and learning. Evaluate whether making a job rotation is right for you. If so, think of the jobs you might move into. Consider jobs in the same field as your own—switching fields entirely makes for a much more difficult and risky transition. Perhaps you can even convince your manager to create a new job which has some of your current responsibilities and some new responsibilities. Use job rotation as another means to get technical depth.

9. Write an article in your field.

You can learn a great deal in your field by writing an article for publication. Writing an article normally requires research in gathering facts and quoting the work of others. By doing this research you will acquire new technical knowledge and skills in your field. Add to this the prestige of being published and making new professional contacts with those who read your article. You should try writing an article if you have never done so before. Identify a likely place to publish your article and find out their publication requirements. Select a subject that you know well and can share with others. Have someone in-house who writes well critique your article and suggest changes. The writing of articles is an excellent way to broaden your technical knowledge and enhance your career.

10. Spend more time with an in-house expert.

Some employees fail to seek out the expertise of someone at their company who is highly knowledgeable in a certain field. These employees miss the opportunity to learn from someone who "knows the ropes." Think of people at your organization who are experts in your field. Seek them out and ask them if they can share out some of their expertise with you. This can be done through meetings or over lunch or other social event. Be certain to reward the person for taking the time to help you. Buying them lunch or its equivalent would be a nice thank you. Think of in-house assistance from an expert as one additional way to increase your technical competence.

11. Brainstorm new innovations impacting your area.

One way to stay more technically current is to anticipate changes in your field. Think of your area right now and how it might change in the next couple of years. What types of new equipment will change the area? Are there new services your competitors are implementing that will change your business? How might your organization be re-structured, or how might your company's products and services change? List out all of the changes you see forthcoming in the next few years.

Next, think of how you can adapt to these changes. What new skills or knowledge might you have to learn? To answer this, you might have to do some homework and study new equipment, procedures, etc. By anticipating this change and how to deal with it you will force yourself to stay more technically current in your field. Try this to broaden your technical knowledge.

12. Interview others with cutting-edge knowledge.

In many professions, some of the leading experts become known through publications, workshops, and other means. You can learn from these individuals not only by reading their articles and attending their workshops, but through personal contact as well. Call up some of the experts you admire in your field. Use as your lead-in the article you read by the person or your attendance at one of their workshops. Try to set up a lunch or breakfast with the person if they live in your area or visit your area. Treat the social get together as an interview, with you asking the person about their area of expertise. By gathering information like this from experts in the field, you can build your technical knowledge and skills.

13. Become the in-house expert in a particular area.

There are two general ways to establish technical expertise, by becoming the in-house expert in a certain area or by broadening out to have general knowledge in a number of areas. You should determine which of the two alternatives you want to be known for, since it is difficult to be known for both. If your choice is to become the in-house expert, then you need to research and develop a very high level of competence in a specific area. Maybe you want to be the accountant who knows more about tax regulations than anyone else, or the attorney who is an expert on employee termination lawsuits, or the production worker who is the best at doing precision drilling.

Whatever your choice, list out the ways you can beef up your knowledge in the area. Go to the library and read all you can on the subject. Interact with other experts, and take seminars or courses where helpful. Communicate what you know to others and establish yourself as the expert in the area. As your expertise grows, more people will seek out your advice, enabling you to learn more, in an endless cycle.

14. Identify jobs that help you with your career plan.

Your technical career is helped by identifying the job you want to be in a few years from now. You should examine the job description for a job of your choosing and other jobs that lead to this position. In particular, note the kinds of technical job knowledge and skills that someone should have in the job. Then figure out what jobs you can rotate into, or promote into, to build the necessary skills for your ultimate job. Next, put together a career plan for getting to the job of interest and building the needed technical skills and knowledge. Review this with your manager or those in human resources to get additional ideas.

15. Volunteer for a "stretch" project.

Departments often get the opportunity to participate in a project with another department. It might involve working with the systems department in designing new software, or the marketing department in designing new literature, or any one of many other possibilities. These projects may be excellent learning experiences since they take you into new areas. Some employees shy away from these projects, regarding them as "add-on" work, and deprive themselves of the opportunity to learn new skills. Do not let that be the case with you. Volunteer to take on such projects and see them as a means to broaden your technical knowledge and skills and make you more valuable to the department.

16. Speak at a professional conference.

Most professional associations hold conferences or seminars. In many cases they seek out employees from a variety of organizations to speak at the get together. You should volunteer to speak at a conference if you have never done so before. In preparing for your talk, you will have to collect additional information on your subject. This will help you broaden your technical knowledge base, and the interchange at the conference itself will be a further learning experience. Start out simple by looking at smaller, local conferences which are attended by small numbers of people. Grow from there to do larger talks.

17. Learn more about your industry.

Technical knowledge can be enhanced by knowing the latest trends in your industry. Each industry has certain unique characteristics and changes in certain ways. By staying current in your industry, you can be much more valuable to an organization from a technical standpoint. Try to seek out more information about your industry. Read industry publications, attend meetings, and network with other professionals in the industry. In particular, note how your company stands up against the competition from a technology standpoint.

Where are you ahead or behind versus other companies? By learning more about this, and making needed changes, you can stay technically competent in your area.

18. Start an informal association of your own.

Many employees find it useful to get together with professionals at other companies in an informal way. For example, a group of human resources directors in the computer industry in a large metro area get together for breakfast once a month. A group of managers in the quality control area have lunch together periodically to trade notes with each other. If this type of informal association does not exist in your area right now, go out and start one.

Identify people who have a job similar to your own at other companies. Contact them to assess their interest, and meet informally over breakfast, lunch, or cocktails. Bring with you some issues you would like to discuss, but let anyone in the group suggest a topic for discussion. By starting an association like this you not only build technical knowledge, but can practice leadership skills as well.

19. Take on a moonlighting project.

Another way to broaden your technical competence is to take on moonlighting projects in your evenings or weekends. For example, you might be responsible for training at your manufacturing company, but know of a local bank that is looking for some training assistance. You might be able to help them by working on the project in your spare time on the evenings or weekends.

You should use a good deal of care in selecting a moonlighting project. First, you want to make sure that you are not doing work with a competitor of your company or this will be a conflict of interest. Also, ensure that the work does not interfere with your job responsibilities. If the factors are favorable, moonlighting work will enable you to learn technical job knowledge and skills that you can bring back to your current job.

20. Add another employee's responsibilities to your own.

Many times in organizations there is a need for someone to cover for another employee. This might be due to illness, vacation, or termination. Examine whether you have ever sought to expand your responsibilities by taking over someone else's area. If not, think of doing this when the opportunity arises. Discuss with your manager your desire to broaden out and learn more. The expansion might be just for a few days or possibly a permanent part of your responsibilities. In either case, it will be an opportunity to learn and become more technically competent. Think of adding another area to your own when the opportunity arises.

21. Join industry associations.

Just as there are professional associations for various occupations, there are industry associations as well. There are manufacturers associations, banking associations, health care associations, and many others. The members may hold many different jobs, but what they have in common is employment in a certain industry. Examine whether there are any industry associations for your industry. You might look into joining them in place of, or in addition to, a professional association. The knowledge gained on what other companies are doing can help you build your technical expertise.

Recommended Readings

There are no specific articles and books provided for this chapter. To do so would require listing technical articles and books in every professional field.

If you are an employee, seek out your manager for articles and books to learn more in your technical field. If you are a manager and uncertain of additional readings for yourself or your employees, contact a professional association or colleagues at another company for their recommendations.

**The remaining chapters in this book are intended for
those currently in supervisory positions,
or those wanting to move into supervisory positions.**

26

Leadership

This chapter helps improve performance in the following areas:

- Developing a more effective management style.
- Showing more leadership and initiative.
- Becoming a participative manager.
- Developing a vision for the department.
- Taking charge and leading the way.

Action Items for Leadership

1. Develop a more participative management style.

A non-participative (autocratic) management style is still dominant in this country. While management style has moved in the participative direction, the movement has been very slow. With the rapid growth of white collar and professional jobs, the non-participative style does not fit as well. It is inappropriate for managers to want to make all decisions, control and legislate the workplace with a white collar work force.

The participative style of management simply involves using the human resources of the company to the fullest degree—letting employees have more authority, decision making responsibility, and involvement in changes in the workplace. That management style fits with today's jobs and today's employees. Assess how you typically make decisions and changes as a manager. If you tend to decide all matters on your own, change your management style to be more participative by involving others. It is the style that fits from here on out.

2. Develop a vision for your area.

Some managers are effective in handling administrative and employee relations responsibilities, but are weak when it comes to developing a vision for their department. As a result, employees may not clearly know where the department is headed, or what the priorities are. As a manager, you need to develop a vision for your department and communicate it to your staff and others. Items to think about in creating the vision include the following:

- Where is the department right now?

- Where should the department be a year from now? Three years from now?

- What is unique about the department?

- What is the department's mission in the company?

- What activities is the department doing well and what activities need to be improved?

- What are the important priorities for employees to concentrate on?

By coming up with the answers to questions like these and others, you can develop a strong vision for your area. By communicating and reinforcing the vision on an ongoing basis, your employees will work as a team to accomplish the vision.

3. Develop a company culture program.

Leading companies take the time to build a strong culture. By culture is meant all of the key elements that make that company unique— its values, management style, place in the marketplace, unique products and services, goals, and many other items. First, these areas need to be clearly defined and written up as a "training course." Then, all existing employees complete the program, with the program being given to all new hires from there on out.

While it is beyond the scope of each manager to create a culture program, managers can escalate the need for such a program to others in the company. They can also develop a small-scale culture program within their own department. With either the company-wide or departmental programs, employees will have a clear understanding of the organization they work for and how to contribute to it.

4. Implement goals and objectives for your department.

Departments that do not use goals and objectives may have a more difficult time in getting employees to achieve a great deal. For how can an employee hit a target if the target is never identified? Using goals and objectives can help employees shoot for, and attain, targets for their area of responsibility. Evaluate whether you are using goals and objectives in your area. If not, work with your staff to define particular goals for the area and write these down on paper with dates for completion. It makes no difference if your system is a formal one (e.g., MBO) or an informal one. The key is to use some sort of system and management style that clearly defines goals for employees. Try using goals and objectives to bolster your leadership capabilities.

5. Reduce the tendency to make decisions on your own.

Some managers have a tendency to make all decisions on their own, even minor decisions. They figure that decision making is what a manager is supposed to do, and that is why they are the manager rather than someone else. This type of attitude and management style can create a disgruntled staff who feels that they do not have any real responsibility. That, in turn, can lead to productivity problems or turnover.

A simple rule to follow with decision making is, "Never make a decision by yourself unless you absolutely have to." Instead, get your staff involved. Delegate some decisions to them or use a collaborative process to shape larger decisions with everyone having a chance to have their say. This will produce better quality decisions since you will be getting a larger number of ideas. It will also leave the staff more satisfied as a result.

6. Lead by strong personal example.

Much of leadership comes from the example set by leaders. Managers who tell their staffs to work long hours yet go home early themselves will have a hard time getting the desired behavior from the staff. As a manager, you should evaluate the example you set in a number of areas. Strong ethics and personal conduct are needed to provide a good role model for others. Areas you should review include:

- Work hours/personal days.
- Down time—breaks, informal conversation, workouts at the health club.
- Honesty and candidness.
- Fairness and objectivity.

- Abuse of management power—e.g., sexual harassment.

- Entering into agreements for personal benefit.

- Playing politics.

Review whether you use a double standard in these and other areas—doing one thing yourself and expecting another from your staff. If so, change that double standard by improving your personal ethics. Regard the personal example you set as having an extremely important effect on others. Make your personal standards the highest to ensure that you get the same from others.

7. Use staff ideas wherever you can.

Any manager has but one perspective and one set of ideas to contribute. That can be a detriment when faced with a tough challenge such as making changes to the department. Strong leaders do not rely solely upon themselves for ideas. They go out and get the ideas of staff, peers, and others who might have something to contribute. They also set up a climate so that employees will feel comfortable in bringing forward ideas at any time. Make that your leadership style as well. Use the ideas of staff and peers to augment your own. You can never be worse off by adding the ideas of others to your own, and can oftentimes come out with new insights and perspectives to enhance your final efforts.

8. Write and post a mission statement.

Employees can benefit by knowing the department mission. Effective leaders will come up with some sort of "theme" or slogan for the department which supports the mission. Think of using this in your department. First, write out a clear mission statement of what your department does and how it contributes to the company's success. Involve your staff in the process if possible. Next, post the mission statement where all can see it and circulate copies. You may even come up with a slogan or key ideas from the mission which can be put on coffee mugs, calendars or other reminder items to give to all employees. Use an effective mission statement to enhance your leadership effectiveness.

9. Figure out the niche of your company or department.

Leaders are often more successful when they identify the niche of their company in the marketplace. For example, it is difficult for a company to be the cheapest, most innovative, have the highest quality, best service, etc. all at the same time. Usually there are a couple of key characteristics that make the company unique in the marketplace that the employees can work toward. The same is true of departments, though in this case the niche pertains to the unique products or services the department provides within the company.

Try to figure out the niche of your company or department. Resist the temptation to make the niche too diverse and a little bit of everything. That can confuse employees, not clarify. Once the niche is defined, see that it gets communicated to all affected by it and supported on an ongoing basis. Defining a niche will greatly enhance your leadership effectiveness.

10. Have high standards for yourself and others.

Effective leaders have very high standards. They expect the best from others and have high personal standards for their own performance as well. Others may merely leave it to employees to set their own standards for themselves. Review whether you maintain high standards for your department. Do you, for example, expect that written materials will be sent out free of errors or that products not be shipped which are faulty? The failure to do this will lead your staff to believe that you do not care about quality, or do not know the difference between high quality and low quality work.

Practice more effective leadership by expecting high quality from others. Set high standards, both for your personal performance and that of others. Inspire people to keep getting better at what they do. The result of using high standards will be reflected in higher department performance.

11. Blaze a trail where no one has gone before.

Some managers are merely content to carry out the basics of their job. They leave changes, innovations, and improvements to someone else and see their role as implementors. Other managers take it upon themselves to blaze a trail where no one has gone before. They see their role as improving upon the past, and changing the workplace to make it more competitive and satisfying. You should evaluate how often you have blazed a trail in your position. How often in the past two years have you developed new procedures, policies, reorganized the area, introduced new equipment, or redesigned jobs in the department? Be certain to count only those activities **you** initiated and not your boss or someone else at the company.

If your list is not a very long one, try to change that. See your role not as an administrator, but as someone who makes changes happen. Start by listing the kinds of changes your department needs now. Brainstorm ways to make the changes, and assign specific people to carry out the plans. On a periodic basis, review your area's needs and have the courage to blaze a new trail where no one else has. It is an excellent way to show leadership.

12. Lead by competency.

There are several ways to establish strong leadership. One of these is to lead by competency. In this case, the manager shows the way by knowing the technical aspects of the department and profession better than most other people. Evaluate how your staff and manager regard your technical skills. If in doubt, ask others for their candid opinion. If the feedback you get is not as strong as you would like it to be, set out to change. Identify ways to build more technical competency in your field. Possible ways include:

- Joining professional associations.

- Read books and articles in your field.

- Attend seminars and workshops in your field.

- Network with professionals at other companies.

- Spend more time with experts in the field.

- Enroll in college courses or training classes.

Set goals and target dates for beefing up your technical skills. Do not quit your technical development until it reaches the level you want, and then try to stay abreast of changes in the field.

13. Lead by having strong people management skills.

Another way to show strong leadership is by having excellent people management skills. The manager who is a technical expert will need people management skills in order to be successful as a manager. Those with superior people skills might even be able to have fewer technical skills and still be a good manager since they are so effective at the people side. Take an honest look at your people management skills. If they need improvement, set up some specific targets to achieve. Read the chapter on interpersonal skills and implement the ideas there. Attend seminars and workshops in the area, and read additional books. People management skills are becoming more and more critical with the movement toward a service economy. Make superior people skills one of the ways you show leadership.

14. Lead by mastering core management skills.

Still yet another way to establish leadership is by having outstanding management skills. By ''management skills'' we are referring to those core management skills such as planning, organizing, prioritizing, problem solving, decision making, and financial skills. Obtain feedback from others on your skills in these management areas. If your skills are weak or average, make improvements as soon as you can. Read the other chapters in this book pertaining to these areas and implement the ideas. Enroll in training classes or workshops to help you build skills where needed. Pursue readings and other forms of development so that you have a high level of competence with core management skills.

15. Develop a stronger results orientation.

Some managers can talk a good game, but are short on action. They seem to be forever talking about the future and how they will improve the department, yet these changes never seem to occur. Other activities such as administrative work eat up all of their time. Make certain this is not the case with you. Do what it takes to get results. Have a bottom-line orientation and ensure that you, and your staff, attain the key results that are needed in the department. Translate your ideas into action. Monitor your area to ensure that day-to-day administrative work does not consume all of the time, with important goals going unmet. Make attaining key results a part of your leadership style.

16. Be more gregarious.

When we envision leaders, we normally think of people who are visible and known to all. While leaders can sometimes lead in a very quiet way, it is more difficult to be a strong people-oriented manager and not be interacting with others. If you are more introverted, try to interact more often with people. Gradually increase the number of people you know in your company. Be more gregarious in introducing yourself to others, and inviting them to lunch or a break. Speak up a bit more in meetings and contact others more often to get their ideas and thoughts. You might also practice more "management by walking around" and find out what employees and customers are thinking about. Increasing your visibility and gregariousness can help you become a stronger leader.

17. Look the part of leader.

Some managers might fail to become leaders because they do not look the part. If managers have poor grooming or do not dress appropriately, we may not accept them as leaders. Their appearance will cause a negative impression and distract others from listening to what they have to say. If you want to establish a stronger leadership role, make certain that you look the part. Note how the senior managers at your company dress, particularly those who are known to be very successful. Try to pattern your own grooming after those you admire, or ask for assistance from those at leading department stores. By projecting a strong image as a leader, you will not only eliminate distractions, but make it easier to command the respect and attention of others.

18. Ask tough questions.

Leaders are known to ask tough questions when interacting with others. They may challenge the numbers or details others are presenting or demand further information. Or they might demand, in a positive way, a more perfect product or service than what they have seen. You should examine whether you will ask the tough questions and demand more of others. If not, you may want to incorporate this into your management style. Do so in a positive way—you want to establish high quality performance, not hurt others in the process. Let others know that you are not an "easy sell" and they have to attain good results for you to be pleased. Reward them when they do an effective job. By demanding high quality and asking tough questions, you will get a higher level of performance from other employees.

19. Convince yourself that you are destined to lead others.

Those who want to lead others need to first convince themselves that they are destined to lead. If you feel you are destined to lead, you are halfway down the road to becoming a leader. Those uncertain of the desire to lead will not likely be very effective leaders.

If you are not convinced of your abilities to lead larger operations, start by changing that right now. Visualize yourself in a more important management position, and the types of activities and status you will enjoy in such a job. A few minutes spent each evening visualizing yourself in such a role will help your subconscious self work towards attaining that role. Being certain of your desire to be in a more responsible management role is first step toward attaining that goal.

20. Expand your span of control.

All organizations go through change of one sort or another. People retire or quit a company, reorganizations take place, or new departments are created because of technology or other reasons. When these changes occur, excellent opportunities are presented for expanding your span of control. When a vacancy occurs, think of whether you can expand your current responsibilities to include the new department. You might even present this as a savings to your manager since your expansion could save replacing the former manager. Leaders take advantage of these opportunities and convince others of their capabilities to handle more responsibility. Look with confidence to expanding your span of control.

21. Invite yourself to the party.

Leaders tend to become involved in a broader range of activities than most other people. Because of curiosity or the desire to influence, they might play a role in shaping the outcome. How do they get this involvement to begin with? Often by inviting themselves to the party. A leader might hear of a meeting to take place that he/she has an interest in. A call might be placed to the meeting coordinator to see if the leader might attend. In subsequent meetings, the leader might be invited as an automatic.

Or a leader might hear of a memo or report that someone wrote which is of interest. A call might be placed to the writer to ask for a copy. Once the copy is obtained, the leader might comment or offer suggestions to help in the area. By inviting yourself to the party in examples like these, you can establish that you are a leader who has a broad interest in what is going on in the company. You will also establish your ability to assist and influence in many areas outside your department, and that increases your leadership role.

22. Link your department's activities to larger goals.

Strong leaders think of their job as more than just carrying out department activities. They see a strong link between what they do and the company's overall goals. This link is communicated to the staff and makes them feel more important and motivated to accomplish a great deal. As a leader, you should evaluate how your department's activities relate to larger company goals. If uncertain of the company-wide goals, ask others in a position to know. Once the link is established, communicate it to others on an ongoing basis. Make them feel that the work they are doing is very important to company success. This is an effective way to communicate leadership to others in the department.

23. Champion the ideas of others.

Leaders are confident enough of themselves that they do not have to bang their own drum continuously. Where appropriate, they will champion the ideas of others. They might take the idea of a staff member or peer and advocate it elsewhere in the company, and give credit to the originator of the idea. By doing this, the leader establishes a high level of trust and respect by pushing someone else's ideas and not only their own. This increases the perceived leadership of the person. Try to do this where appropriate in your company. Go out of your way on occasion to push the ideas of another and give credit where it is due. It is still another way to increase your perceived leadership capabilities.

24. Show pride in your staff's work.

Leaders take a great deal of pride in the work of their staff. They will comment favorably on the work in staff meetings, informal interactions with superiors, and in other settings. That pride in the accomplishments of others makes the person a leader in the eyes of their staff. They see their manager as someone who believes in them and will make others aware of it, and that translates into leadership.

We are not suggesting that the pride and praise be phony. It should be genuine and sincere. The key is to ensure that you take the time to mention this pride to others—that you really feel pleased with the work. Only by letting others know in a visible way will your staff become aware of your feelings. And this will increase their perception of you as a leader.

25. Model yourself after a personal role model.

Increasing leadership can be done by finding and copying a good role model. Think of someone you admire greatly as a leader. What is it that they say or do which makes them stand out as a leader? Perhaps there are several people that you admire as leaders, each with a different set of characteristics. By noting what makes others effective leaders, you can increase your leadership effectiveness. Try to copy those characteristics that you admire in others, incorporating them into your own unique style. By using an effective set of role models, you can improve upon your personal leadership skills.

26. Seek out a mentor.

Many effective leaders mention someone who served as a mentor for them earlier in their careers. This mentor took the person under their wing and helped them develop and grow. While some companies have a formal program to assign young managers a mentor, many do not. If your company does not have a mentor program, think of someone you would like to have as a mentor. Perhaps it is a manager in a more senior position who you admire and is easy to interact with.

Go to this person and explain that you would like them to serve as your mentor. Tell them that you do not want to take up a lot of their time, but merely want to meet with them once every few weeks to get advice. Those meetings might be held over breakfast or lunch to save company time. Listen to your mentor's advice with an open mind, and be certain to implement the developmental suggestions that you receive. The use of a mentor can be very helpful in building strong leadership skills.

27. Seek out feedback on your leadership style.

Leadership can be continually developed by knowing what you are doing well and less well, and improving upon the areas that need development. If you currently do not get much feedback about your leadership style, seek out some feedback from others. Talk to your staff and peers and ask them for candid advice. If that will not work, think of using an anonymous survey of some sort. Look at the feedback you get as a means of learning and developing, not as criticism. Go out and identify ways to improve upon those areas that need changing. Continually learning about and improving upon your leadership style is a very positive way to remain an effective leader.

28. Present your ideas more assertively.

Some managers are reluctant to present their ideas very assertively. They feel that they will be rocking the boat or lose respect by saying what they feel. As a result, they lose the respect and confidence of their staff and are not seen as leaders. While there is always a limit as to how far you should push an idea, leaders do not give up easily on something that they believe in. This should be your leadership style as well.

Be willing to go forward with proposals and ideas that you feel will improve your department. While some risk is always involved in doing this, others will not likely lose any respect for you if you are professional and sincere in presenting your ideas. Persist with the idea a bit longer if appropriate. Others may see it differently if they have a chance to think about it. Being persuasive and assertive in an effective way can contribute to leadership success.

29. Volunteer for leadership roles in the community.

Leadership can be built both away from the job as well as on the job. By volunteering for leadership roles in the community, you can strengthen your leadership capabilities. Think of volunteer organizations that need leadership help. Perhaps this is your church, park board, zoo, condominium association, or hobby club. Take on a leadership role and apply the experience you get back on the job.

Within a company, there are leadership roles of a volunteer basis as well. These include company picnics, retirement parties, special project task forces, and others. Volunteer for some of these activities so you have a chance to test out and develop your leadership skills in new and different areas.

30. Balance you orientations toward people and technical tasks.

It is easy in the workplace to get carried away with the technical aspects of the job and forget about the people side. When this happens, leaders may be seen as technical leaders, but not total leaders. Similarly, someone may concentrate too much on the people side and neglect the technical aspects of the job. What effective leaders do is strike up a nice balance between these two orientations. They focus an equal amount on both technical and people issues and make certain they provide leadership in both areas. You should try to practice this as well. Have an equal balance between technical and people orientations in your leadership role.

31. Have a high level of confidence in people, products, and services.

Strong leaders believe in what they do. That translates into expressing confidence in the people who work for them, and the products and services their organization provides. This is not only felt inside, but mentioned to others in a very open way. Evaluate how much confidence you express in your staff and your organization's products and services. What would you say to a friend or stranger who asked you about them? How about one of your peers at the office? If you do not express faith and confidence in others and the company, you cannot expect the people who work for you to have positive feelings either. They might choose to quit or give up rather than keep working at it, and that is a tragedy for all. Ensure that you believe in your staff and your company and communicate this to others in your informal interactions with them.

Recommended Readings

Albrecht, Karl, and Zemke, Ron. *Service America! Doing Business in the New Economy*. Homewood, IL: Dow Jones-Irwin, 1985.

Allcorn, Seth. Action Skills for Group Leaders. *Management Solutions*, Oct, 1987, 32, p. 25-37.

Allcorn, Seth. Leadership Styles: The Psychological Picture. *Personnel*, April, 1988, p. 46-51.

Bennis, Warren, and Nanus, Burt. *Leaders: The Strategies for Taking Charge*. New York: Harper & Row, 1985.

Blake, R., and Mouton, J. *Managerial Grid III* (3rd ed.). Houston: Gulf, 1984.

Block, Peter. *The Empowered Manager: Positive Political Skills at Work*. San Francisco: Jossey-Bass, 1990.

Bradford, David L., and Cohen, Allan R. *Managing for Excellence: The Guide to Developing High Performance in Contemporary Organizations*. New York: Wiley, 1984.

Cohen, William A., and Cohen, Nurit. *Top Executive Performance: 11 Keys to Success and Power*. New York: Wiley, 1984.

Dumaine, Brian. The New Non-Manager Managers. *Fortune*, February 22, 1993, 80-84.

Gardner, J.W. The Task of Leadership. *Personnel*, Oct, 1986, 63, p. 20-27.

Hamlin, Richard. Choosing Between Directive and Participative Management. *Supervisory Management*, Jan, 1986, 31, p. 14-16.

Kravetz, Dennis J. *The Human Resources Revolution: Implementing Progressive Management Practices for Bottom-Line Success*. San Francisco: Jossey-Bass, 1988.

Lawler, Edward E., III. *High-Involvement Management*. San Francisco: Jossey-Bass, 1986.

Mearles, Larry B. What Good Leaders Do. *Personnel*, Sept, 1988, p. 48-51.

Niehouse, Oliver. Developing a Leadership Strategy. *Management Solutions*, Aug, 1987, 32, p. 21-26.

Peters, Tom. *Thriving on Chaos: A Handbook for a Management Revolution*. New York: Alfred A. Knopf, 1987.

Plunkett, Lorne C. and Fournier, Robert. *Participative Management: Implementing Empowerment*. New York: Wiley and Sons, 1992.

Sargent, Alice and Stupak, Ronald. Managing in the 90s: The Androgynous Manager. *Training and Development*, December, 1989, p. 29-35.

Stuart-Kotze, Robin, and Roskin, Rick. *Success Guide to Managerial Achievement*. Reston, VA: Reston Publishing Company, 1983.

Tichy, Noel M., and DeVanna, Mary Anne. *The Transformational Leader*. New York: Wiley, 1986.

Willis, Suzanne. *The Participative Leader*. Burr Ridge, IL: Irwin Professional Publishing, 1994.

Zenger, John; Musselwhite, Ed; Hanson, Kathleen; and Perrin, Craig. Leadership in a Team Environment. *Training and Development*, October, 1991, 47-52.

27

Coaching and Counseling

This chapter helps improve performance in the following areas:

- Interacting more effectively with employees.

- Improving employee performance.

- Helping employees grow and learn on the job.

- Doing a better job at performance coaching and appraisal.

- Improving counseling and interpersonal skills.

Action Items for Coaching and Counseling

1. Initiate development plans for each of your employees.

Some managers fail to take the time for employee development. They leave development to the employee or only concern themselves with very poor or very effective employees. That attitude can lead to a stagnant work force that does not improve. More effective managers see it as their responsibility to put development plans in place for each of their employees. This includes everyone in the department, regardless of performance level or length of service.

Make an effort to work out development plans with each of your employees and update these plans at least once a year. The development should be very positive and upbeat—you want to help people to learn, grow, and get ahead in their careers. With this type of an approach, development will be seen as positive and desirable by the employee. Use whatever resources you can to help employees execute the plan, be it training courses, job rotation, books, or seminars.

2. Focus on the problem, not the person, in performance coaching.

One mistake that many managers make in employee performance coaching is to focus on the employee. They think they are doing all that is needed if they criticize and blame the employee for past failures and get them to realize this. But by blaming and criticizing, they make the employee feel defensive, threatened, and unlikely to cooperate. The net result is that performance may not change, and the employee may walk away with bitter feelings toward the manager.

An alternative approach is to focus on the problem rather than blaming the employee. If the employee comes in late too often, focus on the problem—how lateness affects department operations and what can be done to solve the problem. If there is a problem with poor filing, a manager might say to the employee, "I've noticed that many of the files have been incorrectly filed. I wonder if you could help me solve this problem." With this focus, cooperation will be obtained, the employee will not become defensive, and solutions will be developed.

3. Coach to share information.

Many managers forget to coach with their employees to share information. When they become aware of company changes, problems, or items of interest, they keep it to themselves. As a result, their employees are uninformed of events that could help them do their jobs better. You should evaluate the degree to which you coach to share information.

To improve coaching to share information, think of others whenever new information comes your way. Would the information help others in doing their jobs? If so, share it out either verbally or in writing. Copy your employees on memos or provide updates on events in staff meetings. Think of informing your staff about problems, new customers, changes in procedures, new people hired, a shift in company goals, financial results, and many other areas. Failing to share information is a much more serious problem than over-communicating. If you must error, error in the direction of sharing out too much information.

4. Make performance coaching a win-win situation.

Some managers see coaching as a win-lose proposition. They share out their feelings about the employee's performance problems, and the employee must accept this and change. The manager wins and the employee loses. Or both lose if the employee comes away from the meeting feeling negative about the meeting and the way it was handled.

More professional managers make performance coaching a win-win situation. Rather than try to make the employee feel bad by dumping the problem on them, they try to focus on positive solutions, and growth and development. That attitude fosters improvement, and makes for a positive working relationship. Make this your attitude when you do performance coaching. See coaching as joint problem solving and helping someone get better at what they do—a joint commitment between you and the employee to make performance better.

5. Have career development discussions at least once a year.

Career development is a growing issue with many employees. With rapid changes in technology, many employees wonder about their career future. Skills that are adequate today could become insufficient tomorrow. Effective managers make career development an important part of their responsibilities. Even if the company has no formal career development program, they take the initiative to do work in this area with their employees. You should make career development an important part of your management activity as well.

Career development meetings should be held with each employee at least once a year. The sessions should be informal and relaxed—you are not there to evaluate job performance or decide someone's future. In the career development session itself, you should focus on what the employee wants to do in the future. Share out your candid feedback on whether they have the skills for the jobs they aspire to. Perhaps you have noted jobs that they are well-suited for and should share these out as well. After discussing the job(s) of interest, the conversation should cover what development should take place to attain subsequent jobs. Here again, be very candid and work with the employee in coming up with a developmental plan. Periodic career development sessions will greatly help with people management.

6. Conduct coaching to reward and motivate.

Another form of coaching which employees need is coaching to reward and motivate. It is important to recognize good employee job performance if you want that performance to continue in the future. If you do not say anything to the employee or provide any other types of rewards, performance may deteriorate. The biggest problem with coaching to reward is doing it often enough. Employees can probably never get enough of praise, but can certainly feel slighted if they do not receive the amount they expect. Review your own practices on coaching to reward, be certain that you say more than a mere "thank you," and that you reward often enough to have an impact.

There are many ways to motivate employees with psychological incentives. Finding the right ones for an individual employee is a key challenge that managers have. You should ensure that you hold periodic coaching sessions to motivate and inspire your staff. These can range from a minor pep talk to very inspiring sessions. For a further discussion on the motivation topic, read the chapter on motivating and inspiring.

7. Make resources available for employee development.

Employees may find it very difficult to develop themselves. If they do not receive improvement coaching from someone else, they may not know where to turn for assistance. As a manager, you have a key responsibility to make resources available to your employees to help them build skills and develop their careers. Such resources include, but are not limited to:

- Articles and books that you are aware of.

- Providing information on seminars and workshops.

- Supporting employee attendance at company training courses.

- Finding in-house "experts" that can help the employee learn new skills.

- Locating self-study programs (cassettes, manuals, etc.).

- Supporting employee participation in professional associations.

- Putting the employee in contact with a network who can assist.

Think through these and other resources that might help your employees with development issues. Make the resources available that will help improve performance and build new skills.

8. Set up a relaxing environment for coaching.

Some managers may fail at coaching by not setting up the right environment. They might coach in a noisy area or let themselves be interrupted several times. As a result, the coaching session will not be as successful as it could be. As a manager you should ensure that your coaching sessions are held in an effective location. Key factors in controlling the environment are as follows:

• Be in a private area (e.g., conference room) where you will not be overheard by others.

• Try to hold phone calls and other interruptions if at all possible.

• Sit in side chairs with the employee—avoid getting behind a desk.

• Use a positive tone in the session—have a friendly, upbeat attitude.

• Be relaxed in style and body language—avoid formal, bureaucratic approaches.

9. See employee development as needed by all.

Managers of the past saw development as only needed by poor performers. That was essential for the poor performer to keep employed. The only other employees to get much developmental attention were the superstars who might be given stretch assignments. Effective managers today recognize that **all** employees can benefit from development. Everyone, regardless of performance level, can benefit from acquiring new skills and strengthening existing skills. With that type of outlook, all employees receive developmental counseling and all benefit from the result. Make that your attitude as well. See employee development as something that all employees can benefit from.

10. Have a joint ownership with employees in the improvement area.

Some managers use the "dump and run" technique for employee improvement—they dump the performance problem in the employees lap, then run away. That sort of technique will not bring about performance improvement. Employee performance problems are jointly shared by manager and employee if for no other reason than the manager is accountable for the employee's area. That means that working out the solution to the problem is also shared between manager and employee.

Effective managers today recognize that performance problems are jointly owned by managers and employees. While employees must ultimately make the improvements, the manager has a role as well. That role might include making other resources available, providing additional coaching, or offering support and assistance. There may even be things the manager can change, such as work loads and job responsibilities, than can help bring about a solution. By doing these activities, managers are much more likely to see change than by using the dump and run technique. See yourself as having a joint ownership for employee improvement as well.

11. Recognize and reward performance improvements.

Part of the performance coaching process involves rewarding performance improvements. It can be very sad for an employee to make significant improvements, only to have the manager fail to recognize and reward the changes. That could very well lead the employee to conclude that the manager is not aware of performance, or does not care about change. When you are coaching employees on performance issues, closely monitor performance after the coaching. Recognize and reward even small changes in performance. If the employee can make a series of small improvements, they can eventually attain the level of performance which is desired. Yet to keep that momentum going, and to build the employee's confidence, the recognition and reward must be there. Make it an integral part of your coaching practices.

12. Practice active listening.

Some managers treat coaching sessions as opportunities for them to talk and for the employee to listen. While managers certainly need to share out their feelings during a coaching session, there needs to be a two-way interaction for the session to be effective. By practicing active listening, managers can ensure that there will be a two-

way dialogue in the coaching session. Managers can practice active listening by doing the following:

- Maintain good eye contact.
- Nod your head to show understanding.
- Let employees say all they want unless they ramble.
- Repeat the employee's main points from time to time.
- Minimize distractions when listening.
- Lean forward to show interest and have a relaxed body posture.
- Read the body language and emotions of the employee.

By practicing active listening, you can ensure that there will be more candidness and open discussion of positive actions. Use active listening in your coaching sessions with employees.

13. Show empathy when needed.

In many coaching sessions employees will make an emotional statement. Perhaps they are dissatisfied with a certain aspect of the job, are upset about a co-worker, or disagree with a certain action that was taken. Whenever there is emotion detected in the employee's comments, empathy statements should be made in return. By showing empathy you are telling the employee that you know how they feel, that you can walk a mile in their shoes. Showing empathy does not mean that you **agree** with the employee, only that you **understand.** Sample empathy statements include the following:

- "I can understand why you feel the way that you do."
- "I know it can be frustrating when you are learning to use new equipment."
- "It must be upsetting to have to work with someone like Ted."

By making empathy statements, you will be showing that you are listening and comprehending what the employee is going through.

From this, you can work toward effective solutions. Remember to use empathy whenever you detect emotion in what someone has said.

14. Utilize effective interpersonal skills.

Coaching can certainly be helped by practicing effective interpersonal skills. This will make employees more comfortable in the coaching session itself, and more likely to seek you out for coaching and advice. There are many aspects to good interpersonal skills, but some of the more important ones are to show more of a personal interest in your employees, to be more friendly and sociable, and to be willing to make with small talk on occasion. You will want to review the chapter on interpersonal skills for more details on how to strengthen your abilities in this area.

15. Practice the open door policy.

Not all coaching sessions are manager initiated. On many occasions, employees may seek out the manager to discuss problems they are having. By effectively nipping the problem in the bud, managers can prevent problems from developing further. The key is to make the employee comfortable enough to seek out the manager for the initial coaching. One of the best ways of doing this is by practicing the open door policy.

Managers who use the open door policy need to think of more than merely keeping their office door open, though that is a key starting point. They also need to be approachable through body language and look for interactions with others by visiting employees on their turf. The open door also means a willingness to listen and react accordingly to what the employee has to say, being candid, and supportive of fixing the problem. It is also a matter of being trusted and respected and doing all you can to establish this. Utilize the open door policy with your employees to be more successful at coaching.

16. Maintain the employee's self-esteem in coaching.

It is extremely important in coaching situations to maintain the employee's self-esteem. If the manager chastises and blames, this can damage self-esteem and will make the employee more defensive and resistant to coaching. On the other hand, when self-esteem is preserved, the employee is more likely to be cooperative and implement the needed changes. How do you maintain self-esteem when you need to bring up a performance problem? First, by reinforcing your belief in the employee's ability to carry out the job and complimenting them for those things that they do well. Second, by not blaming and focusing on the problem instead of the person (see earlier action item). Last, by expressing confidence in the employee's ability to bring about the needed changes. Whenever coaching with employees, try to keep the self-esteem intact for successful coaching results.

17. Use third-party assistance in coaching when needed.

There are several coaching and counseling situations that are sensitive in nature. For example, these might pertain to alcoholism, drug dependency, financial problems, psychological problems, or employee charges of unfairness. When managers are faced with issues like these, they should not attempt to become psychologists, physicians, or financial advisors. The better approach is to listen and understand what the problem is, then refer the employee to an appropriate outside agency. Notifying human resources professionals in the company might also be appropriate since they can be of assistance. After the initial referral, the manager should follow the employee's progress without prying into the details. The key is to get the employee to someone with professional expertise who can help solve the problem.

18. Build trust to increase coaching effectiveness.

For coaching to be effective, the two parties must trust each other. If the employee thinks that the manager cannot be trusted, the coaching session might be ineffective (the same is true with the manager's trust of the employee). As a manager you should ensure that employees trust you. Ways that you can build and maintain trust include:

- Be candid and forthright.

- Have impeccable personal ethics.

- Be honest in dealing with others.

- Avoid using information or people to your advantage.

- Give employees the benefit of the doubt.

- Deliver on promises.

- Trust people until there is unquestionable information that shows they cannot be trusted.

As a manager, you should evaluate how well you build trust with others. Make improvements where necessary. This will help you be more effective at coaching and counseling with your employees.

19. Read body language in coaching sessions.

Some managers fail to pay attention to body language or other clues during a coaching session. They plow ahead even if the employee is uncomfortable or nervous. That may result in a less effective coaching session. As a manager you should pay attention to the body language of employees during coaching sessions. For example, if you see that someone is very nervous, try to relax them before beginning a counseling session. Make some small talk, offer the employee some coffee, or simply tell them to relax. When they look more comfortable, then begin the counseling itself. If the employee looks confused or disturbed by what you say, ask them if they understand or have problems with what you said. By addressing what you see, the session will be more effective than avoiding the issue. Make reading and reacting to body language part of your coaching practices.

20. Learn to recognize the signs of substance abuse.

Many managers will coach employees on performance issues and not be aware of the fact that the employee has a substance abuse problem. The ultimate solution to the employee's problem may never occur since the problem is never surfaced. It is helpful if managers learn to recognize the symptoms of substance abuse. Care must be taken here, for any one of the symptoms may have other causes as well. The more common symptoms of substance abuse are:

• Frequent mood swings for no apparent reason.

• Long lunch hours or being away from the work area for no reason.

• Frequent absence, particularly on Monday and Friday.

• Glazed look in the eyes.

• Slurred or unintelligible speech.

• Frequent depression on the job.

• Complaints of tiredness, not feeling well with no apparent illness.

If one of more of these symptoms is present in your employees, you should try to be attuned to other clues that may indicate a substance abuse problem. We are not suggesting that employees be confronted directly (unless there is obvious use on the job), but in performance coaching you may pursue a bit further what may be causing the absence problem, tardiness problem, etc. The manager has to keep focusing on the performance issues but should be attuned to the real causes and get the employee appropriate help if substance abuse is identified.

21. Work toward solutions and the future in coaching.

Performance coaching sessions can get very bogged down when the focus is on the past and pointing the finger at someone. Managers who are good at coaching do not spend much time debating the past. Instead they focus on the future, and what can be done to improve the problem in a positive, constructive way. The focus is also on solutions, and what both parties can do to help solve the problem itself. With this type of focus, the coaching session will be much more productive and positive. Try to make this your approach as well.

22. Believe employees can learn and change.

Some managers abandon efforts at performance improvement by concluding that employees cannot learn or change. They think people are the way they are and nothing will ever change them. What is important to recognize is that having this attitude will **guarantee** that nothing will change. Managers who feel this way are really just making excuses for not doing performance coaching. And if they enter into coaching with a negative attitude, will the employee be motivated to change?

Your attitude as a manager can have a tremendous impact on the success of performance coaching. If you believe that employees can learn and change, you will express this in coaching and they will be motivated to learn and change. Be certain that your own negative attitude does not ruin performance improvement efforts. We have all learned and developed over the years and have the potential to change more. Recognize this when coaching with your employees.

23. Apply the coaching steps and model presented earlier.

In the introductory chapter to this book we presented a model for conducting performance coaching sessions with your employees. This model should be followed as much as possible for the coaching session to be successful. The steps in the model are as follows:

1. Maintain or strengthen the employee's self-esteem.

2. Describe the problem.

3. Discuss solutions to the problem.

4. Agree on actions.

5. Set follow-up.

6. Express confidence in the employee.

For further details on this model, see the introductory chapter. By utilizing the model, performance coaching sessions will have the proper flow and keep the employee feeling positive throughout the session. Use this process if at all possible.

24. Conduct performance appraisal discussions at least once a year.

Performance coaching should be done on an ongoing basis whenever the need arises. However, there is also a need to look at performance from the "big picture" perspective. All of the employee's achievements from the year and the skill and ability levels should be rolled together into a single appraisal. While many companies have performance appraisal policies, some leave it up to the manager to determine how often to do the appraisal.

Each manager should ensure that appraisals are done at least once a year for each employee, with a written form given to the employee. By doing this, employees will be able to understand their performance from a larger perspective, and focus more clearly on areas for development. They also will benefit from having clear feedback on those areas where they do very well. Make regular performance appraisals a part of your management style.

25. Buy a copy of this book for your employees.

Another way to bring about growth, development, and better performance for your employees is to buy them a copy of this book. While you, as their manager, can suggest actions items for the employee to try, the employee may want to source their own action items. They may have developmental needs in their own minds that you are unaware of or feel are not very important. By giving the employee a copy of the book, they can source their own action items and implement the appropriate ones. Think of this as still yet another resource for your employees. The bottom line is to give them as many tools as possible for bringing about performance change.

26. Give new hires the proper orientation.

One of the most important groups to provide coaching is new hires. Employees who are just hired have many questions and need a support network. The official company orientation may help with filling out benefit forms and providing basic company information, but there are many departmental orientation needs that managers need to fulfill.

See to it that all of your new hires get a proper orientation. If you cannot do this yourself, appoint someone who has a good understanding of the department. Make the employee aware of procedures, policies, goals, values, standards, organization structure, and other necessary information. Provide someone as a "mentor" to look after the new employee if you cannot do it yourself. Provide them with a support network of others to contact should problems come up. A proper orientation is a very important form of coaching that will get employees off to a good start.

27. Make training happen at your company.

Many managers fail to make training happen in their department or their company. They recognize that it is important, but lament that the training department has a limited budget or there are limited courses to pick from. As a result, needed employee development does not take place. Do not fall into this trap at your company.

If you have significant budget authority, encourage the training department to develop the courses you need or develop them on your own. There are many choices to pick from: custom-designed courses, off-the-shelf programs, self-study courses, workshops, seminars, college courses, and other possibilities. The key is to not wait for others to do this for you. If you believe in employee development, you may need to go out on your own and make training happen.

28. Make feedback an ongoing process.

Just as doing an annual appraisal is important, so too is frequent coaching and counseling. Some managers feel they have discharged their responsibilities by doing the once-a-year review. Employees receiving such a limited amount of feedback may express surprise at how they were rated since there was no prior discussion. They may also fail to develop as desired since there is no ongoing coaching and feedback.

As a manager, you should ensure that your employees receive ongoing performance feedback. Try to provide feedback as often as you can, both for a job well done and the need to improve performance in certain areas. Coaching is so much easier when it is done often and early. Make sure that when you do your annual appraisal review that there are no surprises.

29. Keep employees challenged.

Each manager has a responsibility to ensure that employees do not become too complacent on the job. If this happens, boredom may set in and the employee may be thinking of going elsewhere. Evaluate where your employees are in building new skills and taking on new challenges. See it as your job to keep people challenged and growing and learning. Give them special assignments that will require some stretch and growth on the job. When that assignment is complete, think of the next one which will do the same. By continually keeping employees challenged, you will have a more satisfied and productive work force.

30. Share out information on jobs that match employee abilities.

Some managers do not believe in career development. They want to hold on to their own employees and try to keep secret other job opportunities within the company. However, holding people back can be very dangerous. The employee may eventually move on their own to another company. And if that employee was talented, the loss is really tragic.

More progressive managers do not fear losing employees to another department within the company. They feel if the employee gets ahead and becomes more successful, both the employee and the company win, and the employee is likely to stay with the company. You should have this attitude as well. Share out information that will help your employees get ahead. Identify jobs at the company that you think match their interests and abilities, and encourage them to pursue the jobs if appropriate.

31. Cross train your staff.

Employees develop and learn a great deal from cross training. This is still yet another way to provide additional growth, learning, and development. It also is a way to broaden people out and test them in other possible jobs. Last, it can help you as a manager provide better coverage when someone is out ill or on vacation. Evaluate right now the degree of cross training which has occurred in your department. If very little or none, arrange for more to be done in this area. Figure out the best areas to cross train in, and set up some target dates to have the process completed. You need not set up formal training classes. Most employees are capable of training others on what they do with a little extra advice from you. Use cross training as another means to develop your staff.

Recommended Readings

Allenbaugh, G.E. Coaching . . . a Management Tool for a More Effective Work Performance. *Management Review*, May, 1983, 22, p. 21-26.

Cover, William H. Curbstone Coaching. *Training and Development Journal*, Nov, 1980, p. 33-35.

DeBoard, Robert. *Counseling People at Work*. Brookfield, VT: Gower Publishing Company, 1983.

Geber, Beverly. From Manager Into Coach. *Training*, February, 1992, 25-31.

Fournies, F.F. *Coaching for Improved Work Performance*. New York: McGraw-Hill, 1978.

Gilley, Jerry W., and Moore, Herff L. Managers as Career Enhancers. *The Personnel Administrator*, March, 1986, 51-59.

Goodale, James G. *The Fine Art of Interviewing*. Englewood Cliffs, NJ: Prentice-Hall, 1982.

Gordon, Bonnie. Settling Conflicts Among Your Workers. *Nation's Business*, March, 1988, 76, p. 70-71.

Hersey, Paul. *The Situational Leader: The Other 59 Minutes*. New York: Warner Books, 1985.

Hill, N.C. *Counseling at the Workplace*. New York: McGraw-Hill, 1981.

Kinlaw, Dennis. *Coaching for Commitment*. San Diego: University Associates, 1989.

Kirkpatrick, Donald L. *How to Improve Performance Through Appraisal and Coaching*. New York: AMACOM, 1982.

Meckel, Nelson T. The Manager as Career Counselor. *Training and Development*, July, 1981, p. 65-69.

Shore, Lynn McFarlane, and Bloom, Arthur J. Developing Employees Through Coaching and Career Development. *Personnel*, Aug, 1986, 63, p. 34-40.

Stowell, Steven, and Starcevich, Matt M. *The Coach: Creating Partnerships for a Competitive Edge*. Salt Lake City, UT: The Center for Management and Organization Effectiveness, 1987.

Thompson, Brad Lee. An Early Review of Peer Review. *Training*, July, 1991, 42-46.

Tolbert, E.L. *Counseling for Career Development*. Boston: Houghton Mifflin, 1980.

28

Team Building

This chapter helps improve performance in the following areas:

- Building a department team.
- Getting more cooperation and assistance between employees.
- Having group versus individual efforts.
- Building a sense of common goals amongst employees.

Action Items for Team Building

1. Focus on the group, not individuals.

Some managers, out of habit, do not focus on the entire group of individuals in the department. They typically have one-on-one discussions with employees, be it about goals, changes, problems, or other issues. Obviously, there are cases where the discussion is relevant for just one person, but there are many others when the entire group should be involved. You should review how often you, as a manager, focus on the group versus individuals. If you do not have a group perspective, change your outlook right now. Think of the "big picture" in your department and how the work of individuals relates to others, and how the department relates to the company. Having this perspective is an essential starting point in building a team.

2. Hold periodic staff meetings.

This sounds very basic, but many managers fail to realize the team-building potential that staff meetings have. As the meeting leader, you should focus the meeting on larger issues that pertain to all present. Get their involvement and ideas on these issues. Summarize the department's activities such as budget performance, goal attainment, and emphasize how everyone contributes to the success of the department. Have individual members summarize the work they are doing in their individual areas. The purpose of this will be to broaden the understanding of others and make them aware of how each individual contributes to the department's overall mission. Department staff meetings need not be boring, but can be a lively means of doing team building.

3. Use group goals.

Some managers use only individual goals for members of the department. Each employee is individually accountable for achieving certain goals. There are no goals that are worked on jointly by more than one person. While this is fine for individual accountability, it does not to promote teamwork between employees in the department. In fact, they could even be working against each other to accomplish their individual goals.

A more effective practice is to use a mix of individual and group goals. Hold two or more employees jointly accountable for achieving a particular goal, with both equally sharing the success or failure of goal accomplishment. By using some group goals, your staff will be forced to work with each other, get to know each other better, and evolve into a team. We are not advocating that all goals be group goals, but that some be assigned this way with others under the sole responsibility of an individual. Try using more group goals if you have not done so to date.

4. Build the interpersonal skills of your department.

The ability of employees to work together is a function of their **opportunity** to work together and their **interpersonal skills.** By assigning some group goals, you can take care of the opportunity issue. As for interpersonal skills, some additional work may be required. Employees vary tremendously in interpersonal skills. Many can use additional training and assistance in this area. Where this is the case for members of your department, take some initiative to help employees build these skills. Read and have employees apply the ideas in the chapter on interpersonal skills in this book. Find seminars or training courses on interpersonal skills and send one or more members of your department. Keep emphasizing harmony and working together among team members. By building better interpersonal skills in your department, you can build a more effective team.

5. Use cross training amongst your employees.

Some employees focus on their own immediate area to the exclusion of others. This can be due to anything from simple pride to turf problems. When employees are overly focused on their own area, it is difficult for team building to occur. There may be too little knowledge about, or interest in, what other members of the department are doing.

If this problem exists in your department, think of doing more cross training. This need not result in permanent job change, but merely that employees get to know and be able to handle the jobs of their co-workers. By doing this, you will be able to have employees fill in more easily when vacations or illness occur. More importantly, your employees will develop a deeper sense of appreciation and understanding of what their co-workers do. This will result in more teamwork.

6. Train your employees to do peer coaching.

In many organizations, the only person to do performance coaching in the department is the manager. This places a great burden on the manager, particularly in departments where the manager has many direct reports. More progressive companies are now utilizing peer coaching to supplement coaching done by the manager. In peer coaching, employees at the same job level give feedback to each other and may help train and develop each other.

Probably the most important thing to do to make peer coaching work is to ensure that this is the responsibility of every employee. Right now in many companies, employees do not see it as their role to provide feedback or coach a co-worker. Building an understanding that this is a part of the job is a starting point. Next, the manager needs to see that employees have skills at providing feedback in a professional way, and can provide basic training of a co-worker. Peer coaching can go a long way toward building a team amongst your employees.

7. Develop broader jobs and job descriptions.

One of the most aggravating things in building teamwork is to hear an employee say, "It's not my job." This runs completely counter to what a team is supposed to be in helping each other out. One of the contributing factors to this feeling is narrow job responsibilities and narrow job descriptions. Employees who perceive their jobs as narrow are not likely to want to help others out. As a manager you should evaluate the narrowness of your job descriptions since this could be contributing to the "it's not my job" syndrome.

If your jobs are narrowly defined, broaden them out more. Make the jobs more "generalist" oriented. Tell people, either verbally or in writing, that it is a part of their job to help others out and provide coverage. We are not suggesting that this be taken to extremes by having everyone do everything in the department, but that the error is usually in too much narrowness. Try to broaden out your department's jobs as a means of increasing teamwork.

8. Have away-from-work social events.

Team building can also be done away from work when employees are more likely to be relaxed and open. There are many social events that you can schedule together such as picnics, baseball games, luncheons, and trips to zoos. A growing outing for employees in the workplace is "adventure learning." This involves groups of employees climbing small mountains, rafting, taking a desert hike, or mastering tough physical challenges together. As an outcome of the adventure learning, the employees learn that cooperation and assistance—working as a team—made the difference in conquering the challenge. This can then be extended to teamwork back on the job. Plan out the appropriate social event for your department as a means of building a stronger team.

9. Link bonuses and profit-sharing to team success.

In some companies there are bonuses or profit-sharing plans for non-managers. The more effective programs link the amount of financial reward to a department's success (or some combination of department and company success). If at all possible, you should investigate the use of some type of reward for team success in your department. In particular, look for a group reward to add to individual rewards if these are used. When employees share common goals together, and share rewards based upon the attainment of those goals, a new sense of camaraderie and teamwork will evolve. Think of group financial rewards in your department as a means of building teamwork.

10. Use team problem solving.

All companies face their share of problem-solving opportunities. For some, only the managers have their say in solving the problem. Others involve managers and a select number of employees. Still others use team problem solving, where entire work areas or departments have a say in solving the problem. The latter approach permits the group to work together and do team building. You should evaluate the use of team problem solving in your department or area. This does not mean that every employee has to be involved in solving every problem, but that on occasion you involve groups of people to solve problems. Not only will you likely get a large number of ideas and group commitment to carry out the ideas, but a team of people will emerge who know how to work well together.

11. Keep your team balanced.

In many teams, certain individuals will emerge as leaders. While this is normal and desirable, in some cases it can produce resentment, competition, or feelings of not having a say in matters. As a manager, you should ensure that there is balance in your teams. Do not let one person dominate and control others. Alternate team leader positions if feasible. Draw out quieter, more shy employees to make sure that their ideas are heard and listened to in team projects. Rotate team members so that employees have a chance to work with others and learn from them. By balancing and controlling your team, you can ensure that the team remains solid and effective.

12. Let groups make some decisions on their own.

Teams become more effective when they have a sense of controlling their own fate. Team members realize that what they decide and implement will affect them rather than just passing on recommendations to someone else. As a manager, you should evaluate how often you delegate a decision to a group of your employees. If not at all or infrequent, try to do this a bit more often. Let the team have the authority to decide the outcome within certain parameters (e.g., costs) that you give them. This feeling of being able to do something important will heighten the teamwork and feeling of accomplishment among the team members.

13. Make teamwork part of everyone's performance appraisal.

Many performance appraisal systems allow for appraising employees on job knowledge, skills and abilities. If teamwork is an important objective for you, you will want to include teamwork on everyone's performance appraisal. In this way, there will be a clear understanding that working together effectively is a part of everyone's job, and that appraisal ratings (and perhaps salary increases) are partially dependent on teamwork. Measuring teamwork on your performance appraisal system will reinforce the idea that teamwork is important to the department's success. Think of changing your performance appraisal system if necessary to reflect teamwork.

14. Build a common culture and values.

Teams develop a sense of teamness by having common goals, values, and purpose—a common culture. We discussed earlier how to use common goals, but there are other common team elements that need to be addressed as well. Start by defining the mission for your department—what the department does, why it is there, how it relates to the rest of the company. Involve other members of the department as appropriate in defining the culture.

Next, define the values of the department or work area. For example, what is important to be accomplished in your area? What are the priorities? What do you want the department to be known for? After you have defined these culture items, communicate them to your employees as well as the department goals. Reinforce the culture in your staff meetings and one-on-one discussions. When the department understands and supports the common culture, they can work as a unified team to attain the elements in the culture. Make defining the culture a key part of your team building efforts.

15. Link the department's activities to larger company goals.

A team's sense of importance is increased when the members see their activities as related to larger company goals. As a manager, you are in the best position to relate your department's work to larger company goals. Take the time to write out the link between your department and larger company goals if you need to. Then communicate this to your staff on an ongoing basis. Make them feel that the work that they do is important to the success of the company, and helps the company attain its goals for the year. By communicating this link, you can build a stronger sense of pride and teamwork amongst your employees.

16. Avoid playing favorites.

Some managers have an open favoritism to certain members of the staff. In some cases, this might be due to a personal liking and in other cases due to the fact that this employee gets results. While favoritism is understandable, it can be derisive to getting employees to work as part of a team. Team members may be resistant to the fact that one member is getting more attention than they are. Evaluate whether you show any favoritism in your department. You need to eliminate any favoritism should it now exist, particularly the kind that is based on a mere liking of someone else. Try to "spread around" favoritism by relying on the expertise of certain people. Perhaps one staff member is your numbers expert, another your problem solver, another who handles complaints best, etc. If you must push assignments in certain directions, at least make sure that everyone is getting an equal distribution. Keep a check on favoritism to keep the department team's morale up.

17. Focus on cooperation versus competition.

Some managers run the department on a very competitive basis. For example, an employee might be encouraged to "outsell all of the other representatives" or to "work harder than anyone else." While this can help motivate some people, it can also ruin team efforts since co-workers will be seen as competitors who must be beaten to attain the goal. Take a look at your department to see if you have unintentionally fostered a competitive spirit with your employees against each other.

The better approach is to focus on cooperation versus competition. Use words and goals that emphasize working together, reaching consensus, assisting, and being on the same team. If you appeal to the competitive spirit, make the competition another company, not competition within your own company. This will result in a stronger team.

18. Keep the communication flowing to all team members.

To have a department team feel like a department team there needs to be an open sharing of information. Holding back memos, reports, articles, and other materials can make employees feel that there is a "we-they" situation in the department. This can also hamper team efforts to solve problems and attain goals if employees do not know what the problems and goals are. As a manager you are in a key position to control information flow within the department. Try to think of who else would benefit from information that comes your way. Encourage employees to do the same with information that they obtain. The free flow of information can assist in making the team feel there are no secrets and they are all in it together.

19. Make use of job rotation.

Employees can sometimes become overly focused on their own job if they stay in that same job for a long period of time. They may tend to think of themselves as an island and not as part of a team. Job rotation can be a valuable solution to this problem. Not only will employees broaden out and get a breath of fresh air, but rotation can also help with department coverage when someone is absent. While you should never force someone to rotate into another job, bring up the issue with appropriate employees in your department. The rotation need not be permanent, but can be an assignment of several weeks or months. As a result of knowing and working another co-worker's job, your employees will appreciate more of the different roles and how they fit together to make up the department team.

20. Initiate team building training classes.

Another way to build a stronger team among employees is to have them participate in formal training in the team building area. There are commercially available programs in this area which can be done on the outside or brought in-house. You can also custom-design your own programs if feasible. There are many topics that can be covered in team building training. Some of the more common ones are:

- Peer coaching.
- Recognizing and rewarding the performance of a co-worker.
- How to conduct on-the-job training.
- Group dynamics.
- Interpersonal skills.
- Communications skills.
- Group problem solving skills.

Examine the usefulness of courses like these for your department. Remember though, that you must provide support for the skills back on the job and practice the skills yourself. Formal classroom training can help your employees build the skills necessary to function as an effective team. Use this training if you can.

21. Arrange the work area for more easy interactions.

Team building can be difficult if employees are very isolated from each other. This can make day-to-day interactions a challenge, if not impossible. Take a close look at how you department is physically arranged. Is there any way you can change the arrangement to make it easier for employees to see and communicate with each other? If so, discuss alternative space arrangements with your staff. Preserve privacy so people can work on their own where needed, but make it easier for employees to have access to each other's work area. The physical arrangement of the work space can assist in building the team concept.

Recommended Readings

Adair, John. *Effective Teambuilding*. Brookfield, VT: Gower Publishing Company, 1986.

Carr, Clay. *Team Power: Lessons from America's Top Companies on Putting Team Power to Work*. Englewood Cliffs, NJ: Prentice-Hall, 1992.

Galagan, Patricia. Work Teams That Work. *Training and Development Journal*, Nov, 1986, p. 33-35.

Galagan, Patricia. Between Two Trapezes. *Training and Development*, Mar, 1987, p. 40-50.

Guest, Robert H. *Work Teams and Team Building*. New York: Pergamon Press, 1986.

Hardaker, Maurice, and Ward, Bryan K. How to Make a Team Work. *Harvard Business Review*, Nov-Dec, 1987, 65, p. 112-117.

Katzenbach, Jon and Smith, Douglas. *The Wisdom of Teams: Creating the High Performance Organization*. Boston, MA: Harvard Business School Press, 1994.

Kayser, Thomas A. *Building Team Power: How to Unleash the Collaborative Genius of Work Teams*. Burr Ridge, IL: Irwin, 1994.

Kilmann, Ralph H. and Kilmann, Innes. *Making Organizations Competitive: Enhancing Networks and Relationships Across Traditional Boundaries*. San Francisco, Jossey-Bass, 1991.

Littlejohn, Robert F. Team Management: A How-to Approach to Improved Productivity, Higher Morale, and Lasting Job Satisfaction. *Management Review*, Jan, 1982, p. 23-28.

Long, Janet. The Wilderness Lab Comes of Age. *Training and Development*, Mar, 1987, p. 30-39.

Mahoney, Francis X. Team Development, Part 1: What is TD? Why Use It? *Personnel Journal*, Sept-Oct, 1981, 58, p. 13-24.

Mahoney, Francis X. Team Development, Part 2: How to Select the Appropriate TD Approach. *Personnel Journal*, Nov-Dec, 1981, 58, p. 21-38.

Mahoney, Francis X. Team Development, Part 3: Communication Meetings. *Personnel Journal*, Jan-Feb, 1982, 59, p. 49-58.

Mahoney, Francis X. Team Development, Part 4: Work Meetings. *Personnel Journal*, March-April, 1982, 59, p. 45-55.

Mahoney, Francis X. Team development: Its Role in the Work Place. *Personnel Journal*, Sept-Oct, 1982, 59, p. 52-59.

McCan, Dick and Margerison, Charles. Managing High Performance Teams. *Training and Development*, November, 1989, p. 52-60.

Orsbun, Jack; Moran, Linda; Musselwhite, Ed; and Zenger, John. *Self-Directed Work Teams: The New American Challenge*. Homewood, IL: Business One Irwin, 1990.

Schermerborn, John R. Team Development for High Performance Management. *Training and Development*, Nov, 1986, p. 38-41.

Strong, Graham. Taking the Helm of Leadership. *Training and Development*, June, 1986, p. 43-45.

Varney, Glenn H. *Building Productive Teams*. San Francisco: Jossey-Bass, 1989.

Wellins, Richard; Byham, William C.; and Wilson, Jeanne. *Empowered Teams: Creating Self-Directed Work Groups*. San Francisco: Jossey-Bass, 1991.

29

Motivating and Inspiring

This chapter helps improve performance in the following areas:

- Motivating employees to do more.
- Attaining better department productivity results.
- Improving job satisfaction amongst employees.
- Recognizing and rewarding good performance.

Action Items for Motivating and Inspiring

1. Use praise effectively.

Praise for a job well done is perhaps the simplest, and yet most neglected, of all rewards that can be given to employees. It is very common with time pressures in the workplace for managers to forget to praise someone for attaining good results. Or for managers to simply say "thanks" when a few more words would have been appropriate. Every employee likes to hear praise—it's a reward we can never get too much of, but can easily get too little of. As a manager, you should evaluate your use of praise with your employees. Do you use praise as often as you should when your employees deserve it?

In addition to giving praise often, you must give it effectively. Some simple guidelines for giving praise are as follows:

1. Decide the exact form the praise will take (e.g., verbal, letter, award).

2. Give praise for specific incidents (rather than general praise).

3. Link the incidents being praised to department and company goals.

4. Express confidence that the employee can carry out the behavior again.

The use of these guidelines, and giving praise when due, will serve as an excellent motivator for your employees. Keep track of your efforts in this area, keeping a scorecard if necessary.

2. Set the proper example for your employees.

Some managers want their employees to work long hours, yet leave early on their own. Or they want people to be very ethical, yet do not set a good example themselves. This contradiction is easily seen by employees. Not only does the manager set a bad example, but may also be seen as hypocritical. You need to ensure that you never fall into this trap with your work behavior.

Evaluate how good of an example you set for your employees. Do you work long hours? Do you have minimal downtime (long lunches, breaks, trips to health club) on company time? Are you honest? Do you play politics or steer business to friends or associates? Do you ever remove any company property? If your ethics are not perfect, how can you expect your employees to be any better? Set the proper example by having impeccable ethics and work behavior on the job.

3. Set high standards.

Some managers set low standards or no standards at all for their employees. Other managers set high standards and expectations for their employees, and as a result, attain better results. The expectations set by managers have a dramatic affect on employees. Expect and demand a great deal and you will get it. Expect and demand little or nothing and you will get that too.

As a manager you need to evaluate the types of standards and expectations that you set for your employees. If your standards are not very high, then increase them. Demand, in a nice way, higher quality results and higher quantity results and perform in concert with this yourself. Employees look to a manager to set the tone and style of the department. Their motivation will be directly influenced by the standards you set. Make certain your standards are high ones.

4. Link pay increases to performance.

Pay is but one motivational source for employees, and a source that is perhaps over-emphasized. Yet managers should try to get the most motivational impact out of pay as possible since many employees will respond to pay as a motivator. Pay increase systems need to be linked to performance in some direct way, such as a certain performance appraisal rating translating to a certain percentage of salary increase. If your company does not link salary increases to performance, do what you can to encourage this. If pay cannot be linked to performance because of contractual or other issues, then go to the other action items in this chapter.

For those companies that can link pay to performance, this needs to be strongly communicated to your employees. This can be done through memos or guidelines sent to your employees. More importantly, as a manager you need to communicate this link to your employees every time you give out salary increases. Tell employees that the increase was due, all or in part, to the performance rating that they attained. Also explain that higher ratings translate to larger increases within the guidelines that you have to work with. You can emphasize these ideas throughout the year on an ongoing basis. In this way, you will help motivate those who look to pay increases as a source of motivation.

5. Appeal to the individual motives of your staff.

Any project or assignment that an employee works on can serve as a source of motivation. In fact, there are many motives that can be fulfilled with the same project. For example, say you have a project to revise the policies in your area. To successfully complete this project will require research and analysis, writing, working with senior managers, growth, learning, and persuasive skills in selling the final product. This project, like any other, can appeal to different motives depending on how you present it to an employee.

Effective managers present projects and assignments to their staffs keeping in mind the motives of the particular employee. For example, employees who like research and analysis could have the policy project presented to them with that in mind. Status-conscious employees who like to interact with senior managers could have the same project presented to them with that in mind. We are not suggesting that managers deceive employees, but that they merely highlight the project's potential to fulfill the motives of that employee. Similarly, you should appeal to the unique motives of your staff in giving out job assignments.

6. Give credit to your staff where it is due.

Some managers are more than happy to take the credit for the work of their staff. For example, one employee may have worked long and hard on a project only to have the manager receive the praise for it. The manager might fail to inform others of the employee's contribution, or fail to forward compliments to the employee. As a result, employees feel that their work was not recognized and they are less motivated going forward.

As a manager, you should evaluate how effectively you give credit to your staff. Do you present the work of staff members by recognizing who did what or do you merely present it yourself? Do you pass compliments along to those who really deserve them when they are given to you? Effective managers will always give credit to their staffs. In fact, they may go out of their way to see that employees are recognized for their achievements and do not worry about their own egos. That is a style you should have as well. Give credit where credit is due to keep your staff highly motivated.

7. Implement a short-term reward system.

One problem with financial reward systems is that they cannot be given out very often, in the case of pay increases perhaps once a year. That is a long time to expect employees to sustain motivation without any reward. Of course, there are many other kinds of rewards that are discussed in other parts of this chapter, but one set that we want to think of now are short-term financial rewards. Many managers try to make these available to augment other financial rewards such as pay increases. Short-term financial rewards include items such as the following:

- A "night-on-the-town" (movie, dinner, etc.).

- Tickets to theatre, football game, or other event.

- Gift certificate.

- Small cash award.

- Gift such as crystal or clock.

As a manager try to use short-term rewards as a means of recognizing your employees. If an employee does a fine job on a challenging project, give out the reward right then and there. It will come as an unexpected surprise, and help sustain motivation toward other projects and responsibilities. Short-term rewards are an excellent means of helping motivate and inspire employees.

8. Continually stretch employees.

Employees are usually motivated by some new challenge, a challenge which involves learning, growing, developing, and doing something different. The problem is that many employees get into a rut by doing the same activities over and over, and the manager does not work to change the situation. As a manager you should look at your use of stretch activities for your employees. Are you content to let employees merely do more of the same or does each of your employees continually get challenged? Make an effort to stretch employees continually, taking into consideration their skills and learning level so that they do not get in over their heads. Stretch projects will make work exciting and different all of the time and serve as an excellent source of motivation.

9. Institute an employee of the month campaign.

This action item may seem a bit basic, but it can still be an effective motivator. Employees enjoy being recognized for their accomplishments, and seeing your name in the newspaper or posted in the hallway can be a great source of pride. Effective employee of the month campaigns tie in the selection with key elements in the company culture. For example, if a key element in the company culture is to provide excellent customer service, then the employee of the month may be that person who best provided service. Of course there may be many items in the culture beyond service, but the point is to link the award to company culture rather than give it for "outstanding service," which is vaguely defined. Implement an employee of the month campaign at your company (or division if it is large enough) and take advantage of this additional source of motivation.

10. Trust and believe that employees want to work hard.

Some managers create their own problems with regard to employee motivation. They believe that employees cannot be trusted and do not want to work hard and they manage with this in mind. Other managers feel people can be trusted and do want to work hard. They, in turn, delegate more and their employees perform at a higher level in return for being trusted and treated as professionals. The initial beliefs of the manager cause employees to behave in a certain way.

You should assess for the moment your management beliefs and trust. When a new employee calls in sick, do you trust them or do you think they might not really be ill? Do you trust your employees to work hard when you are away or do you think they will loaf? Your employees become what you believe they are. Get on the positive cycle, if you are not there now, by believing in your employees and showing trust. It will result in harder work and motivation.

11. Encourage employee ownership in the company.

Employees identify with a company more strongly when they feel they own a piece of the company. This can lead to greater motivation to work hard and see the company be successful. Leading companies try to encourage their employees to own a part of the company. This is accomplished through stock ownership, profit sharing or some other similar plan. Evaluate whether your company promotes employee ownership or profit sharing amongst **all** employees. If not, set up programs to encourage more active participation by the employees. This can increase their psychological identification with the company, and be a source of motivation since it is **our** company, not **your** company.

12. Treat your staff as professionals and give them meaningful assignments.

Some managers lament about the lack of employee motivation, yet may be the source of the problem. Employees work hardest and best when they are given responsible assignments, when they feel challenged and treated like professionals and responsible adults. If they are given repetitive tasks over and over again, with all of the "fun stuff" reserved for the manager, then motivation will wane. The solution is to change the treatment of employees. As a manager you should treat your employees as responsible professionals who can carry out meaningful assignments. This is regardless of the employee's education, job title, or length of experience. Try to broaden the jobs of your employees, and delegate part of your activities to them. This will not only create a source of motivation for the employees, but enable you to free up more time for yourself.

13. Use a variety of non-monetary rewards.

Some managers erroneously conclude that the only thing employees care about is money. While everyone needs to earn money, there are many other types of rewards as well. Under this action item, we would like to discuss other material rewards (psychological rewards are discussed in other places). One effective material reward is a letter of commendation for effective employee job performance. Such a letter might be sent to the employee's boss, senior managers, or placed in the employee's file. While the importance is more psychological than material, it is important in that there is a long-lasting physical memento of a job well done. Similarly, many effective managers drop employees handwritten notes of a job well done, and more than one employee has saved these to look at in the future. Plaques or certificates are other rewards that are a source of pride for employees as well. Think of adding these non-monetary rewards to your system to provide recognition and to help motivate outstanding job performance.

14. Build a sense of accomplishment in your staff.

It seems so obvious that employees should feel a sense of accomplishment when completing a particular job. Yet many employees feel that they are merely doing tasks and do not get a sense of accomplishment from their work. That is one of the most important responsibilities for a manager, building a sense of achievement in your staff. Take the time to assess whether you do this right now. Do you make comments to your staff reflecting how proud they should feel about their accomplishments or how their work contributes to company success? Make more comments to this effect if you are not doing so now.

You need not build this sense of accomplishment daily or even weekly, but at least once a month make some comment about how good the employee should feel about what they just accomplished. And how this accomplishment helps the company to be more successful. You role in communicating this sense of accomplishment is very critical to sustaining employee motivation at a high level.

15. Understand what motivates each member of your staff.

Employees differ in what motivates them. Some might be very receptive to praise; others might value most a surprise award like a night on the town. There are many other sources as well, as suggested in other parts of this chapter. The important point is that you, as a manager, need to know and understand what motivates your employees. Take the time to write this out on paper if you have not already done so. If you are uncertain, simply ask your employees what makes them feel good about working—what motivates them each day. Once you understand the motivation sources for each employee, you can try to make these motivators available to them. Of course, you need not restrict yourself to just one motivator, but can use multiple ones based upon the employees preferences. Knowing what motivates each member of your staff is a big step toward motivating them on an ongoing basis.

16. Provide support for your staff.

Many employees are motivated to execute their responsibilities, but get bogged down along the way. They run into a company policy, an uncooperative co-worker, a lack of resources, or some other problem. The roadblock drains their motivation. Evaluate whether you have motivated employees who express frustration at getting the job done. If this is the case, you need to clear a path and provide support for your staff.

As a manager, you should have the ability to open doors for your employees. You may be able to persuade an uncooperative colleague to be more helpful, escalate the need to revise a company policy, or make additional resources available. At the very least, you should become a "cheerleader" in encouraging the employee to keep on trying despite the initial difficulties. This role of providing support for your staff is essential for them to sustain the motivation that they have.

17. Implement a system of goals and objective.

Employee motivation is best directed at specific targets rather than vague ideas. For example, a goal of increasing sales to $1.5 MM per year is much more targeted than telling someone to work harder or work smarter. If your department does not have a system of goals and objectives right now, think of changing over to one. It makes no difference if this is a formal system such as MBO's or an informal one where you list out targets at the beginning of the year. The point is to give the employee specific areas to work toward accomplishing. This will enable them to focus their attention and their motivation in a specific direction. The net result will be a greater achievement than with no specific targets. Use goals and objectives as another means of motivating your staff, regardless of their jobs or level in the organization.

18. Build a strong team spirit.

A department can be inspired to accomplish more when there is a strong team spirit, where employees feel that others will help them out and the entire group wins. That team spirit has to be built by the manager of the department. Evaluate whether or not a team spirit has evolved in your department. If not, initiate some team building efforts on your own. Read the chapter in this book on team building and apply the ideas to your department. Ensure that there is a sense of group identity and that employees help each other out in working toward common goals. When this "esprit de corps" evolves, it can help generate additional motivation on the part of each team member.

19. Link individual and group goals to larger company goals.

If you are using a system with goals and objectives, it is helpful to link those goals and objectives to larger company goals. This "linking pin" concept must be done by the manager, the person who is in the best position to know what else is going on in the company. The basic way to make the link is to first communicate to the staff the company goals for the year, then those goals for the business unit and department. The individual employee goals are then linked with the department activities, and in turn, linked to the rest of the company.

As an example, the company might have a goal to increase sales by twenty percent in the coming year. A human resources recruiter might have a goal to hire twenty new sales representatives in the first six months of the year. After a formal link is made between company and individual goals, managers should verbally reinforce the idea as the year progresses. Linking individual and group goals to larger company goals is an excellent way to emphasize the importance of the goal and build employee motivation.

20. Establish a culture and vision for your department.

Employee motivation and inspiration is greatly affected by the culture and vision that are defined for a department. The culture and vision tell employees where the department is going, what the key goals are, the values, priorities, and "niche" that the department has in the company. Also defined are the mission, the purpose, and the services that the department is to be know for. The manager must have a key role in defining and communicating the culture and vision for the department. No one else can take on this role. Have you developed a culture and vision for your department?

If not, make this a personal goal. It helps if the culture and vision are written down so employees can refer to them on an ongoing basis, but verbal reinforcement is needed as well. Make defining these items one way that you use to inspire your staff.

21. Give employees more responsibility and autonomy.

Employee motivation can often be affected by the amount of responsibility and autonomy in the job, particularly for employees who feel they are not being challenged. It is increasingly common for employees in all types of jobs to want to be able to control the pace of work, to make decisions on their own, and to have freedom in how to carry out the job. Managers who reserve all of these activities for themselves will find their staffs bored, uninspired, and not motivated. The fault lies not in the employee, but in job design. Review how much responsibility, autonomy, and decision making authority you have given your staff. If not much, work on increasing this. The net result can relieve some of the administrative burden from you, and be a source of motivation for your employees.

22. Open up communications.

Some departments run in a very secretive way. Not much information gets shared beyond the manager level. This can make employees suspicious and uncertain of what is going on in the company and can stifle motivation. The fact is, there are many things going on in every company that employees should be aware of. When successes are attained such as key sales, everyone can feel inspired by knowing that the company is going to be more successful.

Even problems can be a source of inspiration. When employees know of a problem, they will often work toward solving the problem even if the manager does not ask them to do so. The difficulty results when managers hide the problem or feel that they are the only person who can solve it. In running your department, use open communications. Share out information that comes your way with others, be the information good or bad. Recognize that being in-formed makes employees feel like a part of the team and can in-spire them to do more.

23. Increase employee self-esteem.

Some employees are not motivated to work hard because they have low self-esteem. They lack confidence in themselves, do not feel they have good skills and abilities, or do not believe they can suc-ceed. With this type of attitude, it is no wonder that they are not motivated to achieve much. As a manager, you need to be attuned to these signs in any of your employees. If you recognize it, try to build up the employee's self-esteem. Note activities that they do well and provide feedback in this area. Encourage them to stretch themselves a bit further and take on new responsibilities. When they succeed in this area, be certain to provide reinforcement. By gradually building the employees self-esteem, you will increase their confidence and motivation.

24. Show pride in your staff's work.

Some managers fail to bang the drum for their staff. They spend very little time, if any, citing the achievements of their staff to others. As a result, the staff may feel neglected, unappreciated, and not motivated. Reflect back on how often you speak out favorably about your staff. How often do you mention their achievements to your boss or other managers? Do you champion their ideas? Express pride in them in staff meetings or other situations? Do more here if you can. For the pride you show in your staff can make them feel in-spired and appreciated by others. You are a great deal more likely to work diligently, even on boring work, if you know that somebody up there notices and recognizes your good work. Show pride in your staff whenever you can.

Recommended Readings

Bardwick, Judith M. If One of Your Employees Has Plateaued. *Managing Solutions*, Dec, 1986, 31, p. 4-10.

Bradford, David L., and Cohen, Allan R. *Managing for Excellence: The Guide to Developing High Performance in Contemporary Organizations*. New York: Wiley, 1987.

Clark, Charles H. *Idea Management: How to Motivate Creativity and Innovation*. New York: AMACOM, 1980.

Grant, Philip C. *Employee Motivation: Principles and Practices*. New York: Vantage Press, 1984.

Herzberg, Frederick. One More Time: How Do You Motivate Employees? *Harvard Business Review*, Sept-Oct, 1987, 65, p. 109-120.

Hickman, Craig R. and Silva, Michael A. *Creating Excellence: Managing Corporate Culture, Strategy and Change in the New Age*. New York: New American Library, 1985.

Kouzes, James M. and Posner, Barry Z. *The Leadership Challenge: How Get Extraordinary Things Done in Organizations*. San Francisco: Jossey-Bass, 1987.

Kravetz, Dennis J. *The Human Resources Revolution: Implementing Progressive Management Practices for Bottom-Line Success*. San Francisco: Jossey-Bass, 1988.

Lawler, Edward E. III. *High Involvement Management*. San Francisco: Jossey-Bass, 1987.

Lehrer, Sande. Motivating Subordinates: Making It Work. *Bureaucrat*, Summer, 1986, 15, p. 49-52.

Nelson, Bob. *1001 Ways to Reward Employees*. New York: Workman Publishing, 1994.

Quick, Thomas L. *The Manager's Motivation Desk Book*. New York: Wiley, 1985.

Rodgers, Buck. *Getting the Best Out of Yourself and Others*. New York: Harper & Row, 1987.

Rosenbaum, Bernard L. *How to Motivate Today's Workers: Motivational Models for Managers and Supervisors*. New York: McGraw-Hill, 1982.

Tissue, Gayle L. Empowering the Secretarial Workforce. *Personnel*, March, 1986, 65, p. 50-54.

Ulrich, Robert A. *Motivation Methods that Work*. Englewood Cliffs, NJ: Prentice-Hall, 1981.

Ziglar, Zig. *Top Performance*. New York: Berkley Books, 1982.

30

Delegating

This chapter helps improve performance in the following areas:

- Making the best use of staff.

- Developing staff to fullest potential.

- Avoiding doing too much individually.

- Freeing up management time for planning, organizing, and people management.

- Making management style compatible with flat organizations.

Action Items for Delegating

1. Delegate responsibility, not just the task.

Some managers think that they are delegating to employees when they delegate a task to someone. These managers may reserve all decision making for themselves but merely let the employee gather some information in their behalf. Technically speaking, this is delegating, but it is not all that there is to delegation. For employees will grow, learn, and ultimately be able to better assist the manager only by having **responsibility** delegated to them.

Examine your actions when you delegate to someone on your staff. Do you delegate only the task, or both the responsibility and the task? Develop your employees more fully and make a better use of your time by delegating both responsibility and the task when appropriate. Recognize that this is what delegation is really all about, not merely giving the employee a task to do.

2. Trust your staff to carry out delegated assignments.

Some managers are reluctant to delegate to their staff because they do not trust the staff. They feel the employees do not have the skills, initiative, or traits to do the assignment, and therefore they do the assignment themselves. While it is always possible that this is true, in many cases it reflects that the manager does not want to delegate to others, or is reluctant to train the staff to handle the assignment. The problem is more with the manager than with the staff.

If you have a lack of trust in certain members of your staff, list out the reasons why you feel this way. Are the reasons objective and valid or merely guesses and opinions? Are your reasons based on recent experiences or dated information? If the trust issue is due more to you than the employee, change your attitude and give the employee a chance. If the trust is due to a problem with skills, motivation, etc., then work on changing this so you can delegate to the employee. Get to the point where you have trust in each member of your staff.

3. Delegate only tasks for new employees.

It was mentioned in the first action item that delegation ultimately involves delegating the responsibility to an employee as well as the task. There can, however, be exceptions to the rule. Exceptions might include new or inexperienced employees who are not familiar with the department or the job. While delegating responsibility all at once can be a great way to learn, it might make the employee feel uncomfortable when they are new.

When delegating to a new employee who is inexperienced, start by just delegating the task. Assess how quickly they learn and are ready to take on more. You may be able to broaden them into taking on the responsibility as well as the task within a short period of time. Move them as fast as you can without creating too much anxiety. Most employees today will like to have the increased responsibility early on.

4. Involve others in decision making.

Some managers reserve all decisions for themselves. They are reluctant to delegate decision making to either individuals or groups of employees. As a result, their staffs never get to develop decision making skills, and decision making quality may suffer since only one person, the manager, is involved in making decisions. A more effective approach today is to involve many of the staff in making the decision. By doing so, the ideas of others can be added to the managers to produce a better quality decision. You can never be worse off by involving others in decision making, but can often gain other ideas that you did not think of yourself. Involve others in your decision making process.

5. Use group brainstorming techniques.

Problem solving is another activity that can be delegated to employees in the department. Rather than have the manager solve all problems personally, others are involved in the process as well. Group problem solving is best handled through the use of brainstorming techniques. After the problem is clearly defined, the entire group tries to come up with as many solutions as possible. None of these solutions is evaluated at this stage, but merely listed for all to see. After possible solutions have been exhausted, the group goes back to evaluate the suggested solutions and narrows down the list to the best alternatives. Fully involving your staff in problem solving will generate many more ideas than you could on your own. Use group brainstorming techniques where appropriate as another means of delegating and developing your staff.

6. Delegate important assignments, not just routine work.

Some managers are quick to say that they delegate all of the time, yet analyzing **what** they delegate yields some surprises. In these cases, the assignments delegated are routine information requests or other "busywork" that the manager does not want to be bothered with. The really important projects and assignments are all kept by the manager.

Assess not only how often you delegate, but what you delegate. If it is routine work you do not want to be bothered with, change your approach. You would not feel happy with this type of delegation and neither does your staff. Be willing to delegate a meaty project once in a while so the staff member can be challenged by it and learn from it. What you delegate to others is just as important as how often you delegate.

7. Match delegation to your employees.

For delegation to work really well, a manager needs to delegate according to the unique abilities of the staff. It may not be appropriate to delegate a particular project to just anyone on the staff, but rather someone who is suited for it. Give some thought to who is capable of handling a particular project before delegating it out. Consider delegating a project to more than one person on occasion, perhaps one employee who is an "expert'in the area and another who shows promise in the area but is inexperienced. By matching your delegation to employee skills, abilities, and knowledge, you are more likely to ensure successful completion.

8. Do not try to do it all on your own.

Some managers have the unrealistic expectation that they can do it all on their own. This includes the planning, organizing, people issues, administrative burdens, meetings, travel, and countless other things. As a result, some activities do not get done or they get done in a less than thorough way. It is unrealistic for any manager to do everything on their own, yet some try. The starting point toward being a good delegator is to first recognize that you cannot do it all by yourself, and it makes better sense to delegate some of the responsibility to your staff. Make sure that you have this attitude as well. Be willing to delegate in order to be a more effective manager.

9. Assess workloads when delegating.

It is tempting at times to delegate quickly without considering employee workloads. However, at times employees may be too busy to take on the delegated work. The net result is a project that does not get done, or gets done late. Before delegating to a member of your staff, assess how busy the person is. If the employee is quite busy, you may have to consider delegating to someone else or altering priorities for the employee so they can take on the new project. The important point is to know the workloads of your staff and to take this into consideration before delegating. Make sure that you are currently doing this.

10. Delegate more as you flatten or decentralize the company.

In recent years many companies have flattened the management hierarchy by taking out certain levels of management and increasing the number of direct reports to any manager. Similarly, many companies have decentralized by pushing out responsibilities to the field. If these organizations did not change their way of delegating, they could find the new structure does not work well. For example, when a given manager has more direct reports, he/she must delegate more or will be unable to get everything done. And you would not want to centralize decision making in a decentralized company, would you?

If your company has been through a flattening of the management hierarchy or done more decentralizing, take stock of delegation. Managers need to delegate even more than before under these circumstances to be effective. If you or your colleagues are not delegating thoroughly, change that right now. Delegating extensively must go hand in hand with flat or decentralized companies.

11. List out the activities you do that can be done by others.

It can be helpful to evaluate what you currently do to determine delegation possibilities. Start by listing all of the key activities that you do frequently, paying attention to those that come up time and time again. Which of these are **essential** for you to do given your unique skills and experience? Which could just as easily be delegated to someone else to free up time for your other activities.

For those activities that can be delegated, list out the appropriate employee(s), considering their skills, time, and other factors. Rather than dump all at once, take the time to train them to take on these new responsibilities. Present the new responsibilities as challenges and growth, not items you are trying to unload. You can be a more effective manager by understanding what you need to do personally and delegating other responsibilities to others.

12. Do not regard delegation as a loss of power.

Some managers are reluctant to delegate because they see delegation as a loss of power and control. They think they will be less valuable, or maybe even unneeded, if employees take on significant responsibilities. Actually, nothing could be further from the truth. Managers who delegate are still very much in control of the department. By delegating effectively they can spend more time on important tasks such as planning, and increase their success as managers. Delegating, rather than causing a loss in power, can actually increase power by increasing the manager's effectiveness. Ensure that you have no fears regarding delegation to others. See delegation as a smarter, more effective way for you to manage.

13. Improve employee abilities if you do not have confidence in the person.

Some managers may be reluctant to delegate due to a lack of confidence in some of their employees. They may correctly assess that a particular employee may not be capable of carrying out a certain task. However, unless the manager works to change the situation, this will turn into a vicious cycle. Because the employee lacks abilities, the task is not delegated, which prevents the employee from developing the abilities, which prevents. . .

The way to break out of this cycle is to provide the needed development for the employee. You need to make this happen for it cannot happen by itself. Coach and counsel with the employee and make resources available such as training so that they can develop the needed abilities. Once these abilities are present to some degree, show trust and confidence by delegating an assignment to the employee which will enable them to further develop their abilities. Do not let a lack of confidence or lack of abilities stop you from delegating. Take the necessary actions so your confidence in the individual is increased.

14. Use due dates for delegated work.

Managers need to maintain some control over work that is delegated. Without doing so, there is the danger that work may go unmonitored and not be completed as expected. The starting point for controlling delegated work is to make sure the assignment is clearly understood and that there is a target date for completion (unless the work is ongoing). If the assignment is lengthy, the manager and employee should work out the steps and resources needed to complete the assignment. As with other assignments, there should be check points to review what has been completed to date. By using due dates and other work planning procedures, delegated work is more likely to be carried out as desired. Make sure that you use these procedures.

15. Do not let "there's not enough time to train" prevent delegation.

Some managers do not delegate because they feel they do not have the time to train someone to do the task. While this might be a good reason for one-time projects that are complex in nature, it is not a good reason for recurring work. When the task is likely to come up again and again, the manager is much better off training the individual on what to do. The few minutes or few hours spent training an employee will lead to a long-term **savings** in time over the manager's doing the task over and over again. Assess whether or not you have ever used the "there's not enough time to train" reason from delegating recurring tasks. If so, change that by making time (early or late in the day, weekends) for training the employee on what to do.

16. Recognize that delegating is a smart use of employees.

One of the major benefits of delegating to employees is that it makes a smart use of employee abilities and skills. Rather than have employees do repetitive and limited tasks, the effective manager provides additional stretch for employees. They take on something new, and learn and grow from it, resulting in more satisfaction on the job. The manager, in turn, by delegating to the lowest possible level, frees up more time for important activities. When looked at from a distance, delegation is a smart use of employees and a smart use of the manager's time. See delegation this way as well, not something to be skeptical of, but an effective management technique.

17. Discourage delegating upwards.

Some employees have mastered the technique of delegating upwards. They bring tasks they should be doing to the manager and dump them. Many managers then do the tasks instead of giving them back to employees. You should discourage delegating upwards in your staff. Encourage them to discuss with you the proper way to do a task if they are stumped. Demonstrate the proper way if appropriate, but do not merely do the task if it is dumped in your lap. Instead, give it back to the employee, providing the additional training if needed. Tell the employee you have confidence in their abilities to handle the task and ask them to carry it out. Do not let delegating upwards take away from your managerial effectiveness.

18. Recognize that your employees may not do a task as well as you can.

Some managers are perfectionists. They have performed a certain task over and over again for many years and have become experts at it. They are reluctant to delegate the task away because they fear that an employee will not do it as well as they can. That fear may be very real, at least for the first few times that the employee does the task

However, managers only need to remember that they were not always experts at the task themselves. They had to learn how to do it, and would never have become so good at it if their manager had not been willing to delegate. Review whether you have ever been reluctant to delegate because a staff member could not do the task as well as you can. If so, change this by delegating the task. Recognize that the employee will get better as they do the task more, just as you did. Do not let your desire for perfection get in the way of developing your staff and making the best use of your time.

19. Recognize that delegation does not mean abandonment.

For some managers, delegation means the last they ever want to hear of a certain task. Their delegation is total, and they see their activity ending as soon as they explain the task. While that may work on some occasions, there are many others where the manager should have some continued involvement. That involvement might include review meetings with an employee, providing guidance, helping make a decision on the delegated task, or at least being made aware of the final outcome. Managers should not regard delegation as a total end to their activity. For many tasks, there will be some continued involvement, though the employee will be carrying out the majority of the task. Make ongoing involvement of some sort your practice when delegating to your staff.

20. Do not delegate key management activities to others.

There is a temptation for some managers to go too far with delegation. Perhaps they do not like doing performance coaching, so they decide to get someone else to do it. While there are many tasks in the workplace that can be delegated, some must be kept by managers. The more common areas that should **not** be delegated include:

- Performance coaching.

- Performance appraisals.

- Recognizing and rewarding employees.

- Developing a vision and culture for the department.

- Salary increases and other compensation practices.

- Department plan and goals.

If you have ever tried to delegate these tasks, recognize that they should be kept within your domain as a manager. While employees might have input or thoughts on these matters, managers should actually carry out these responsibilities.

21. Use delegation to test out employees for other jobs.

Delegation should not be done to merely make an effective use of employees and free up management time. There are other reasons for delegating as well, which include delegating to test out an employee for another job. This is a safe and easy way to find out if the employee has the potential to take on another assignment without actually making a job change. Certain tasks from the new job can be given to the employee on an interim basis to see how they do.

When using delegation to test out employees for other jobs, recognize that the employee is at the early stages of a learning curve. They will not be as proficient as someone who has done the task for quite a while. Yet their early performance can provide excellent information on promotional potential. Use delegation as one means to test out your employees for other jobs.

22. Use delegation to free up time for other important management activities.

It is a common lament of many managers that there is just not enough time for everything. They cannot find the hours to train an employee, complete performance appraisals, do coaching, or carry out the necessary planning and organizing to run the department. One of the reasons these important tasks do not get done is that the manager does not delegate other tasks to employees in the department.

If you feel you do not have enough time for important management tasks, see delegation as a very helpful solution to your problem. You simply may be working on lower priority tasks while high priority items go undone, a situation that will eventually catch up with you. Change the situation by listing out which activities you can delegate and to whom. Then carry out the delegation effectively and see if it does not free up more of your time for more important management activities.

23. Sell delegated tasks positively.

Some managers get delegation off to a bad start with employees. Rather than sound optimistic about the soon-to-be-delegated task, they act like it is a chore they are glad to be rid of. These managers describe the task as time-consuming, or boring, or beneath their capabilities. The net result is that the employee sees the task as menial work, not a new challenge.

Review how you present a new task to one of your employees. Are you positive and upbeat about the task or you describe it as something that you dislike or is unimportant? Remember, that even a routine task for you might be a new, exciting learning experience for one of your employees who has never done the task before. But you have to present the task in a positive light or it will never be seen this way. Sell the tasks you are about to delegate in a positive, upbeat way.

Recommended Readings

Dessler, Gary. *Organization and Management*. Englewood Cliffs, NJ: Prentice-Hall, 1982.

Dumaine, Brian. The New Non-Manager Managers. *Fortune*, February 22, 1993, 80-84.

Engle, Herbert M. *How to Delegate: A Guide to Getting Things Done*. Houston: Gulf Publishing, 1983.

Kirkpatrick, Donald. The Power of Empowerment. *Training and Development*, September, 1992, 29-34.

Krein, Theodore J. How to Improve Delegation Habits. *Management Review*, May, 1982, p. 58-61.

Matthews, Stephen. The Gentle Art of Delegation. *Accountancy*, Oct, 1980, p. 120-122.

McConkey, Dale D. *No-Nonsense Delegation* (rev. ed.). New York: AMACOM, 1986.

Plunkett, Lorne C. and Fournier, Robert. *Participative Management: Implementing Empowerment*. New York: Wiley, 1992.

Quick, Thomas L. *The Manager's Motivation Desk Book*. New York: Wiley, 1985.

Taylor, Harold. *Delegate: The Key to Successful Management*. New York: Beauford Books, 1984.

Vinton, Donna. Delegation for Employee Development. *Training and Development*, Jan, 1987, p. 65-67.

Willis, Suzanne. *The Participative Leader*. Burr Ridge, IL: Irwin Professional Publishing, 1994.

31

Staff Selection

This chapter helps improve performance in the following areas:

- Selecting highly qualified job candidates.
- Making better promotional decisions.
- Sourcing and identifying job candidates.
- Doing a better job at interviewing and hiring employees.

Action Items for Staff Selection

1. List out requirements for the job.

No manager should attempt to select employees for a job until the job is clearly defined. Without a clear understanding of the job's requirements, it will be impossible to find the right person. Manager's should develop a list of the job requirements before beginning a search for job candidates. Requirements to be listed out include:

- Job knowledge.

- Suggested educational background.

- Skills and abilities.

- Suggested experience.

- Personal traits and "style" (e.g., flexibility, participative manager).

Once developed, the job requirements become a yardstick to measure candidates against. Whether or not someone is the "right" candidate will depend upon how well they stack up against the requirements. Use the listing of job requirements as your starting point for selecting employees.

2. Use a rating system for evaluating job candidates.

When interviewing job candidates, it is helpful to use some sort of rating system. This helps sort out all of the information that you are collecting through interviews and other means. The simplest system is to assess a rating on a five-point scale on how the candidate's background stacks up against each job requirement. A sample rating scale might be the following:

5—Greatly above job requirements.

4—Above job requirements.

3—Meets job requirements.

2—Below job requirements.

1—Unacceptable.

By making a 1-5 rating on each candidate for each job requirement, you can better profile the candidate. This also makes it easier to compare job candidates and the relative strengths and weaknesses of each. Use some sort of rating system each time you select or promote employees.

3. Use a charting system to improve selection decisions.

Interviewing job candidates and collecting other information on them can lead to information overload. When the time comes to make a final decision, some managers fall back upon a "gut feeling" rather than the objective information they have collected. One way to avoid this, as discussed in the above action item, is to make a rating on each job candidate. A logical next step from this is to chart out the ratings on all job candidates. This chart would have the candidates names listed as rows and the job requirements listed as columns. The rating of each candidate on each requirement would make up the cell entries on the chart. If multiple interviewers were used, the cell entries might be the averages of all raters combined.

The use of a charting system such as this will help managers compare job candidates and the relative merits of each. There is a tremendous benefit from being able to see on one chart all of the candidates compared on the key requirements. When it comes time to make the final decision, there will be a more objective means of doing this. Use a charting system in your selection decisions.

4. Make your final selection decision a fair, objective decision.

All managers owe it to themselves to make a fair, objective decision when selecting or promoting someone. It is tempting at times to hire someone who has some characteristics similar to your own, is a friend, or comes across in the interview as a "nice person." Yet these factors may not having any bearing on the candidate's success on the job. They could, in fact, result in selecting people who are not particularly qualified and that will reflect poorly on the manager and the department.

The suggestions presented in the above action items help ensure fairness in the selection process. Implement them whenever you make a selection decision. Also make sure that you roll together the ratings into some sort of composite and are hiring a highly qualified person. By focusing on the important job requirements, and each candidate's unique qualifications, factors such as race, sex, and marital status will not enter into the judgment process. This ensures fairness and that the person hired is chosen because of their background and skills, not irrelevant factors.

5. Use assessments or job simulations to select employees.

For many jobs today, it is difficult to assess the candidate's qualifications through a mere interview. For example, how do you assess a manager's employee relations skills in an interview? Or someone's decision making style? Or sales presentation skills? These areas, and many others, are difficult to get at through traditional interview questions. The solution is to utilize an assessment process or develop job simulations. The assessment involves having an in-house or outside expert get at those skills that you need to evaluate. This expert, usually having a degree in industrial psychology or related area, can use a variety of "role-play" and other assessment techniques in addition to an interview to get at these areas of interest. This information, when coupled with your own, can lead to a good selection decision.

Job simulations are exercises that any candidate can complete that simulate a portion of the targeted job. For example, say you are hiring someone to be a sales representative and the person in this job must make sales presentations. A simulation exercise in this area would give candidates background information that would enable them to put together, and deliver, a presentation. They would then be evaluated on how well they did this. While designing this requires technical expertise, the important point is that managers may want to use more than just an interview when making their decisions. Use outside experts to help you make better hiring decisions. Have assessments done or get job simulations designed.

6. Have high standards when hiring.

Some managers do not maintain high standards when hiring replacements. They feel the pressure of having a vacant job, and want to get a replacement (nearly anyone) as quickly as possible. However, the short-term benefit of getting a quicker replacement may turn into a long-term loss if the candidate is unskilled or does not work out. Then the job is vacant again or there are performance problems with the incumbent. This presents a bigger problem for the manager. You should evaluate whether or not you have ever compromised your hiring standards to get someone on board quickly.

The effective manager will not compromise standards to hire a replacement. Instead they will continue to look, using other sources if need be to find the right candidate. If the vacant job is creating problems, the manager may reassign another employee on a temporary basis or bring in a temporary person from the outside (there are temporary agencies now for even professional and managerial personnel). Ensure that you do not compromise your hiring standards for a short-term fix. Continue to search for a high quality replacement that will benefit you, and the company, for a number of years.

7. Post or advertise your jobs internally.

Some managers, and companies, are reluctant to post or advertise vacant jobs. They fear the administrative work from processing applications and the need to consider perhaps a large number of job candidates. While that additional work is no doubt needed, there is a great benefit from posting jobs internally. First, it is a means of surfacing a larger number of candidates than might be known to any manager. Second, it is a way of communicating your department and opportunities to employees in other parts of the company, and getting them interested in the department. Third, the posting of jobs ensures more fairness and objectivity will go into the selection process since more candidates have a chance to nominate themselves and are looked at. That, in turn, should lead to a better selection decision. Post or advertise your vacant jobs within the company.

8. Be willing to give up one of your employees to another department.

Some managers are reluctant to allow one of their employees to interview for, or be chosen for, a job in another department. These managers want to keep their employees, and figure that the other department needs to take care of their own hiring problems. While it is desirable to try and keep your good employees, this only creates additional problems. A highly talented employee might feel that they are being held back, and perhaps end up leaving the company to advance their career somewhere else. The manager has not only lost the employee, but the company has lost a valuable resource that could have been retained.

Evaluate your openness in allowing your employees to move to other jobs within the company. Do you support and encourage this or discourage it? If you discourage it, try to change your behavior. Recognize that the key is for the company to retain its good employees, and that holding someone back hurts the company and the employee. Remember also that this is a two-way street, and you may gain employees from other departments. Allow your employees more freedom to pursue other jobs, and even encourage this where you can. It is a better selection philosophy to have.

9. Communicate the company values and culture to job candidates.

All companies have a unique culture and values. Many have formally defined the culture while others have an informal culture. Regardless of whether the culture is formally defined or not, it is important to communicate the culture to prospective employees. Job candidates want to know what the company is like that they will be joining—what are the company's values, goals, management style, mission, niche in the industry, and other factors. By knowing this information, the candidate can make a more intelligent decision on whether they fit the company. Where some companies and managers go wrong is that they fail to communicate the company's values and culture to job candidates. They then find out the hard way that the employee does not fit.

As a manager, you should do all you can to communicate the culture of your organization. Be candid in letting prospective employees know what the company is all about. Just as you assess candidates, candidates assess companies. When the both of you are convinced that you have a match, it is to your mutual benefit.

10. Develop a "niche" for your employees.

Just as all companies have a certain niche in their industry, so too, can employees or individual departments. For example, employees may be known in the industry as being the hardest working, the brightest, most innovative, or the best at customer service. While it is tempting to want employees to stand out in every area, it is unrealistic to expect this. The company is better off defining a niche and then communicating this.

As a manager you should define a niche for the employees in your department if there is no niche for the entire company. Think of what you want your employees to be known for both within and outside the company. Communicate this to your current employees and prospective new hires. Evaluate job candidates against the niche and make it a part of your selection process.

11. Set up a career development program.

Employees today want more than a job; they want a career. Companies need to address this in their hiring practices and career development practices. Take a moment to think of your practices. Do you hire for only the job which is open or for long-term careers? Do you provide career development assistance for your employees after hire? If your activities need improvement, start by focusing on the employees that you hire.

When hiring, ask employees where they want to go in the future. Assess whether your company can fulfill their plans if the employees show potential. Then, after hire, provide ongoing career development assistance. Match up employee skills and abilities with job opportunities and help employees develop themselves further for jobs that are a match. Development assistance you can provide includes the following:

- Internal or outside training courses.

- College tuition reimbursement assistance.

- Job rotation assignments.

- Special projects.

- Attendance at seminars and workshops.

- Membership in professional associations.

12. Set up an incentive system for employee referrals.

When job vacancies occur, many companies rely upon traditional means of filling the jobs, such as newspaper advertising and agencies. While this works in many cases, it can also be a costly way to recruit. Many companies have a gold mine available in their own employees. Rather than run newspaper ads or use agencies, they can tap their own employees for referrals. Since each employee has a network, this can be an effective way to recruit and be cost effective. Employees are generally candid in describing their place of employment to someone else since they know this person in the outside world.

Think of setting up an incentive system for your employees to encourage job candidate referrals. Give employees a cash reward for each person who is hired as a result of their referral. Prohibit the referring of close relatives should you feel that this is necessary. The use of an incentive system for employee referrals adds another recruiting source to your company and results in a cost saving.

13. Ask open-ended questions when interviewing.

Some managers fail to ask open-ended questions when interviewing job candidates. As a result, they find out relatively little about the job candidate and cannot make an accurate selection decision. Open-ended questions such as the following would yield a great deal of information:

- "Tell me about your work experience at the XYZ Company."

- "What sort of career goals do you have for the future."

- "What type of job do you enjoy most."

- "How do you handle performance problems with your staff."

By contrast, closed-ended questions, which can be answered yes-no, are used only to verify information. Practice the use of open-ended questions by writing several down that you can use in interviews. They will help you collect more information and do a better job at interviewing.

14. Practice active listening.

Some managers make the mistake of doing all of the talking in the interview. They are so anxious to explain what the job and company are like that they fail to interview the candidate. As a result, the selection decision will not be a good one. Evaluate how much time you spend talking and listening in an interview. If you spend more than half the time talking, change your practices.

Interviews go best when the interview is split into two parts, information collecting and information sharing. In the first part, information collecting, you should ask open-ended questions and sit back and listen, making good eye contact, taking notes, nodding, and having a proper body language. In the second part, information sharing, you should tell as much as you can about the job, the company, and the company culture. Active listening will add a great deal to the information gathering part of your interview. Make sure you make it a part of your process.

15. Use "role-play" questions to evaluate style.

Nearly every company wants to evaluate the fit between the employee and the company. By "fit" we are referring not to technical skills, but the employee's style and personality traits in comparison to the company. There are many cases where the employee has the right technical skills but does not have the appropriate style for the company. For example, a manager may be technically competent but too autocratic for a particular company. The question is, how do you evaluate fit?

The best way to assess the fit is through role-play questions. Role-play questions are those that describe a scenario to the candidate, then ask the person what to do. For example, you might describe a scenario where an employee storms into a manager's office and threatens to leave the company because of insufficient pay. You then ask the manager job candidate, "What would you do? How would you handle this?" Answers shed light on the manager's style in comparison to the company style. Use role-play questions as an aid in making better selection decisions.

16. Check references of outside job candidates.

It is tempting to eliminate the checking of job references of a candidate since this takes additional time and the decision to hire has already been made. Yet studies have shown that perhaps twenty-five percent or more of job candidates misstate their backgrounds. They might list a college degree they never obtained, fill in gaps in employment, or invent a job they never held. While slight exaggerations may not be serious, outright falsification would probably cause an employer to not hire the person.

This problem can be avoided by doing reference checks on each candidate before the offer is made. Normally, candidates are asked to sign a brief form or letter giving former employers and schools permission to release information. While a written request may be needed for certain types of information, phone reference checks can be made as well. These are particularly important to conduct with the former supervisors of the employee to check on job responsibilities, strengths, and other factors. Conduct reference checks (or get the human resources group to do so) for all job candidates that you plan to hire. It can make your selection process a more accurate one.

17. Experiment with different recruiting sources.

Some companies get into the habit of using the same means to fill jobs (e.g., newspaper ads). This may not necessarily be the most effective technique, leading to a shortage of good job candidates or poor quality job candidates. Where possible, managers and human resources departments should evaluate the effectiveness of different recruiting sources and select the most effective one for the available job. Possible recruiting sources to keep in mind include:

- Newspaper ads.
- Employee referrals.
- College recruiting.
- College placement offices (alums and students).
- Search firms.
- Employment agencies.
- Professional association magazine ads or placement facilities.
- Networking through professionals at other companies.

By identifying which source is best for your job, you can focus your efforts. This will permit you to identify high quality job candidates in the most effective way. Experiment and evaluate different recruiting sources to improve your staff selection efforts.

18. Use multiple interviewers.

It is risky in any employment situation to have just one or two people interview job candidates. Selection efforts are improved by having multiple interviewers who each probe in depth. This yields more information that can be rolled together. Evaluate how many people you currently have a job candidate interview with. Ensure that the number is at least six or more to get a good picture of the candidate and enable the candidate to get to know more people and the company.

When using multiple interviewers, it is best to divide up the areas to probe. For example, some interviewers might probe only technical skills while others might try to get a handle on management skills. After the interviews are concluded, get your interviewers together to combine the ratings on each candidate. The use of multiple interviewers can help you increase the accuracy of your selection process.

19. Attend a workshop on interviewing skills.

Some managers are comfortable at interviewing, but not necessarily good at probing and evaluating job candidates. They would benefit from interviewing training classes. Many organizations offer workshops in the area, particularly professional associations in the human resources/training area and continuing education programs at universities. Most offer effective skill-building classes in the area, with ample opportunity to practice. Candidly assess your interviewing skills and ability to probe in depth. If you could benefit from training in the area, seek out a workshop that can help you. It can improve your effectiveness at selecting a better staff.

20. Use job rotation and special assignments for testing employees.

One way to make better selection decisions is to eliminate some of the risk. If you want to know whether an employee has potential for another job, give them a brief chance to perform the job. This could be through a temporary job rotation or special assignment to carry out some of the responsibilities of the targeted job. Information gained from this assignment can help greatly in making the selection decision. Care must be taken to ensure that the employee is not "given"the job, then removed, causing bitter feelings. Also, an evaluation of their performance must take into consideration that the employee is still learning the responsibilities. Despite these factors, job rotation and special assignments can yield valuable information on employee potential for other jobs. Use these options to help you plan for the future and make better selection decisions.

21. Resist the tendency to hire in your own image.

It is very tempting to hire someone in your own image. Since most of us like ourselves, who better to hire than someone who is similar to us? Similarities might show up in schools attended, majors in college, common hobbies, residence in the same neighborhood, or age. You should evaluate whether you have consciously or subconsciously tried to hire others like yourself. If so, try to be more open-minded in your evaluation of other people. Recognize that someone can get to be very talented via a different route than you followed, and that factors like the school attended may not have that much bearing on the decision to hire.

Care needs to be taken that the job requirements (see earlier action item) are not written to reflect backgrounds only like your own. If this bias can be eliminated, the use of an objective rating system as described earlier can keep the selection process accurate throughout.

22. Interview for more than technical job skills.

Many managers focus their interviewing on only technical job skills. They probe a great deal on accounting knowledge or whatever the specialty is, and disregard other factors. Six months later the new employee with all of the right technical knowledge is seen as not fitting the organization, and the manager does not know what to do. While there are many ways to rationalize about it (e.g., the candidate "just does not fit"), the real problem was with the selection process.

When you are interviewing job candidates, resist the temptation to select only on technical knowledge. Do not assume that the employees in human resources or the employment agency have probed the candidate's personality and goodness of fit. You must do this on your own. Ask role-play or other types of questions to get at the candidate's style, personality, and fit. Spend approximately fifty percent of your time probing non-technical areas. It will help you see the total picture of what each candidate is like and reach a better decision.

23. Look for typos and unclear ideas in job candidate written materials.

Some managers are surprised when new employees have difficulty writing, spelling, typing, or filling out forms. Yet these same employees may have shown this tendency in their cover letters, resumes, or completed application blanks. Evaluate whether you closely scrutinize written materials submitted by job candidates. If errors are evident in these materials, there is every reason to believe they will be present on the job as well. Treat written materials as a job sample when they come across your desk. Ask yourself if you want to hire someone who is unable to spell or write clear sentences. Use written materials as one other means to evaluate job candidates.

24. Be candid and upbeat in communicating your company to others.

All job candidates want to know about the job and company they are thinking of joining. Candid information is wanted. Some managers, however, take candidness to the extreme by making a great deal of negative comments about the job or the company. They fail to balance this with the positive side. The net result is that the candidate runs for the door.

When describing your job opportunity and company, be candid with job candidates, yet upbeat and optimistic. You are selling your opportunity so it is best to think of it this way. Mention the tough challenges or changes which might be negatives but share out optimism that these problems can be handled by the right person. Also share out what is good about the company and the job so that the candidate walks away feeling good about the opportunity. Make your approach one with candidness and optimism to attract and keep good job candidates in the running.

25. Use flexibility in salary negotiations.

Some managers and companies are overly rigid in handling salary negotiations with job candidates. They will let an outstanding job candidate walk away from the job over a few dollars in starting salary. While there have to be ultimate limits on what a company will spend in filling a particular job, inflexible, rigid policies work to the detriment of all. The few extra dollars spent on the outstanding job candidate might be made back for the company within a few weeks in the form of high performance. That high performance might be attained for years to come, making the small investment in extra salary seem like a very good one.

When handling salary negotiations with job candidates, try to keep flexibility in mind. If you really cannot meet someone's starting salary demands, maybe there is a way around the situation. Perhaps the candidate can be given a guaranteed bonus, either at the time of hire or after a certain time period. Or given shares of company stock in the form of options or a grant to be exercised later. There are many other possibilities as well. The point is, do not lose that outstanding job candidate over a few dollars in compensation. Have flexibility and negotiate a package that is acceptable to all.

Recommended Readings

American Society for Personnel Administration. *Recruitment/ Selection*. Alexandria, VA: American Society for Personnel Administration, 1986.

Arthur, Diane. *Recruiting, Interviewing, Selecting and Orienting New Employees*. New York: AMACOM, 1986.

Beatty, Richard W., and Schneier, Craig. *Personnel Administration: An Experiential Skill-Building Approach* (2nd ed.). Reading, MA: Addison-Wesley, 1981.

Dickerson, Elizabeth. The Hiring Decision: Assessing Fit into the Workplace. *Management Solutions*, Jan, 1987, 32, p. 24-30.

Goodale, James G. *The Fine Art of Interviewing*. Englewood Cliffs, NJ: Prentice-Hall, 1982.

Half, Robert. *Finding, Hiring and Keeping the Best Employees*. New York: Wiley, 1993.

Hendrickson, J. Hiring the Right Stuff. *The Personnel Administrator*, Nov, 1987, 32, p, 70-74.

Heneman, Herbert G. III; Schwab, Donald; Fossum, John; and Dyer, Lee. *Personnel/ Human Resource Management*. Homewood, IL: Irwin, 1980.

Kennedy, Jim. *Getting Behind the Resume*. Englewood Cliffs, NJ: Prentice-Hall, 1987.

Loretto, Vincent. Effective Interviewing is Based on More than Intuition. *Personnel Management*, Dec, 1986, 65, p. 10-14.

Manter, Marcia and Janice, Benjamin. How to Hold On to First Careerists. *The Personnel Administrator*, September, 1989, p. 44-48.

Moore, Laurence V. Maps to a Good Match. *The Personnel Administrator*, May, 1988, p. 102-105.

Pinsker, Richard J. *Hiring Winners*. New York: AMACOM Books, 1994.

Smart, Bradford D. Progressive Approaches for Hiring the Best People. *Training and Development*, Sept, 1987, p. 46-53.

Swan, William S. *Swan's How to Pick the Right People Program*. New York: Wiley, 1989.